A FAMILY CHRISTMAS

A FAMILY CHRISTMAS

SELECTED AND INTRODUCED BY

Caroline Kennedy

Illustrated by Jon J Muth

and Laura Hartman Maestro

HYPERION

NEW YORK

Library of Congress Cataloging-in-Publication Data has been applied for.

ISBN: 978-1-4013-2227-4

Hyperion books are available for special promotions and premiums.
For details contact Michael Rentas, Proprietary Markets, Hyperion,
77 West 66th Street, 12th floor, New York, New York 10023, or call
212-456-0133.

Chapter and selected pictures © 2007 Jon J Muth
Text illustrations © 2007 Laura Hartman Maestro
Book design by Richard Oriolo

First Edition

10 9 8 7 6 5 4 3 2 1

We Need a Little Christmas

JERRY HERMAN

Haul out the holly
Put up the tree before my spirit falls again
Fill up the stocking
I may be rushing things, but deck the halls again now

For we need a little Christmas
Right this very minute
Candles in the window
Carols at the spinet

Yes, we need a little Christmas
Right this very minute
It hasn't snowed a single flurry
But Santa, dear, we're in a hurry

So climb down the chimney
Turn on the brightest string of lights I've ever seen
Slice up the fruitcake
It's time we hung some tinsel on that evergreen bough

For I've grown a little leaner
Grown a little colder
Grown a little sadder
Grown a little older

And I need a little angel
Sitting on my shoulder
Need a little Christmas now

For we need a little music
Need a little laughter
Need a little singing
Ringing through the rafter

And we need a little snappy
"Happy ever after"
Need a little Christmas now

Contents

O COME, ALL YE FAITHFUL   279

WINTER WONDERLAND   311

Letter to Santa

CAROLINE KENNEDY

December 19, 1962

Dear Santa,

    I would like a pair of silver skates—and one of those horse wagons with lucky dips—and Susie Smart and Candy Fashion dolls and a real pet reindeer and a clock to tell time and a covered wagon & a farm and you decide anything else—

    And interesting planes or bumpy thing he can ride in or some noisy thing or something he can push or pull for John.

Love from
Caroline

    PS I would like a basket for my bicycle

INTRODUCTION

CHRISTMAS IS A HOLIDAY OF HOPE. As children, we wait all year for the chance to wish for whatever we want most. Frequently, these wishes take the form of toys, but often we ask for more profound gifts, such as a reunited family or a world at peace. Children possess a spiritual curiosity that is sometimes underestimated or overlooked in the holiday hustle and bustle. Yet children ponder the mysteries of life and of faith that Christmas makes real. Later on, as parents, we reconnect with our own childhood sense of hope, reaffirm our faith, and recognize the power of love and family.

For each of us, there are aspects of Christmas that remain magical throughout our lives. Looking back on my childhood, I can now see it was unusual, though it did not seem so at the time. One of my earliest memories comes from living in the White House. Every morning before I went to school, I would go into my father's room and talk to him as he was getting ready to go to the office. We spent most of the time discussing topics of interest to me, including my hamsters and parakeets, or my cousins and their adventures. We often used to call my grandparents on the phone together. It wasn't like making a normal phone call. All I had to do was pick up the phone and tell the White House operator who we wanted to speak with, and she would get them on the line. Of course, my favorite person to call was Santa Claus. The fact that he had the same soft Southern accent common to many White House workers of the day escaped me completely.

As I grew older, preparing for the holidays continued to be a special time for me, and traditions were important in our family. Like my grandmother, my mother had a special dress that she always wore on Christmas Eve, because her mother had done the same, and she taught us the carol that she and her sister used to sing, "Carol Carol Children." My brother and I put on a little pageant every year until we outgrew our Mary and Joseph costumes, and my children did the same.

Whether we were gluing sequins onto construction-paper ornaments, sticking cloves into oranges until our thumbs hurt to make pomander balls, or bringing home an art project from school, Christmas brought us the chance to think about the people who were special to us. Making and giving gifts, collecting toys, and volunteering to help those less fortunate are meaningful and creative ways to experience the joy of loving others, which can help shape our adult lives.

In our family, with the exception of a few Christmas cookies, preparations tended to the literary rather than the culinary. My mother used to write poems for her mother, and my brother and I illustrated Bible verses, wrote poems, and decorated cards for her. She collected them in a special scrapbook or framed them, just as her mother had done. My children have continued the tradition, and when I hang our multi-generational efforts around the house at Christmastime, they demonstrate the continuity of family life in a tangible and comforting way.

I grew up in a Catholic family and attended Catholic school, so the emphasis was on the religious aspects of the holiday: the birth of Jesus, the desire to be worthy of Him, and the importance of faith in our lives. There was a tacit disapproval of the commercial aspects of Christmas, and a feeling that although we had been encouraged to ask Santa for presents, if we actually wanted anything, somehow we weren't being true to the Christmas spirit—all somewhat contradictory. Our house was a last bastion of the Victorian era, when a fresh orange was considered a special treat, and my mother was certainly alone in her view that walnuts were appropriate stocking stuffers. My brother and I were constantly pointing out that American society had moved beyond such homespun delights, and by the time my children were writing letters to Santa, even my mother had embraced the era of plastic—presenting them with a miniature plastic kitchen, a pink plastic shopping cart with plastic vegetables, and a talking plastic telephone.

The genius of Christmas is that it has meaning on so many levels. It allows each child to connect with the Divine and with others. There is also room for each family to create its own traditions while, at the same time, participating in a larger cultural and civic festival. Although America was founded on the separation of church and state, and Christmas has developed with regional and sectarian differences, in some ways, this national celebration intertwines the secular and the sacred, as it strengthens the bonds between individuals and the larger social community. It wasn't always this way.

In colonial times, Christmas was less important than New Year's Day, and neither was celebrated in a religious manner. In fact, in 1659, the Puritans in Massachusetts passed a law banning the celebration of Christmas, which had become known for public drunkenness, licentious sex, and gambling. There was no basis for Christmas as a religious holiday, they claimed, since nowhere in the Bible did it say on which day Jesus was born. However, popular sentiment rejected this narrow view, and over time the commemoration of the Nativity has become the largest holiday of the year.

There is some truth, but more legend, in the popularly held belief that various traditions came to America with different European immigrant groups. While it may be true that Martin Luther decorated the first Christmas tree for his own children, and that German immigrants brought the custom to America, it seems clear that Christmas trees became widely adopted after the publication of pictures of Queen Victoria and her family gathered around a tabletop tree decorated with cookies and candles. Similarly, we are told that the Dutch brought their patron saint, St. Nicholas, to New Amsterdam, but in fact there is no mention of him until the nineteenth century. The English contribution of mince pies, the Yule log, and the custom of tipping were actually popularized in America through *A Christmas Carol* by Charles Dickens and the stories of Washington Irving, author of "Rip van Winkle" and "The Legend of Sleepy Hollow." In early America, Christmas was a day like any other—shops and businesses remained open, and it wasn't until after the Civil War that Christmas was declared a holiday in most states.

In fact, it was in the 1820s that America began to invent the celebration that we recognize today. American society was changing—waves of poor and uneducated immigrants were beginning to arrive at the same time that the agricultural way of life was being replaced by a more urban and upper-middle-class society, especially in the North. A group of civic fathers in New York, concerned about the drunkenness and gunfire used to ring in Christmas and New Year's Day, set about civilizing the celebration. They founded the St. Nicholas Society, urged the transfer of the holiday from the streets to the home, and placed children at its center. Their efforts coincided with, and were influenced by, larger social transformations of the Victorian era, with its emphasis on domestic propriety and economic prosperity.

Undoubtedly, their most important contribution was the creation of the modern Santa Claus. In 1822, one of the founders of the Society, Clement Clarke Moore, a wealthy farmer and professor of ancient languages and divinity, wrote the poem "A Visit from St. Nicholas." Moore's St. Nick drew upon older Germanic traditions of elves and trolls, and transformed the severe and judgmental St. Nicholas into a beneficent, kindly soul who fulfilled the wishes of children with the tacit approval of their parents. This image of Santa was published throughout the nineteenth century, most famously in Thomas Nast's annual illustrations for *Harper's Magazine,* one of which featured Santa wearing a star-spangled shirt and striped pants while addressing a camp of Union soldiers. The process of intertwining a secular and patriotic holiday tradition had begun.

In the late nineteenth and early twentieth centuries, America "invented" the department store, which contributed greatly to the economic growth of Christmas. In New York, Macy's began decorating its holiday windows in the 1870s and inaugurated its Thanksgiving Day Parade in 1924. The annual Christmas Eve carol service for 14,000 at Wanamaker's in Philadelphia was accompanied by the world's largest pipe organ, and the lighting of the Christmas tree at Marshall Field's flagship Chicago store became a meaningful civic ritual. Over the next century, as American culture spread internationally, advertising, particularly by the Coca-Cola company, helped export the American image of Santa worldwide.

Rooted in the Nativity and the teachings of Jesus, the desire for peace and the obligation to share one's blessing with those less fortunate have always been integral parts of Christmas. One of the most powerful examples of the Christmas spirit is the spontaneous truce of World War I in which the British and German soldiers stopped fighting and came out of their trenches to shake hands, collect their dead and wounded, and sing carols.

In the later nineteenth century, churches and social-welfare organizations began institutionalizing large-scale Christmas charity and volunteerism in ways that continue to this day. For example, in 1899, a Salvation Army Banquet in Madison Square Garden served a sit-down dinner to 20,000 of the city's poor.

The invention of the lightbulb in 1879 had major implications for the holiday celebration. The first electric Christmas-tree lights, eighty hand-blown red, white, and blue glass bulbs, festooned the 1882 tree of Edward Johnson, an executive in the Edison Illuminating Company. But tree lights remained far too expensive for the average family. Even after General Electric began mass producing lights in 1903, they were used primarily in stores and public spaces.

Civic celebrations also began in the years before World War I. In our family, we take great pride in the fact that my great grandfather Mayor John F. Fitzgerald of Boston, after whom my father was named, led the carol singing and lit the first Christmas tree on Boston Common in 1912. Growing up, I understood this to be the first public Christmas tree in America, but when I was researching this book, I came across articles suggesting otherwise. They asserted that, in fact, the first public Christmas tree was erected in New York City's Madison Square by a Mrs. J. B. F. Herreshoff and her group of wealthy friends. Although I was sure she would prove no match for Honey Fitz, the fourth of twelve children, who supported his brothers and sisters after the death of both his parents, this apparent misconception was alarmingly widespread. I feared I was entering a Yankees–Red Sox type rivalry, and resolved to get to the bottom of these competing claims.

Combing through the archives of the *Boston Globe* and the *New York Times,* I discovered that in 1912, due to a violent infestation of the gypsy moth, the Agriculture Department instituted a quarantine on the transport of most New England and Adirondack Christmas trees. Some suggest this led to the idea of public celebrations. But I knew in my heart that children, not moths, would have motivated Honey Fitz, who also put up the first carousel in Boston. My faith was vindicated when a careful comparison of the articles revealed that although the bells of New York began to chime at 4:50 p.m., the 1,500 lights on the Boston tree were illuminated at 5:00, a full half-hour before the New York tree lights went on. The custom spread across the country, and in 1923, Calvin Coolidge lit the first national Christmas tree on the White House lawn.

But to even things out, I also discovered that the true relics of the real-life St. Nicholas are kept in a Greek Orthodox church in New York City.

Before I began working on this collection, I was skeptical that I would learn anything new, but reading and reflecting brought back many memories and taught me a great deal. I learned about the history of Christmas in America, the layers of meaning and experience, and the powerful and often conflicting emotions that are wound up in the holiday. Hope can bring disappointment. Love can be painful. Families fracture and recombine. And the powerful emotions of the holidays are not always easy to manage. Yet the liturgy and literature teaches us that Christmas encompasses the miraculous and the tragic, the profound and the ridiculous, and always represents the connection to something larger than ourselves. If we are open to the gifts of understanding, hope, and faith in others and in God, the spirit of Christmas can help make real the way we want to live our lives.

This book has been a gift to me. I hope it will give other families the chance to reflect on their own personal observances, as well as our shared heritage, and that they too will enjoy the chance to "keep Christmas" all year long.

THE
GRACIOUS
TIME

THE GRACIOUS TIME

from *Hamlet*, Act I, Scene i

WILLIAM SHAKESPEARE

Some say that ever 'gainst that season comes
Wherein our Saviour's birth is celebrated,
The bird of dawning singeth all night long:
And then, they say, no spirit dares stir abroad;
The nights are wholesome; then no planets strike,
No fairy takes, nor witch hath power to charm,
So hallow'd and so gracious is the time.

Psalm 8

O LORD our Lord, how excellent is thy name in all the earth! who hast set thy glory above the heavens.

Out of the mouth of babes and sucklings hast thou ordained strength because of thine enemies, that thou mightest still the enemy and the avenger.

When I consider thy heavens, the work of thy fingers, the moon and the stars, which thou hast ordained;

What is man, that thou art mindful of him? and the son of man, that thou visitest him?

For thou hast made him a little lower than the angels, and has crowned him with glory and honour.

Thou madest him to have dominion over the works of thy hands; thou hast put all things under his feet:

All sheep and oxen, yea, and the beasts of the field;

The fowl of the air, and the fish of the sea, and whatsoever passeth through the paths of the seas.

O LORD our Lord, how excellent is thy name in all the earth!

CREDO

EDWIN ARLINGTON ROBINSON

I cannot find my way: there is no star
In all the shrouded heavens anywhere;
And there is not a whisper in the air
Of any living voice but one so far
That I can hear it only as a bar
Of lost, imperial music, played when fair
And angel fingers wove, and unaware,
Dead leaves to garlands where no roses are.

No, there is not a glimmer, nor a call,
For one that welcomes, welcomes when he fears,
The black and awful chaos of the night;
For through it all—above, beyond it all—
I know the far-sent message of the years,
I feel the coming glory of the Light.

Letter to Fred Allen

GROUCHO MARX

December 23, 1953

Dear Freddie:

Now the melancholy days have come. The department stores call it Christmas. Other than for children and elderly shut-ins the thing has developed to such ridiculous proportions—well, I won't go into it. This is not an original nor novel observation and I am sure everyone in my position has similar emotions. Some of the recipients are so ungrateful. For example, yesterday I gave the man who cleans my swimming pool $5.00. This morning I found two dead fish floating in the drink. Last year I gave the mailman $5.00. I heard later he took the five bucks, bought two quarts of ratgut and went on a three week bender. I didn't get any mail from December 24th to January 15th. . . . For Christmas I bought the cook a cookbook. She promptly fried it and we had it for dinner last night. It was the first decent meal we had in three weeks. From now on I am going to buy all my food at the bookstore.

So you see, the life of a rich man isn't all beer and skittles (whatever the hell that means). We, too, have our troubles just the same as the lowly commoner and the shepherd in the hills.

I hope you and the kid in the tights are enjoying the Yule season and that you place a small wager on Tom Fool the next time he goes to the post.

My best,
Groucho

Mr. Fred Allen
180 West 58th Street
New York 19, New York.

RELATIVE PRONOUNS

E. B. WHITE

December 25, 1948

WE HAD A SCROOGE IN OUR office a few minutes ago, a tall, parched man,* beefing about Christmas and threatening to disembowel anyone who mentioned the word. He said his work had suffered and his life been made unbearable by the demands and conventions of the season. He said he hated wise men, whether from the East or from the West, hated red ribbon, angels, Scotch Tape, greeting cards depicting the Adoration, mincemeat, dripping candles, distant and near relatives, fir balsam, silent nights, boy sopranos, shopping lists with check marks against some of the items, and the whole yuletide stratagem, not to mention the low-lying cloud of unwritten thank-you letters hanging just above the horizon. He was in a savage state. Before he left the office, though, we saw him transfigured, just as Scrooge was transfigured. The difference was that whereas Scrooge was softened by visions, our visitor was softened by the sight of a small book on our desk—a copy of Fowler's "Modern English Usage."

"Greatest collection of essays and opinions ever assembled between covers," he shouted, "including a truly masterful study of *that* and *which*."

He seized the book and began thumbing through it for favorite passages, slowly stuffing a couple of small gift-wrapped parcels into the pocket of his greatcoat.

"Listen to this," he said in a triumphant voice. "'Avoidance of the obvious is very well, provided that it is not itself obvious, but, if it is, all is spoilt.' Isn't that beautiful?"

We agreed that it was a sound and valuable sentiment, perfectly expressed. He then began a sermon on *that* and *which*, taking as his text certain paragraphs from Fowler, and warming rapidly to his theme.

*Harold Ross, editor of *The New Yorker* from its founding in 1925 to his death in 1951

"Listen to this: 'If writers would agree to regard *that* as the defining relative pronoun, and *which* as the non-defining, there would be much gain both in lucidity and in ease. Some there are who follow this principle now; but it would be idle to pretend that it is the practice either of most or of the best writers.'"

"It was the practice of St. Matthew," we put in hastily. "Or at any rate he practiced it in one of the most moving sentences ever constructed: 'And, lo, the star, which they saw in the east, went before them, till it came and stood over where the young child was.' You've got to admit that the *which* in that sentence is where it ought to be, as well as every other word. Did you ever read a more satisfactory sentence than that in your life?"

"It's good," said our friend, cheerfully. "It's good because there isn't a ten-dollar word in the whole thing. And Fowler has it pegged, too. Wait a minute. Here. 'What is to be deprecated is the notion that one can improve one's style by using stylish words.' See what I mean about Fowler? But let's get back to *that* and *which*. That's the business that really fascinates me. Fowler devotes eight pages to it. I got so excited once I had the pages photostatted. Listen to this: 'We find in fact that the antecedent of *that* is often personal.' Now, that's very instructive."

"Very," we said. "And if you want an example, take Matthew 2:1: ' . . . there came wise men from the east to Jerusalem, saying, Where is he that is born King of the Jews?' Imagine how that simple clause could get loused up if someone wanted to change *that* to *who*!"

"Exactly," he said. "That's what I mean about Fowler. What was the sentence again about the star? Say it again."

We repeated, "And, lo, the star, which they saw in the east, went before them, till it came and stood over where the young child was."

"You see?" he said, happily. "This is the greatest damn book ever written." And he left our office transfigured, a man in excellent spirits. Seeing him go off merry as a grig, we realized that Christmas is where the heart is. For some it is in a roll of red ribbon, for some in the eyes of a young child. For our visitor, we saw clearly, Christmas was in a relative pronoun. Wherever it is, it is quite a day.

KEEPING CHRISTMAS

HENRY VAN DYKE

IT IS A GOOD THING TO observe Christmas day. The mere marking of times and seasons when men agree to stop work and make merry together is a wise and wholesome custom. It helps one to feel the supremacy of the common life over the individual life. It reminds a man to set his own little watch, now and then, by the great clock of humanity.

But there is a better thing than the observance of Christmas day, and that is, keeping Christmas.

Are you willing to forget what you have done for other people and to remember what other people have done for you; to ignore what the world owes you and to think what you owe the world; to put your rights in the background and your duties in the middle distance and your chances to do a little more than your duty in the foreground; to see that your fellow men are just as real as you are, and try to look behind their faces to their hearts, hungry for joy; to own that probably the only good reason for your existence is not what you are going to get out of life, but what you are going to give to life; to close your book of complaints against the management of the universe and look around you for a place where you can sow a few seeds of happiness—are you willing to do these things even for a day? Then you can keep Christmas.

Are you willing to stoop down and consider the needs and the desires of little children; to remember the weakness and loneliness of people who are growing old; to stop asking how much your friends love you and ask yourself whether you love them enough; to bear in mind the things that other people have to bear on their hearts; to try to understand what those who live in the same house with you really want, without waiting for them to tell you; to trim your lamp so that it will give more light and less smoke, and to carry it in front so that your shadow will fall behind you; to make a grave for your ugly thoughts and a garden for your kindly feelings, with the gate open—are you willing to do these things even for a day? Then you can keep Christmas.

Are you willing to believe that love is the strongest thing in the world,—stronger than hate, stronger than evil, stronger than death,—and that the blessed life which began in Bethlehem nineteen hundred years ago is the image and brightness of the Eternal Love? Then you can keep Christmas.

And if you keep it for a day, why not always?

But you can never keep it alone.

WHITE CHRISTMAS

IRVING BERLIN

I'm dreaming of a white Christmas
Just like the ones I used to know
Where the treetops glisten,
and children listen
To hear sleigh bells in the snow

I'm dreaming of a white Christmas
With every Christmas card I write
May your days be merry and bright
And may all your Christmases be white

I'm dreaming of a white Christmas
With every Christmas card I write
May your days be merry and bright
And may all your Christmases be white

Deck the Halls

DECK THE HALLS

WELSH TRADITIONAL CAROL

Deck the halls with boughs of holly,
Fa la la la la la la la la.
'Tis the season to be jolly,
Fa la la la la la la la la.
Don we now our gay apparel,
Fa la la la la la la la la.
Troll the ancient Yuletide carol,
Fa la la la la la la la la.

See the blazing Yule before us,
Fa la la la la la la la la.
Strike the harp and join the chorus,
Fa la la la la la la la la.
Follow me in merry measure,
Fa la la la la la la la la.
While I tell of Yuletide treasure,
Fa la la la la la la la la.

Fast away the old year passes,
Fa la la la la la la la la.
Hail the new, ye lads and lasses,
Fa la la la la la la la la.
Sing we joyous all together,
Fa la la la la la la la la.

Heedless of the wind and weather,
Fa la la la la la la la la.

Deck the halls with boughs of holly,
Fa la la la la la la la la.

Under the Mistletoe

COUNTEE CULLEN

I did not know she'd take it so,
Or else I'd never dared:
Although the bliss was worth the blow,
I did not know she'd take it so.
She stood beneath the mistletoe
So long I thought she cared;
I did not know she'd take it so,
Or else I'd never dared.

MESSIAH
(CHRISTMAS PORTIONS)

*A little heat caught
in gleaming rags,
in shrouds of veil,
    torn and sun-shot swaddlings:*

*over the Methodist roof,
two clouds propose a Zion
of their own, blazing
    (colors of tarnish on copper)*

*against the steely close
of a coastal afternoon, December,
while under the steeple
    the Choral Society*

*prepares to perform
Messiah, pouring, in their best
blacks and whites, onto the raked stage.
    Not steep, really.*

*but from here,
the first pew, they're a looming
cloudbank of familiar angels:
    that neighbor who*

fights operatically
with her girlfriend, for one,
and the friendly bearded clerk
    from the post office.

    —tenor trapped
in the body of a baritone? Altos
from the A&P, soprano
    from the T-shirt shop:

    today they're all poise,
costume and purpose
conveying the right note
    of distance and formality.

    Silence in the hall,
anticipatory, as if we're all
about to open a gift we're not sure
    we'll like;

    how could they
compete with sunset's burnished
oratorio? Thoughts which vanish,
    when the violins begin.

    Who'd have thought
they'd be so good? Every valley,
proclaims the solo tenor,
    (a sleek blonde

    I've seen somewhere before
—the liquor store?) shall be exalted,
and in his handsome mouth the word
    is lifted and opened

into more syllables
than we could count, central ah
dilated in a baroque melisma,
    liquefied; the pour

    of voice seems
to make the unplaned landscape
the text predicts the Lord
    will heighten and tame.

    This music
demonstrates what it claims:
glory shall be revealed. If art's
    acceptable evidence,

    mustn't what lies
behind the world be at least
as beautiful as the human voice?
    The tenors lack confidence,

    and the soloists,
half of them anyway, don't
have the strength to found
    the mighty kingdoms

    these passages propose
—but the chorus, all together,
equals my burning clouds,
    and seems itself to burn,

    commingled powers
deeded to a larger, centering claim.
These aren't anyone we know;
    choiring dissolves

familiarity in an up-
pouring rush which will not
rest, will not, for a moment,
    be still.

    aren't we enlarged
by the scale of what we're able
to desire? Everything,
    the choir insists,

    might flame;
inside these wrappings
burns another, brighter life,
    quickened, now,

    by song: hear how
it cascades, in overlapping,
lapidary waves of praise? Still time.
    Still time to change.

LITTLE TREE

E. E. CUMMINGS

little tree
little silent Christmas tree
you are so little
you are more like a flower

who found you in the green forest
and were you very sorry to come away?
see   i will comfort you
because you smell so sweetly

i will kiss your cool bark
and hug you safe and tight
just as your mother would,
only don't be afraid

look   the spangles
that sleep all the year in a dark box
dreaming of being taken out and allowed to shine,
the balls the chains red and gold the fluffy threads,

put up your little arms
and i'll give them all to you to hold
every finger shall have its ring
and there won't be a single place dark or unhappy

then when you're quite dressed
you'll stand in the window for everyone to see
and how they'll stare!
oh but you'll be very proud

and my little sister and i will take hands
and looking up at our beautiful tree
we'll dance and sing
"Noel Noel"

THE CHRISTMAS TREE

EMMA LAZARUS

Crusted with silver, gemmed with stars of light,
  Topaz and ruby, emerald, sapphire, pearl,
The enchanted tree within a world of white
Uplifts her myriad crystal branches bright
  Against the pale blue skies. The keen winds whirl
Her globèd jewels on the sheeted snow,
That hard and pure as marble lies below.

Yet even as the radiant fruitage falls,
  Touching the solid earth, it melts to air.
Gold-glimmering rings and clear, flame-hearted balls,—
These be the magic keys to elfin halls.
  The outstretched hands of greed are void and bare,
But elfin hands may clasp, elf eyes may see,
The mystic glories of the wondrous tree.

Lo, as beneath the silver boughs I stood,
  And watched the gleaming jewel in their heart,
Blue as a star, the subtle charm held good:
  I touched and clasped a dropping diamond dart,
  And, rapt from all the snowy world apart,
Alone within the moist, green woods of May,
I wandered ere the middle hour of day.

And over me the magic tree outspread
    Her rustling branches like a silken tent;
An azure light the balmy heavens shed;
Rose-white with odorous bloom above my head,
    Scarce 'neath their burden soft the wreathed sprays bent.
Through them went singing birds, and once on high
Surely a blindfold, winged boy-god flew by.

In the cool shade two happy mortals stood
    And laughed, because the spring was in their veins,
Coursing like heavenly fire along their blood,
To see the sunbeams pierce the emerald wood,
    To hear each other's voice, to catch the strains
Of sweet bird-carols in the tree-tops high;
And laughed like gods, who are not born to die.

A spirit murmured in mine ear unseen,
    "Rub well the dart thou holdest." I obeyed,
And all the tree was swathed in living green,
Veiled with hot, hazy sunshine, and between
    The ripe, dark leaves plump cherries white and red,
Swaying on slender stalks with every breeze,
Glowed like the gold fruits of Hesperides.

Once more I rubbed the talisman. There came
Once more a change: the rusty leaves outshone
With tints of bronze against a sky of flame,
Weird with strange light, the same yet not the same.
    But brief the glory, setting with the sun:
A fog-white wraith uprose to haunt the tree,
And shrill winds whistled through it drearily.

From out my hand the mystic arrow fell:
　Like dew it vanished, and I was aware
Of winter-tide and death. Ah, was it well,
Ye mocking elves, to weave this subtle spell,
　And break it thus, dissolving into air
The fairy fabric of my dream, and show
Life a brief vision melting with the snow?

CHRISTMAS TREES

A Christmas Circular Letter

ROBERT FROST

The city had withdrawn into itself
And left at last the country to the country;
And when between whirls of snow not come to lie
And whirls of foliage not yet laid, there drove
A stranger to our yard, who looked the city,
Yet did in country fashion in that there
He sat and waited till he drew us out
A-buttoning coats to ask him who he was,
He proved to be the city come again
To look for something it had left behind
And could not do without and keep its Christmas.
He asked if I would sell my Christmas trees,
My woods—the young fir balsams like a place
Where houses are all churches and have spires.
I hadn't thought of them as Christmas trees.
I doubt if I was tempted for a moment
To sell them off their feet to go in cars
And leave the slope behind the house all bare,
Where the sun shines now no warmer than the moon
I'd hate to have them know it if I was.
Yet more I'd hate to hold my trees except
As others hold theirs or effuse for them,
Beyond the time of profitable growth,
The trial by market everything must come to
I dallied so much with the thought of selling

Then whether from mistaken courtesy
And fear of seeming short of speech, or whether
From hope of hearing good of what was mine,
I said, "There aren't enough to be worth while."
"I could soon tell how many they would cut,
You let me look them over."

"You could look
But don't expect I'm going to let you have them."
Pasture they spring in, some in clumps too close
That lop each other of boughs, but not a few
Quite solitary and having equal boughs
All round and round. The latter he nodded "Yes" to,
Or paused to say beneath some lovelier one,
With a buyer's moderation, "That would do."
I thought so too, but wasn't there to say so.
We climbed the pasture on the south, crossed over,
And came down on the north.

He said, "A thousand."

"A thousand Christmas trees!—at what apiece?"

He felt some need of softening that to me:
"A thousand trees would come to thirty dollars."

Then I was certain I had never meant
To let him have them. Never show surprise!
But thirty dollars seemed so small beside
The extent of pasture I should strip, three cents
(For that was all they figured out apiece),
Three cents so small beside the dollar friends
I should be writing to within the hour
Would pay in cities for good trees like those,

Regular vestry-trees whole Sunday Schools
Could hang enough on to pick off enough.
A thousand Christmas trees I didn't know I had!
Worth three cents more to give away than sell,
As may be shown by a simple calculation.
Too bad I couldn't lay one in a letter.
I can't help wishing I could send you one,
In wishing you herewith a Merry Christmas.

A CHRISTMAS TREE

PIRI THOMAS

TWO MORE WEEKS AND IT WOULD come around again. Christmas. The year was 1938. I was ten years old and living with my family in Harlem. Las Navidades was a sacred time for all the devout Christians regardless of color, for it was in honor of Jesus Christ, who had not even known the comfort of being born in a hospital, since there had been no room at the inn. Instead he had been born in a manger in the stable. Popi, who was a death-bed Catholic, would only see a priest when he was ready to kick the bucket, but when anybody asked him what his faith was, he would proudly boom out, "Me, I'm *católico*."

For kids in El Barrio, Christmas was a time of great expectations and nighttime dreams of a beautiful yellow bicycle with balloon tires or a brand-new pair of ice skates. I dropped hints all over the place hoping to receive at least one or the other. I would write to Santa Claus asking for what I wanted, always sending my best regards to Mrs. Claus with the hope of establishing a better connection. But the truth of the matter was that nobody heard me. We Thomas children always got something, although not exacly what we had asked for. Our brave, tight smiles with the glimmer of a tear were meant to pass as the happy joy of receiving pretty close to what we wanted, but we sure didn't fool Mami, who, in gentle tones, would tell us that we ought to be thankful that we had received something, at least, since a lot of ghetto children had not gotten anything because of the great unemployment. The lines at Catholic Charities were long and not everybody in them was Catholic. The Twenty-third precinct on 104th Street gave out toys to the kids in our community, and then some of the cops proceeded to bust our chops for the rest of the year. La Casita María in El Barrio on 110th Street gave out warm blankets and clothes and bags of groceries and the Heckscher Foundation on 104th Street was there for us, too, and gave shoes and warm clothing to the very poor. Mami gave each of us a kiss and a tight hug and told us we should give thanks to God that our father had had a job at the toy warehouse for the past two years. I smiled in agreement, but with my thoughts I responded, "*Sí*, Mami, but they don't have yellow bikes with balloon tires and pro ice skates."

Popi's boss was named Mr. Charles. Popi worked as a toy inspector who checked the toys, separating out the damaged ones as rejects. Popi also served with distinction as packer and porter. Popi had told us that his boss considered himself to be a good guy and so at Christmastime he allowed his workers to take home damaged toys as presents for their children. But all the toys Popi had brought home last Christmas were brand-new with the exception of one single reject among them. As it came out years later, Popi, who like many other parents wanted the best for his children, wanted brand-new toys instead of rejects, and had simply put prime-condition toys into a large potato sack and then placed a damaged one right on top, bringing them all home in one sack, which made us kids very happy on Christmas morning. Of course Popi didn't want Mami to know, because she, as a good Christian, would disapprove of any action that smacked of dishonesty.

It was four days before Christmas and we still had not gotten our tree. Popi had waited until he got his few dollars' Christmas bonus and then announced that it was time to buy our tree and asked us who wanted to come. Of course all four kids began to squeal and jump around, using any excuse for creating joy. I looked out the window of the living room which faced the street. The barrio was covered by a soft white blanket of snow that kept falling gently. "Dress warmly," Mami admonished, and in no time at all the four of us looked like Eskimos, complete with warm scarves that swallowed our faces. As we ran out into the dimly lit hallway and noisily descended the stairs two at a time, I heard Mami call down to Popi about not going crazy and spending too much money on the Christmas tree.

The five of us stepped out into a white world of falling snow and muffled sounds. The snow looked good enough to eat. We could make snowballs and then pour on flavored syrup and eat the balls like *piraguas*. Popi exclaimed, "*Vaya* kids, look at all the snow, is this not a most beautiful sight?" We all shivered in agreement. Lots of *familias* with their children were heading toward Third Avenue. We turned the corner on 104th Street and Third and the avenue was ablaze on both sides of the street with millions of multicolored Christmas lights blinking at each other all the way up to 125th Street. Loudspeakers hooked to the outside walls of well-stocked stores blared Christmas songs like "I'm Dreaming of a White Christmas," "Joy to the World," and "Hark the Herald Angels Sing," with commercial breaks in English and Spanish that promised tremendous bargains with 50 percent off and instant credit.

José was anxious to get to the empty lot near Second Avenue, because he had been chosen to be the one to pick the tree. We all entered the huge lot full of all sizes and kinds of trees. Popi led us to where the regular-sized trees were trying to look their scrawny best, and we followed right behind him—that is, all except José, who was nowhere to be seen. Everybody took a point on the compass and frantically went José-hunting. I hoped he had not been kidnapped and held for ransom. Sis ended those lousy thoughts by waving at all of us to come over. We joined her and as she pointed to the more expensive, taller, and fuller trees, there was little José lost in wonder, looking up at one of the tallest and most expensive trees in the lot! I saw Popi's face like he was remembering what Mami had said about not going crazy and spending too much money. We all stared at José, who turned to us with a big grin on his small face and pointed to what from his vantage point must have seemed like a giant redwood straight from California. Popi smiled at little José, and we all followed suit as Popi tried to persuade José that he had to be kidding, trying to steer our little brother toward some Christmas trees more his size, but to no avail. José held his ground without a grin and kept his tiny forefinger pointed at the gorgeous tree of his choice. Popi offered him a delicious hot dog from a nearby stand, knowing that José (and us along with him) loved hot dogs with a passion, but José was determined not to be moved. His little lips started to quiver and his tiny forefinger was getting tired of pointing and just before the first tears formed, Frankie, my sister, and I were practically glaring at poor Popi, who was hung up in the middle with no place to go. Popi did what he had to do and snatched José up in his arms and raised him onto his shoulder and shouted out for José and all to hear, "Hey Mista, how much you want for this tree?" Popi's eyes pleaded with the Negro brother that the price not be too high, so that he could please his youngest child along with the rest of the family.

The brother, who was an old man of about thirty, looked the tree over, lips pursed like he was into a real heavy decision. Popi finally said, "Well, Mista, what's your price?" and added under his breath, "You know, if it's too high, I won't be able to deal with it." I watched everyone closely. Their faces were somber. José had some tears ready just in case the price was out of the question.

"Well, sir, this tree is worth about ten dollars." We gasped. Ten dollars in 1938 was like two months' rent and food for months and months. Rice and beans were about five cents a pound. Popi shook his head grimly and did not dare look straight at José, who was nibbling his upper lip with his lower. "How much do you have, sir?" asked the mista. "I got a five-dollar bill from which I gotta bring home at least two for the Christmas dinner." Popi squatted down to José's size and offered him a whispered deal of how about us getting a smaller tree and José could have a whole dollar all of his own. José just shook his head and pointed his tiny forefinger up at his personal Christmas tree. Popi got up and whispered to the mista, "Say brother, what's the best you can do?"

"Wal, I sez if you don't mind giving me a hand tomorrow night, you got the tree for three bucks. Whatta ya say?"

"Done deal." Popi shook hands with the mista and said, "My name is Juan but I'm known as Johnny."

"My name is Matt," and that was that. Popi gave Matt the worn five-dollar bill and got two bucks in return. José put on one of his famous grins and we all broke out in a victorious cheer.

The five of us struggled through the snow until we were across the street in front of our building at 112 East 104th Street. We were living on the top floor and it suddenly dawned on Popi that the hallway was too narrow and the turns up the steps were even worse. We tried getting the tree into the hallway, but to no avail unless we wanted to scrape the branches clean. By this time a small crowd of neighbors had gathered around us, some of whom stopped to greet Popi and admire José's great choice of Christmas tree. Then the debate began on how in the heck were we going to get that twelve-foot tree up to our apartment, where the ceiling was only nine feet high. Some suggested we bind the tree firmly and squeeze and bend it around the banister. Popi was listening to the suggestions of the men when Mami, full of curiosity, came downstairs and out onto the street where the small crowd had gotten larger. Mami quickly sized up the situation and brightly suggested, "Why don't we pull it up the side of the building to the fifth floor and then

haul it in through the front win-
dow?" Everybody smiled and
agreed that Mami's way was the
best, and soon Pancho, who had a
small truck, came back with a long
strong rope and a small pulley. He
and Popi went up to our apartment
and quickly secured the pulley to the
side of the fire escape and then ran the
rope through it to the street below. By
this time neighbors were serving
hot coffee to whoever wanted some
and small shots of rum to those
who might be extra cold.
Everybody seemed to be extra cold.
The tall, full Christmas tree was
then tied to the rope and with Popi
on the fifth-floor fire escape directing the
hauling, Mami took charge below, with Sis
and Frankie watching José, who took in the
whole scene with a tremendous grin.
Tenants appeared on each fire escape and
hands from each of the fire escapes carefully
helped guide the tall tree upward until it reached
the fifth floor without the loss of a single branch.
Popi and Pancho pulled the big tree in amidst a
mighty cheer that rose up from the muffled street
below—the sound of victory brought about by the unity
of neighbors.

    After all that, the tree did not fit in our apartment. But
Popi was not to be defeated, so he measured it carefully and
Pancho sawed off three feet, finally making it the right size. Then
Mami had us carry the three feet of Christmas tree down to Abuela

Santiago, who lived alone but had almost everybody in the building for an adopted family. Mami took some lights and trimmings and went down to her apartment with José so he could be the one to do most of the decorating, and Abuela blessed us after we finished. I thought that this promised to be a fine Christmas, indeed.

When Christmas morning finally dawned, my siblings and I dashed out of our bedrooms to look under José's tree, which was now brightly decorated with multi-colored Christmas lights blinking on and off. Lo and behold, underneath the tree, in full view of the world, was a pair of ice skates just like the pros used, and on closer look, who the heck cared if they were second-hand, fresh from the Salvation Army thrift store? They were professional skates and that was all I cared about. *Vaya*, next year might just bring the beautiful yellow bike with balloon tires. "Merry Christmas," I began to shout and my siblings followed my example. Soon we were joined by happy kids in the hallway stomping up and down the stairs, shouting Merry Christmas and *Feliz Navidad* to one another. *Punto*.

CHRISTMAS PARTY AT THE SOUTH DANBURY CHURCH

DONALD HALL

December twenty-first
we gather at the white Church festooned
red and green, the tree flashing
green-red lights beside the altar.
After the children of Sunday School
recite Scripture, sing songs,
and scrape out solos,
they retire to dress for the finale,
to perform the pageant
again: Mary and Joseph kneeling
cradleside, Three Kings,
shepherds and shepherdesses. Their garments
are bathrobes with mothholes,
cut down from the Church's ancestors.
Standing short and long,
they stare in all directions for mothers,
sisters and brothers,
giggling and waving in recognition,
and at the South Danbury
Church, a moment before Santa
arrives with her ho-hos
and bags of popcorn, in the half-dark
of whole silence, God
enters the world as a newborn again.

THE LOUDEST VOICE

GRACE PALEY

THERE IS A CERTAIN PLACE WHERE dumb-waiters boom, doors slam, dishes crash; every window is a mother's mouth bidding the street shut up, go skate somewhere else, come home. My voice is the loudest.

There, my own mother is still as full of breathing as me and the grocer stands up to speak to her. "Mrs. Abramowitz," he says, "people should not be afraid of their children."

"Ah, Mr. Bialik," my mother replies, "if you say to her or her father 'Ssh,' they say, 'In the grave it will be quiet.'"

"From Coney Island to the cemetery," says my papa. "It's the same subway; it's the same fare."

I am right next to the pickle barrel. My pinky is making tiny whirlpools in the brine. I stop a moment to announce: "Campbell's Tomato Soup. Campbell's Vegetable Beef Soup. Campbell's S-c-otch Broth . . ."

"Be quiet," the grocer says, "the labels are coming off."

"Please, Shirley, be a little quiet," my mother begs me.

In that place the whole street groans: Be quiet! Be quiet! but steals from the happy chorus of my inside self not a tittle or a jot.

There, too, but just around the corner, is a red brick building that has been old for many years. Every morning the children stand before it in double lines which must be straight. They are not insulted. They are waiting anyway.

I am usually among them. I am, in fact, the first, since I begin with "A."

One cold morning the monitor tapped me on the shoulder. "Go to Room 409, Shirley Abramowitz," he said. I did as I was told. I went in a hurry up a down staircase to Room 409, which contained sixth-graders. I had to wait at the desk without wiggling until Mr. Hilton, their teacher, had time to speak.

After five minutes he said, "Shirley?"

"What?" I whispered.

He said, "My! My! Shirley Abramowitz! They told me you had a particularly loud, clear voice and read with lots of expression. Could that be true?"

"Oh yes," I whispered.

"In that case, don't be silly; I might very well be your teacher someday. Speak up, speak up."

"Yes," I shouted.

"More like it," he said. "Now, Shirley, can you put a ribbon in your hair or a bobby pin? It's too messy."

"Yes!" I bawled.

"Now, now, calm down." He turned to the class. "Children, not a sound. Open at page 39. Read till 52. When you finish, start again." He looked me over once more. "Now, Shirley, you know, I suppose, that Christmas is coming. We are preparing a beautiful play. Most of the parts have been given out. But I still need a child with a strong voice, lots of stamina. Do you know what stamina is? You do? Smart kid. You know, I heard you read 'The Lord is my shepherd' in Assembly yesterday. I was very impressed. Wonderful delivery. Mrs. Jordan, your teacher, speaks highly of you. Now listen to me, Shirley Abramowitz, if you want to take the part and be in the play, repeat after me, 'I swear to work harder than I ever did before.'"

I looked to heaven and said at once, "Oh, I swear." I kissed my pinky and looked at God.

"That is an actor's life, my dear," he explained. "Like a soldier's, never tardy or disobedient to his general, the director. Everything," he said, "absolutely everything will depend on you."

That afternoon, all over the building, children scraped and scrubbed the turkeys and the sheaves of corn off the schoolroom windows. Goodbye Thanksgiving. The next morning a monitor brought red paper and green paper from the office. We made new shapes and hung them on the walls and glued them to the doors.

The teachers became happier and happier. Their heads were ringing like the bells of childhood. My best friend Evie was prone to evil, but she did not get a single demerit for whispering. We learned "Holy Night" without an error. "How wonderful!" said Miss Glacé, the student teacher. "To think that some of you don't even speak the language!" We learned "Deck the Halls" and "Hark! The Herald Angels." . . . They weren't ashamed and we weren't embarrassed.

Oh, but when my mother heard about it all, she said to my father: "Misha, you don't know what's going on there. Cramer is the head of the Tickets Committee."

"Who?" asked my father. "Cramer? Oh, yes, an active woman."

"Active? Active has to have a reason. Listen," she said sadly, "I'm surprised to see my neighbors making tra-la-la for Christmas."

My father couldn't think of what to say to that. Then he decided: "You're in America! Clara, you wanted to come here. In Palestine the Arabs would be eating you alive. Europe you had pogroms. Argentina is full of Indians. Here you got Christmas. . . . Some joke, ha?"

"Very funny, Misha. What is becoming of you? If we came to a new country a long time ago to run away from tyrants, and instead we fall into a creeping pogrom, that our children learn a lot of lies, so what's the joke? Ach, Misha, your idealism is going away."

"So is your sense of humor."

"That I never had, but idealism you had a lot of."

"I'm the same Misha Abramovitch, I didn't change an iota. Ask anyone."

"Only ask me," says my mama, may she rest in peace, "I got the answer."

Meanwhile the neighbors had to think of what to say too.

Marty's father said: "You know, he has a very important part, my boy."

"Mine also," said Mrs. Sauerfeld.

"Not my boy!" said Mrs. Klieg. "I said to him no. The answer is no. When I say no! I mean no!"

The rabbi's wife said, "It's disgusting!" But no one listened to her. Under the narrow sky of God's great wisdom she wore a strawberry-blond wig.

Every day was noisy and full of experience. I was Right-hand Man. Mr. Hilton said: "How could I get along without you, Shirley?"

He said: "Your mother and father ought to get down on their knees every night and thank God for giving them a child like you."

He also said: "You're absolutely a pleasure to work with, my dear, dear child."

Sometimes he said: "For God's sakes, what did I do with the script? Shirley! Shirley! Find it."

Then I answered quietly: "Here it is, Mr. Hilton."

Once in a while, when he was very tired, he would cry out: "Shirley, I'm just tired of screaming at those kids. Will you tell Ira Pushkov not to come in till Lester points to that star the second time?"

Then I roared: "Ira Pushkov, what's the matter with you? Dope! Mr. Hilton told you five times already, don't come in till Lester points to that star the second time."

"Ach, Clara," my father asked, "what does she do there till six o'clock she can't even put the plates on the table?"

"Christmas," said my mother coldly.

"Ho! Ho!" my father said. "Christmas. What's the harm? After all, history teaches everyone. We learn from reading this is a holiday from pagan times also, candles, lights, even Chanukah. So we learn it's not altogether Christian. So if they think it's a private holiday, they're only ignorant, not patriotic. What belongs to history, belongs to all men. You want to go back to the Middle Ages? Is it better to shave your head with a secondhand razor? Does it hurt Shirley to learn to speak up? It does not. So maybe someday she won't live between the kitchen and the shop. She's not a fool."

I thank you, Papa, for your kindness. It is true about me to this day. I am foolish but I am not a fool.

That night my father kissed me and said with great interest in my career, "Shirley, tomorrow's your big day. Congrats."

"Save it," my mother said. Then she shut all the windows in order to prevent tonsillitis.

In the morning it snowed. On the street corner a tree had been decorated for us by a kind city administration. In order to miss its chilly shadow our neighbors walked three blocks east to buy a loaf of bread. The butcher pulled down black window shades to keep the colored lights from shining on his chickens. Oh, not me. On the way to school, with both my hands I tossed it a kiss of tolerance. Poor thing, it was a stranger in Egypt.

I walked straight into the auditorium past the staring children. "Go ahead, Shirley!" said the monitors. Four boys, big for their age, had already started work as prop-men and stagehands.

Mr. Hilton was very nervous. He was not even happy. Whatever he started to say ended in a sideward look of sadness. He sat slumped in the middle of the first row and asked me to help Miss Glacé. I did this, although she thought my voice too resonant and said, "Show-off!"

Parents began to arrive long before we were ready. They wanted to make a good impression. From among the yards of drapes I peeked out at the audience. I saw my embarrassed mother.

Ira, Lester, and Meyer were pasted to their beards by Miss Glacé. She almost forgot to thread the star on its wire, but I reminded her. I coughed a few times to clear my throat. Miss Glacé looked around and saw that everyone was in costume and on line waiting to play his part. She whispered, "All right . . ." Then:

Jackie Sauerfeld, the prettiest boy in first grade, parted the curtains with his skinny elbow and in a high voice sang out:

> *"Parents dear*
> *We are here*
> *To make a Christmas play in time.*
> *It we give*
> *In narrative*
> *And illustrate with pantomime."*

He disappeared.

My voice burst immediately from the wings to the great shock of Ira, Lester, and Meyer, who were waiting for it but were surprised all the same.

"I remember, I remember, the house where I was born . . ."

Miss Glacé yanked the curtain open and there it was, the house—an old hayloft, where Celia Kornbluh lay in the straw with Cindy Lou, her favorite doll. Ira, Lester, and Meyer moved slowly from the wings toward her, sometimes pointing to a moving star and sometimes ahead to Cindy Lou.

It was a long story and it was a sad story. I carefully pronounced all the words about my lonesome childhood, while little Eddie Braunstein wandered upstage and down with his shepherd's stick, looking for sheep. I brought up lonesomeness again, and not being understood at all except by some women everybody hated. Eddie was too small for that and Marty Groff took his place, wearing his father's prayer shawl. I announced twelve friends, and half the boys in the fourth grade gathered round Marty, who stood on an orange crate while my voice harangued. Sorrowful and loud, I declaimed about love and God and Man, but because of the terrible deceit of Abie Stock we came suddenly to a famous moment. Marty, whose remembering tongue I was, waited at the foot of the cross. He stared desperately at the audience. I groaned, "My God, my God, why hast thou forsaken me?" The soldiers who were sheiks grabbed poor Marty to pin him up to die, but he wrenched free, turned again to the audience, and spread his arms aloft to show despair and the end. I murmured at the top of my voice, "The rest is silence, but as everyone in this room, in this city—in this world—now knows, I shall have life eternal."

That night Mrs. Kornbluh visited our kitchen for a glass of tea.

"How's the virgin?" asked my father with a look of concern.

"For a man with a daughter, you got a fresh mouth, Abramovitch."

"Here," said my father kindly, "have some lemon, it'll sweeten your disposition."

They debated a little in Yiddish, then fell in a puddle of Russian and Polish. What I understood next was my father, who said, "Still and all, it was certainly a beautiful affair, you have to admit, introducing us to the beliefs of a different culture."

"Well, yes," said Mrs. Kornbluh. "The only thing . . . you know Charlie Turner—that cute boy in Celia's class—a couple others? They got very small parts or no part at all. In very bad taste, it seemed to me. After all, it's their religion."

"Ach," explained my mother, "what could Mr. Hilton do? They got very small voices; after all, why should they holler? The English language they know from the beginning by heart. They're blond like angels. You think it's so important they should get in the play? Christmas . . . the whole piece of goods . . . they own it."

I listened and listened until I couldn't listen any more. Too sleepy, I climbed out of bed and kneeled. I made a little church of my hands and said, "Hear, O Israel . . ." Then I called out in Yiddish, "Please, good night, good night. Ssh." My father said, "Ssh yourself," and slammed the kitchen door.

I was happy. I fell asleep at once. I had prayed for everybody: my talking family, cousins far away, passersby, and all the lonesome Christians. I expected to be heard. My voice was certainly the loudest.

Peace and Goodwill to Managers

GEORGE BERNARD SHAW

A review of *The Babes in the Wood*. The Children's Grand Pantomime.
By Arthur Sturgess and Arthur Collins. Music by J. M. Glover.
Theatre Royal, Drury Lane, 27 December 1897.

January 1, 1898

I AM SORRY TO HAVE TO introduce the subject of Christmas in these articles. It is an indecent subject; a cruel, gluttonous subject; a drunken, disorderly subject; a wasteful, disastrous subject; a wicked, cadging, lying, filthy, blasphemous, and demoralizing subject. Christmas is forced on a reluctant and disgusted nation by the shopkeepers and the press: on its own merits it would wither and shrivel in the fiery breath of universal hatred; and anyone who looked back to it would be turned into a pillar of greasy sausages. Yet, though it is over now for a year, and I can go out without positively elbowing my way through groves of carcases, I am dragged back to it, with my soul full of loathing, by the pantomime.

The pantomime ought to be a redeeming feature of Christmas, since it professedly aims at developing the artistic possibilities of our Saturnalia. But its professions are like all the other Christmas professions: what the pantomime actually does is to abuse the Christmas toleration of dullness, senselessness, vulgarity, and extravagance to a degree utterly incredible by people who have never been inside a theatre. The manager spends five hundred pounds to produce two penn'orth of effect. As a shilling's worth is needed to fill the gallery, he has to spend three thousand pounds for the "gods," seven thousand five hundred for the pit, and so on in proportion, except that when it comes to the stalls and boxes he caters for the children alone, depending on their credulity to pass off his twopence as a five-shilling piece. And yet even this is not done systematically and intelligently. . . . The rough rule is to spend money recklessly on whatever can be seen and heard and recognized as costly, and to economize on invention, fancy, dramatic faculty—in short, on brains. It is only when the brains get thrown in gratuitously through the accident of some of the contracting parties happening to possess them—a contingency which managerial care cannot always avert—that the entertainment acquires sufficient form or purpose to make it humanly apprehensible. . . .

THE OLD SCOUT: THE SEASON OF LETTER-PERFECT FAMILIES

GARRISON KEILLOR

December 12, 2006

I LOVE READING CHRISTMAS NEWSLETTERS IN which the writer bursts the bonds of modesty and comes forth with one gilt-edged paragraph after another: "Tara was top scorer on the Lady Cougars soccer team and won the lead role in the college production of *Antigone*, which by the way they are performing in the original Greek. Her essay on chaos theory as an investment strategy will be in the next issue of *Fortune* magazine, the same week she'll appear as a model in *Vogue*. How she does what she does and still makes Phi Beta Kappa is a wonderment to us all. And, yes, she is still volunteering at the homeless shelter."

I get a couple dozen Christmas letters a year, and I sit and read them in my old bathrobe as I chow down on Hostess Twinkies. Everyone in the letters is busy as beavers, piling up honors hand over fist, volunteering up a storm, traveling to Beijing, Abu Dhabi and Antarctica; nobody is in treatment or depressed or flunking out of school, though occasionally there is a child who gets shorter shrift. "Chad is adjusting well to his new school and making friends. He especially enjoys the handicrafts." How sad for Chad. There he is in reform school learning to get along with other little felons and making belts and birdhouses, but he can't possibly measure up to the goddess Tara. Or Lindsay or Meghan or Madison, each of whom is also stupendous.

This is rough on us whose children are not paragons. Most children aren't. A great many teenage children go through periods when they loathe you and go around slamming doors and playing psychotic music and saying things like "I wish I had never been born," which is a red-hot needle stuck under your fingernail. One must be very selective, writing about them for the annual newsletter. "Sean is becoming very much his own person and is unafraid to express himself. He is a lively presence in our family and his love of music is a thing to behold."

I come from Minnesota, where it's considered shameful to be shameless, where modesty is always in fashion, where self-promotion is looked at askance. Give us a gold trophy and we will have it bronzed so you won't think that we think we're special. There are no Donald Trumps in Minnesota: We strangled them all in their cribs. A football player who likes to do his special dance after scoring a touchdown is something of a freak.

The basis of modesty is winter. When it's ten below zero and the wind is whipping across the tundra, there is no such thing as stylish and smart, and everybody's nose runs. And the irony is, if you're smart and stylish, nobody will tell you about your nose. You look in the rearview mirror and you see a gob of green snot hanging from your left nostril and you wonder, "How long have I been walking around like that? Is that why all those people were smiling at me?"

Yes, it is.

So we don't toot our own horns. We can be rather ostentatious in our modesty and can deprecate faster than you can compliment us. We are averse to flattery. We just try to focus on keeping our noses clean.

So here is my Christmas letter:

Dear friends. We are getting older but are in fairly good shape and moving forward insofar as we can tell. We still drink strong coffee and read the paper and drive the same old cars. We plan to go to Norway next summer. We think that this war is an unmitigated disaster that will wind up costing a trillion dollars and we worry for our country. Our child enjoys her new school and is making friends. She was a horsie in the church Christmas pageant and hunkered down beside the manger and seemed to be singing when she was supposed to. We go on working and hope to be adequate to the challenges of the coming year but are by no means confident. It's winter. God is around here somewhere but does not appear to be guiding our government at the moment. Nonetheless we persist. We see kindness all around us and bravery and we are cheered by the good humor of young people. The crabapple tree over the driveway is bare, but we have a memory of pink blossoms and expect them to return. God bless you all.

THE COMPUTER'S FIRST CHRISTMAS CARD

EDWIN MORGAN

jollymerry
hollyberry
jollyberry
merryholly
happyjolly
jollyjelly
jellybelly
bellyberry
hollyheppy
jollyMolly
merryJerry
merryHarry

hoppyBarry
heppyJarry
boppyheppy
berryjorry
jorryjolly
moppyjelly
Mollymerry
Jerryjolly
bellyboppy
jorryhoppy
hollymoppy
Barrymerry

Jarryheppy
happyboppy
boppyjolly
jollymerry
merrymerry
merrymerry
merryChris
ammeryasa
Chrismerry
asMERRY CHR
YSANTHEMUM

Lynch v. Donnelly, 465 U.S. 668 (1984)

THE CHIEF JUSTICE DELIVERED THE OPINION of the court.

We granted certiorari to decide whether the Establishment Clause of the First Amendment prohibits a municipality from including a crèche, or Nativity scene, in its annual Christmas display.

Each year, in cooperation with the downtown retail merchants' association, the City of Pawtucket, Rhode Island, erects a Christmas display as part of its observance of the Christmas holiday season. The display is situated in a park owned by a non-profit organization and located in the heart of the shopping district. The display is essentially like those to be found in hundreds of towns or cities across the Nation—often on public grounds—during the Christmas season. The Pawtucket display comprises many of the figures and decorations traditionally associated with Christmas, including, among other things, a Santa Claus house, reindeer pulling Santa's sleigh, candy-striped poles, a Christmas tree, carolers, cutout figures representing such characters as a clown, an elephant, and a teddy bear, hundreds of colored lights, a large banner that reads "SEASONS GREETINGS," and the crèche at issue here. All components of this display are owned by the City.

The crèche, which has been included in the display for 40 or more years, consists of the traditional figures, including the Infant Jesus, Mary and Joseph, angels, shepherds, kings, and animals, all ranging in height from 5" to 5'. In 1973, when the present crèche was acquired, it cost the City $1365; it now is valued at $200. The erection and dismantling of the crèche costs the City about $20 per year; nominal expenses are incurred in lighting the crèche. No money has been expended on its maintenance for the past 10 years. . . .

In every Establishment Clause case, we must reconcile the inescapable tension between the objective of preventing unnecessary intrusion of either the church or the state upon the other, and the reality that, as the Court has so often noted, total separation of the two is not possible. . . .

When viewed in the proper context of the Christmas Holiday season, it is apparent that, on this record, there is insufficient evidence to establish that the inclusion of the crèche is a purposeful or surreptitious effort to express some kind of subtle governmental advocacy of a particular religious message. In a pluralistic society a variety of motives and purposes are implicated. The City, like the Congress and Presidents, however, has principally taken note of a significant historical religious event long celebrated in the Western World. The crèche in the display depicts the historical origins of this traditional event long recognized as a National Holiday.

The narrow question is whether there is a secular purpose for Pawtucket's display of the crèche. The display is sponsored by the City to celebrate the Holiday and to depict the origins of that Holiday. These are legitimate secular purposes. . . .

We are satisfied that the City has a secular purpose for including the crèche, that the City has not impermissibly advanced religion, and that including the crèche does not create excessive entanglement between religion and government. . . .

The crèche, like a painting, is passive; admittedly it is a reminder of the origins of Christmas. Even the traditional, purely secular displays extant at Christmas, with or without a crèche, would inevitably recall the religious nature of the Holiday. The display engenders a friendly community spirit of good will in keeping with the season.

The crèche may well have special meaning to those whose faith includes the celebration of religious masses, but none who sense the origins of the Christmas celebration would fail to be aware of its religious implications. That the display brings people into the central city, and serves commercial interests and benefits merchants and their employees, does not, as the dissent points out, determine the character of the display. That a prayer invoking Divine guidance in Congress is preceded and followed by debate and partisan conflict over taxes, budgets, national defense, and myriad mundane subjects, for example, has never been thought to demean or taint the sacredness of the invocation.

Of course the crèche is identified with one religious faith but no more so than the examples we have set out from prior cases in which we found no conflict with the Establishment Clause. It would be ironic, however, if the inclusion of a single symbol of a particular historic religious event, as part of a celebration acknowledged in the Western World for 20 centuries, and in this country by the people, by the Executive Branch, by the Congress, and the courts for two centuries, would so "taint" the City's exhibit as to render it violative of the Establishment Clause. To forbid the use of this one passive symbol—the crèche—at the very time people are taking note of the season with Christmas hymns and carols in public schools and other public places, and while the Congress and Legislatures open sessions with prayers by paid chaplains would be a stilted over-reaction contrary to our history and to our holdings. If the presence of the crèche in this display violates the Establishment Clause, a host of other forms of taking official note of Christmas, and of our religious heritage, are equally offensive to the Constitution. . . .

We hold that, notwithstanding the religious significance of the crèche, the City of Pawtucket has not violated the Establishment Clause of the First Amendment.

THE HOLLY AND THE IVY

ENGLISH TRADITIONAL CAROL

The holly and the ivy,
When they are both full grown,
Of all the trees that are in the wood,
The holly bears the crown.
O, the rising of the sun,
And the running of the deer,
The playing of the merry organ,
Sweet singing in the choir.

The holly wears a blossom
As white as the lily flower;
And Mary bore sweet Jesus Christ
To be our sweet Saviour.
O, the rising of the sun,
And the running of the deer,
The playing of the merry organ,
Sweet singing in the choir.

The holly bears a berry
As red as any blood;
And Mary bore sweet Jesus Christ
To do poor sinners good.
O, the rising of the sun,
And the running of the deer,

The playing of the merry organ,
Sweet singing in the choir.

The holly bears a prickle
As sharp as any thorn;
And Mary bore sweet Jesus Christ
On Christmas Day in the morn.
O, the rising of the sun,
And the running of the deer,
The playing of the merry organ,
Sweet singing in the choir.

The holly bears a bark
As bitter as any gall;
And Mary bore sweet Jesus Christ
For to redeem us all.
O, the rising of the sun,
And the running of the deer,
The playing of the merry organ,
Sweet singing in the choir.

The holly and the ivy
Now both are full well grown,
Of all the trees that are in the wood,
The holly bears the crown.
O, the rising of the sun,
And the running of the deer,
The playing of the merry organ,
Sweet singing in the choir.

Santa Claus Is
Comin' to Town

Santa Claus Is Comin' to Town

WORDS BY HAVEN GILLESPIE
MUSIC BY J. FRED COOTS

You better watch out,
You better not cry,
Better not pout,
I'm telling you why:
Santa Claus is comin' to town.

He's making a list
And checking it twice,
Gonna find out who's naughty and nice:
Santa Claus is comin' to town.

He sees you when you're sleepin'
He knows when you're awake.
He knows if you've been bad or good,
So be good for goodness sake.

Oh! you better watch out,
You better not cry,
Better not pout,
I'm telling you why:
Santa Claus is comin' to town.

A Visit from St. Nicholas

CLEMENT CLARKE MOORE

'Twas the night before Christmas, when all through the house
Not a creature was stirring, not even a mouse;
The stockings were hung by the chimney with care,
In hopes that St. Nicholas soon would be there;
The children were nestled all snug in their beds,
while visions of sugar-plums danced in their heads,
And mamma in her kerchief, and I in my cap,
Had just settled down for a long winter's nap,—
When out on the lawn there arose such a clatter,
I sprang from the bed to see what was the matter.
Away to the window I flew like a flash,
Tore open the shutters and threw up the sash.

The moon on the breast of the new-fallen snow
Gave the lustre of midday to objects below;
When what to my wondering eyes should appear,
But a miniature sleigh and eight tiny reindeer,
With a little old driver, so lively and quick
I knew in a moment it must be St. Nick.
More rapid than eagles his coursers they came,
And he whistled and shouted, and called them by name:
"Now, Dasher! now, Dancer! now, Prancer and Vixen!
On, Comet! on, Cupid! on, Donder and Blitzen!
To the top of the porch! to the top of the wall!
Now dash away! dash away! dash away all!"
As dry leaves that before the wild hurricane fly,
When they meet with an obstacle mount to the sky,
So up to the house-top the coursers they flew,
With the sleigh full of toys,—and St. Nicholas too.
And then, in a twinkling I heard on the roof
The prancing and pawing of each little hoof.
As I drew in my hand, and was turning around,
Down the chimney St. Nicholas came with a bound.
He was dressed all in fur from his head to his foot,
And his clothes were all tarnished with ashes and soot;
A bundle of toys he had flung on his back,
And he looked like a peddler just opening his pack.
His eyes, how they twinkled! his dimples, how merry!
His cheeks were like roses, his nose like a cherry;
His droll little mouth was drawn up like a bow,
And the beard of his chin was as white as the snow.
The stump of a pipe he held tight in his teeth,
And the smoke it encircled his head like a wreath.
He had a broad face and a little round belly
That shook, when he laughed, like a bowl full of jelly.

He was chubby and plump,—a right jolly old elf;
And I laughed, when I saw him, in spite of myself,
A wink of his eye and a twist of his head
Soon gave me to know I had nothing to dread.
He spoke not a word, but went straight to his work,
And filled all the stockings; then turned with a jerk,
And laying his finger aside of his nose,
And giving a nod, up the chimney he rose.
He sprang to his sleigh, to his team gave a whistle,
And away they all flew like the down of a thistle;
But I heard him exclaim, ere he drove out of sight,
"Happy Christmas to all, and to all a good-night!"

Is There a Santa Claus? ("Yes, Virginia")

FRANCIS P. CHURCH,
Editor, *The New York Sun*

September 21, 1897

WE TAKE PLEASURE IN ANSWERING AT once and thus prominently the communication below, expressing at the same time our great gratification that its faithful author is numbered among the friends of THE SUN:

"Dear Editor: I am 8 years old.

"Some of my little friends say there is no Santa Claus.

"Papa says 'If you see it in THE SUN it's so.'

"Please tell me the truth: is there a Santa Claus?

"Virginia O'Hanlon.

"115 West Ninety-fifth Street."

Virginia, your little friends are wrong. They have been affected by the skepticism of a skeptical age. They do not believe except they see. They think that nothing can be which is not comprehensible by their little minds. All minds, Virginia, whether they be men's or children's, are little. In this great universe of ours man is a mere insect, an ant, in his intellect, as compared with the boundless world about him, as measured by the intelligence capable of grasping the whole of truth and knowledge.

Yes, Virginia, there is a Santa Claus. He exists as certainly as love and generosity and devotion exist, and you know that they abound and give to your life its highest beauty and joy. Alas! how dreary would be the world if there were no Santa Claus. It would be as dreary as if there were no Virginias. There would be no child-like faith then, no poetry, no romance to make tolerable this existence. We should have no enjoyment, except in sense and sight. The external light with which childhood fills the world would be extinguished.

Not believe in Santa Claus! You might as well not believe in fairies! You might get your papa to hire men to watch in all the chimneys on Christmas Eve to catch Santa Claus, but even if they did not see Santa Claus coming down, what would that prove! Nobody sees Santa Claus, but that is no sign that there is no Santa Claus. The most real things in the world are those that neither children nor men can see. Did you ever see fairies dancing on the lawn? Of course not, but that's no proof that they are not there. Nobody can conceive or imagine all the wonders there are unseen and unseeable in the world.

You may tear apart the baby's rattle and see what makes the noise inside, but there is a veil covering the unseen world which not the strongest man, nor even the united strength of all the strongest men that ever lived, could tear apart. Only faith, fancy, poetry, love, romance, can push aside that curtain and view and picture the supernal beauty and glory beyond. Is it all real? Ah, Virginia, in all this world, there is nothing else real and abiding.

No Santa Claus! Thank God! he lives, and he lives forever. A thousand years from now, Virginia, nay, ten times ten thousand years from now, he will continue to make glad the heart of childhood.

Letter to
Michelle Rochon

JOHN F. KENNEDY

October 28, 1961

The White House

Dear Michelle:

I was glad to get your letter about trying to stop the Russians from bombing the North Pole and risking the life of Santa Claus.

I share your concern about the atmospheric testing of the Soviet Union, not only for the North Pole but for countries throughout the world; not only for Santa Claus but for people throughout the world.

However, you must not worry about Santa Claus. I talked with him yesterday and he is fine. He will be making his rounds this Christmas.

Sincerely,

John Kennedy

Miss Michelle Rochon
Marine City, Michigan

Letter from Santa Claus

MARK TWAIN

SANTA CLAUS, WHOM PEOPLE SOMETIMES CALL THE MAN IN THE MOON:

My dear Susy Clemens:

I have received and read all the letters which you and your little sister
have written me by the hand of your mother and your nurses; I have also read
those which you little people have written me with your own hands—for
although you did not use any characters that are in grown people's alphabet,
you used the characters that all children in all lands on earth and in the twin-
kling stars use; and as all my subjects in the moon are children and use no
character but that, you will easily understand that I can read your and your
baby sister's jagged and fantastic marks without any trouble at all. But I had
trouble with those letters which you dictated through your mother and the
nurses, for I am a foreigner and cannot read English writing well. You will
find that I made no mistakes about the things which you and the baby
ordered in your own letters—I went down your chimney at midnight when
you were asleep and delivered them all myself—and kissed both of you, too,
because you are good children, well-trained, nice-mannered, and about the
most obedient little people I ever saw. But in the letters which you dictated
there were some words which I could not make out for certain, and one or
two orders which I could not fill because we ran out of stock. Our last lot of
kitchen-furniture for dolls has just gone to a very poor little child in the
North Star away up in the cold country above the Big Dipper. Your mama
can show you that star and you will say: "little Snow Flake" (for that is the
child's name) "I'm glad you got that furniture, for you need it more than I."
That is, you must write that, with your own hand, and Snow Flake will write

you an answer. If you only spoke it she wouldn't hear you. Make your letter light and thin, for the distance is great and the postage very heavy.

There was a word or two in your mama's letter which I couldn't be certain of. I took it to be "trunk full of doll's clothes." Is that it? I will call at your kitchen door about nine o'clock this morning to inquire. But I must not see anybody and I must not speak to anybody but you. When the kitchen doorbell rings George must be blindfolded and sent to open the door. Then he must go back to the dining-room or the china closet and take the cook with him. You must tell George he must walk on tiptoe and not speak—otherwise he will die some day. Then you must go up to the nursery and stand on a chair or the nurse's bed and put your ear to the speaking-tube that leads down to the kitchen and when I whistle through it you must speak in the tube and say, "Welcome, Santa Claus!" Then I will ask whether it was a trunk you ordered or not. If you say it was, I shall ask you what color you want the trunk to be. Your mama will help you to name a nice color and then you must tell me every single thing in detail which you want the trunk to contain. Then when I say "Goodbye and Merry Christmas to my little Susy Clemens," you must say "Goodbye, good old Santa Claus, I thank you very much and please tell that little Snow Flake I will look at her star tonight and she must look down here—I will be right in the West bay-window; and every fine night I will look at her star and say, 'I know somebody up there and like her, too.'" Then you must go down into the library and make George close all the doors that open into the main hall, and everybody must keep still for a little while. I will go to the moon and get those things and in a few minutes I will come down the chimney that belongs to the fireplace that is in the hall—if it is a trunk you want—because I couldn't get such a thing as a trunk down the nursery chimney, you know.

People may talk if they want, until they hear my footsteps in the hall. Then you tell them to keep quiet a little while till I go back up the chimney. Maybe you will not hear my footsteps at all—so you may go now and then and peep through the dining-room doors, and by and by you will see that thing which you want, right under the piano in the drawing-room—for I shall put it there. If I should leave any snow in the hall, you must tell George to sweep it into the fireplace, for I haven't time to do such things. George must not use a broom, but a rag—else he will die some day. You must watch George and not let him run into danger. If my boot shall leave a stain on the marble, George must not holy-stone it away. Leave it there always in memory of my visit; and whenever you look at it or show it to anybody you must let it remind you to be a good little girl. Whenever you are naughty and somebody points to that mark which your good old Santa Claus's boot made on the marble, what will you say, little Sweetheart?

Goodbye for a few minutes, till I come down to the world and ring the kitchen door-bell.

> Your loving Santa Claus
> Palace of St. Nicholas in the Moon,
> Christmas Morning

SANTA'S STOCKING

KATHERINE LEE BATES

Dame Snow has been knitting all day
With needles of crystal and pearl
To make a big, beautiful stocking
For Santa, her merriest son;
And now in some wonderful way
She has hung it, by twist and by twirl,
On the tip of the moon, and sits rocking,
Old mother, her day's work done.

How long and how empty it flaps,
Like a new, white cloud in the sky!
The stars gleam above it for candles;
But who is to fill it and trim?
Dame Snow in her rocking-chair naps.
When Santa comes home by and by,
Will he find—O scandal of scandals! —
No Christmas at all for him? . . .

His pack is bursting with toys;
The dollies cling round his neck;
And sleds come slithering after
As he takes the roofs at a run.
Blithe lover of girls and boys,
Bonbons he pours by the peck;
Holidays, revels and laughter,
Feasting and frolic and fun.

Who would dream that his kind heart aches
—Heart shaped like a candied pear,
Sweet heart of our housetop rover—
For the homes where no carols resound,
For the little child that wakes
To a hearth all cold and bare,
For Santa, his white world over,
Finds Christmas doesn't go round!. . .

Let us bring the dear Saint from our store
Fair gifts wrapped softly in love;
Let all gentle children come flocking,
Glad children whose Christmas is sure;
Let us bring him more treasures and more,
While the star-candles glisten above,
For whatever we put in his stocking,
Santa Claus gives to the poor.

MR. EDWARDS
MEETS SANTA CLAUS

from *Little House on the Prairie*

LAURA INGALLS WILDER

THE DAYS WERE SHORT AND COLD, the wind whistled sharply, but there was no snow. Cold rains were falling. Day after day the rain fell, pattering on the roof and pouring from the eaves.

Mary and Laura stayed close by the fire, sewing their nine-patch quilt blocks, or cutting paper dolls from scraps of wrapping-paper, and hearing the wet sound of the rain. Every night was so cold that they expected to see snow next morning, but in the morning they saw only sad, wet grass.

They pressed their noses against the squares of glass in the windows that Pa had made, and they were glad they could see out. But they wished they could see snow.

Laura was anxious because Christmas was near, and Santa Claus and his reindeer could not travel without snow. Mary was afraid that, even if it snowed, Santa Claus could not find them, so far away in Indian Territory. When they asked Ma about this, she said she didn't know.

"What day is it?" they asked her, anxiously. "How many more days till Christmas?" And they counted off the days on their fingers, till there was only one more day left.

Rain was still falling that morning. There was not one crack in the gray sky. They felt almost sure there would be no Christmas. Still, they kept hoping.

Just before noon the light changed. The clouds broke and drifted apart, shining white in a clear blue sky. The sun shone, birds sang, and thousands of drops of water sparkled on the grasses. But when Ma opened the door to let in the fresh, cold air, they heard the creek roaring.

They had not thought about the creek. Now they knew they would have no Christmas, because Santa Claus could not cross that roaring creek.

Pa came in, bringing a big fat turkey. If it weighed less than twenty pounds, he said, he'd eat it, feathers and all. He asked Laura, "How's that for a Christmas dinner? Think you can manage one of those drumsticks?"

She said, yes, she could. But she was sober. Then Mary asked him if the creek was going down, and he said it was still rising.

Ma said it was too bad. She hated to think of Mr. Edwards eating his bachelor cooking all alone on Christmas day. Mr. Edwards had been asked to eat Christmas dinner with them, but Pa shook his head and said a man would risk his neck, trying to cross that creek now.

"No," he said. "That current's too strong. We'll just have to make up our minds that Edwards won't be here tomorrow."

Of course that meant that Santa Claus could not come, either.

Laura and Mary tried not to mind too much. They watched Ma dress the wild turkey, and it was a very fat turkey. They were lucky little girls, to have a good house to live in, and a warm fire to sit by, and such a turkey for their Christmas dinner. Ma said so, and it was true. Ma said it was too bad that Santa Claus couldn't come this year, but they were such good girls that he hadn't forgotten them; he would surely come next year.

Still, they were not happy.

After supper that night they washed their hands and faces, buttoned their red-flannel nightgowns, tied their night-cap strings, and soberly said their prayers. They lay down in bed and pulled the covers up. It did not seem at all like Christmas time.

Pa and Ma sat silent by the fire. After a while Ma asked why Pa didn't play the fiddle, and he said, "I don't seem to have the heart to, Caroline."

After a longer while, Ma suddenly stood up.

"I'm going to hang up your stockings, girls," she said. "Maybe something will happen."

Laura's heart jumped. But then she thought again of the creek and she knew nothing could happen.

Ma took one of Mary's clean stockings and one of Laura's, and she hung them from the mantel-shelf, on either side of the fireplace. Laura and Mary watched her over the edge of their bed-covers.

"Now go to sleep," Ma said, kissing them good night. "Morning will come quicker if you're asleep."

She sat down again by the fire and Laura almost went to sleep. She woke up a little when she heard Pa say, "You've only made it worse, Caroline." And she thought she heard Ma say: "No, Charles. There's the white sugar." But perhaps she was dreaming.

Then she heard Jack growl savagely. The door-latch rattled and someone said, "Ingalls! Ingalls!" Pa was stirring up the fire, and when he opened the door Laura saw that it was morning. The outdoors was gray.

"Great fishhooks, Edwards! Come in, man! What's happened?" Pa exclaimed.

Laura saw the stockings limply dangling, and she scrooged her shut eyes into the pillow. She heard Pa piling wood on the fire, and she heard Mr. Edwards say he had carried his clothes on his head when he swam the creek. His teeth rattled and his voice shivered. He would be all right, he said, as soon as he got warm.

"It was too big a risk, Edwards," Pa said. "We're glad you're here, but that was too big a risk for a Christmas dinner."

"Your little ones had to have a Christmas," Mr. Edwards replied. "No creek could stop me, after I fetched them their gifts from Independence."

Laura sat straight up in bed. "Did you see Santa Claus?" she shouted.

"I sure did," Mr. Edwards said.

"Where? When? What did he look like? What did he say? Did he really give you something for us?" Mary and Laura cried.

"Wait, wait a minute!" Mr. Edwards laughed. And Ma said she would put the presents in the stockings, as Santa Claus intended. She said they mustn't look.

Mr. Edwards came and sat on the floor by their bed, and he answered every question they asked him. They honestly tried not to look at Ma, and they didn't quite see what she was doing.

When he saw the creek rising, Mr. Edwards said, he had known that Santa Claus could not get across it. ("But you crossed it," Laura said. "Yes," Mr. Edwards replied, "but Santa Claus is too old and fat. He couldn't make it, where a long, lean razor-back like me could do so.") And Mr. Edwards reasoned that if Santa Claus couldn't cross the creek, likely he would come no farther south than Independence. Why should he come forty miles across the prairie, only to be turned back? Of course he wouldn't do that!

So Mr. Edwards had walked to Independence. ("In the rain?" Mary asked. Mr. Edwards said he wore his rubber coat.) And there, coming down the street in Independence, he had met Santa Claus. ("In the daytime?" Laura asked. She hadn't thought that anyone could see Santa Claus in the daytime. No, Mr. Edwards said; it was night, but light shone out across the street from the saloons.)

Well, the first thing Santa Claus said was, "Hello, Edwards!" ("Did he know you?" Mary asked, and Laura asked, "How did you know he was really Santa Claus?" Mr. Edwards said that Santa Claus knew everybody. And he had recognized Santa at once by his whiskers. Santa Claus had the longest, thickest, whitest set of whiskers west of the Mississippi.)

So Santa Claus said, "Hello, Edwards! Last time I saw you you were sleeping on a cornshuck bed in Tennessee." And Mr. Edwards well remembered the little pair of red-yarn mittens that Santa Claus had left for him that time.

Then Santa Claus said: "I understand you're living now down along the Verdigris River. Have you ever met up, down yonder, with two little young girls named Mary and Laura?"

"I surely am acquainted with them," Mr. Edwards replied.

"It rests heavy on my mind," said Santa Claus. "They are both of them sweet, pretty, good little young things, and I know they are expecting me. I surely do hate to disappoint two good little girls like them. Yet with the water up the way it is, I can't ever make it across that creek. I can figure no way whatsoever to get to their cabin this year. Edwards," Santa Claus said, "would you do me the favor to fetch them their gifts this one time?"

"I'll do that, and with pleasure," Mr. Edwards told him.

Then Santa Claus and Mr. Edwards stepped across the street to the hitching-posts where the pack-mule was tied. ("Didn't he have his reindeer?" Laura asked.

"You know he couldn't," Mary said. "There isn't any snow." Exactly, said Mr. Edwards. Santa Claus traveled with a pack-mule in the southwest.)

And Santa Claus uncinched the pack and looked through it, and he took out the presents for Mary and Laura.

"Oh, what are they?" Laura cried; but Mary asked, "Then what did he do?"

Then he shook hands with Mr. Edwards, and he swung up on his fine bay horse. Santa Claus rode well for a man of his weight and build. And he tucked his long, white whiskers under his bandana. "So long, Edwards," he said, and he rode away on the Fort Dodge trail, leading his pack-mule and whistling.

Laura and Mary were silent an instant, thinking of that.

Then Ma said, "You may look now, girls."

Something was shining bright in the top of Laura's stocking. She squealed and jumped out of bed. So did Mary, but Laura beat her to the fireplace. And the shining thing was a glittering new tin cup.

Mary had one exactly like it.

These new tin cups were their very own. Now they each had a cup to drink out of. Laura jumped up and down and shouted and laughed, but Mary stood still and looked with shining eyes at her own tin cup.

Then they plunged their hands into the stockings again. And they pulled out two long, long sticks of candy. It was peppermint candy, striped red and white. They looked and looked at the beautiful candy, and Laura licked her stick, just one lick. But Mary was not so greedy. She didn't take even one lick of her stick.

Those stockings weren't empty yet. Mary and Laura pulled out two small packages. They unwrapped them, and each found a little heart-shaped cake. Over their delicate brown tops was sprinkled white sugar. The sparkling grains lay like tiny drifts of snow.

The cakes were too pretty to eat. Mary and Laura just looked at them. But at last Laura turned hers over, and she nibbled a tiny nibble from underneath, where it wouldn't show. And the inside of the little cake was white!

It had been made of pure white flour, and sweetened with white sugar.

Laura and Mary never would have looked in their stockings again. The cups and the cakes and the candy were almost too much. They were too happy to speak. But Ma asked if they were sure the stockings were empty.

Then they put their hands down inside them, to make sure.

And in the very toe of each stocking was a shining bright, new penny!

They had never even thought of such a thing as having a penny. Think of having a whole penny for your very own. Think of having a cup and a cake and a stick of candy and a penny.

There never had been such a Christmas.

Now of course, right away, Laura and Mary should have thanked Mr. Edwards for bringing those lovely presents all the way from Independence. But they had forgotten all about Mr. Edwards. They had even forgotten Santa Claus. In a minute they would have remembered, but before they did, Ma said, gently, "Aren't you going to thank Mr. Edwards?"

"Oh, thank you, Mr. Edwards! Thank you!" they said, and they meant it with all their hearts. Pa shook Mr. Edwards' hand, too, and shook it again. Pa and Ma and Mr. Edwards acted as if they were almost crying, Laura didn't know why. So she gazed again at her beautiful presents.

She looked up again when Ma gasped. And Mr. Edwards was taking sweet potatoes out of his pockets. He said they had helped to balance the package on his head when he swam across the creek. He thought Pa and Ma might like them, with the Christmas turkey.

There were nine sweet potatoes. Mr. Edwards had brought them all the way from town, too. It was just too much. Pa said so. "It's too much, Edwards," he said. They never could thank him enough.

Mary and Laura were too excited to eat breakfast. They drank the milk from their shining new cups, but they could not swallow the rabbit stew and cornmeal mush.

"Don't make them, Charles," Ma said. "It will soon be dinner-time."

For Christmas dinner there was the tender, juicy, roasted turkey. There were the sweet potatoes, baked in the ashes and carefully wiped so that you could eat the good skins, too. There was a loaf of salt-rising bread made from the last of the white flour.

And after all that there were stewed dried blackberries and little cakes. But these little cakes were made with brown sugar and they did not have white sugar sprinkled over their tops.

Then Pa and Ma and Mr. Edwards sat by the fire and talked about Christmas times back in Tennessee and up north in the Big Woods. But Mary and Laura looked at their beautiful cakes and played with their pennies and drank their water out of their new cups. And little by little they licked and sucked their sticks of candy, till each stick was sharp-pointed on one end.

That was a happy Christmas.

A Chaparral Christmas Gift

O. HENRY

THE ORIGINAL CAUSE OF THE TROUBLE was about twenty years in growing.

At the end of that time it was worth it.

Had you lived anywhere within fifty miles of Sundown Ranch you would have heard of it. It possessed a quantity of jet-black hair, a pair of extremely frank, deep-brown eyes and a laugh that rippled across the prairie like the sound of a hidden brook. The name of it was Rosita McMullen; and she was the daughter of old man McMullen of the Sundown Sheep Ranch.

There came riding on red roan steeds—or, to be more explicit, on a paint and a flea-bitten sorrel—two wooers. One was Madison Lane, and the other was the Frio Kid. But at that time they did not call him the Frio Kid, for he had not earned the honors of special nomenclature. His name was simply Johnny McRoy.

It must not be supposed that these two were the sum of the agreeable Rosita's admirers. The broncos of a dozen others champed their bits at the long hitching rack of the Sundown Ranch. Many were the sheeps'-ewes that were cast in those savannas that did not belong to the flocks of Dan McMullen. But of all the cavaliers, Madison Lane and Johnny McRoy galloped far ahead, wherefore they are to be chronicled.

Madison Lane, a young cattleman from the Nueces country, won the race. He and Rosita were married one Christmas day. Armed, hilarious, vociferous, magnanimous, the cowmen and the sheepmen, laying aside their hereditary hatred, joined forces to celebrate the occasion.

Sundown Ranch was sonorous with the cracking of jokes and sixshooters, the shine of buckles and bright eyes, the outspoken congratulations of the herders of kine.

But while the wedding feast was at its liveliest there descended upon it Johnny McRoy, bitten by jealousy, like one possessed.

"I'll give you a Christmas present," he yelled, shrilly, at the door, with his .45 in his hand. Even then he had some reputation as an offhand shot.

His first bullet cut a neat underbit in Madison Lane's right ear. The barrel of his gun moved an inch. The next shot would have been the bride's had not Carson, a sheepman, possessed a mind with triggers somewhat well oiled and in repair. The guns of the wedding party had been hung, in their belts, upon nails in the wall when they sat at table, as a concession to good taste. But Carson, with great promptness, hurled his plate of roast venison and frijoles at McRoy, spoiling his aim. The second bullet, then, only shattered the white petals of a Spanish dagger flower suspended two feet above Rosita's head.

The guests spurned their chairs and jumped for their weapons. It was considered an improper act to shoot the bride and groom at a wedding. In about six seconds there were twenty or so bullets due to be whizzing in the direction of Mr. McRoy.

"I'll shoot better next time," yelled Johnny; "and there'll be a next time." He backed rapidly out the door.

Carson, the sheepman, spurred on to attempt further exploits by the success of his plate-throwing, was first to reach the door. McRoy's bullet from the darkness laid him low.

The cattlemen then swept out upon him, calling for vengeance, for, while the slaughter of a sheepman has not always lacked condonement, it was a decided misdemeanor in this instance. Carson was innocent; he was no accomplice at the matrimonial proceedings; nor had any one heard him quote the line "Christmas comes but once a year" to the guests.

But the sortie failed in its vengeance. McRoy was on his horse and away, shouting back curses and threats as he galloped into the concealing chaparral.

That night was the birthnight of the Frio Kid. He became the "bad man" of that portion of the State. The rejection of his suit by Miss McMullen turned him to a dangerous man. When officers went after him for the shooting of Carson, he killed two of them, and entered upon the life of an outlaw. He became a marvelous shot with either hand. He would turn up in towns and settlements, raise a quarrel

at the slightest opportunity, pick off his man and laugh at the officers of the law. He was so cool, so deadly, so rapid, so inhumanly blood-thirsty that none but faint attempts were ever made to capture him. When he was at last shot and killed by a little one-armed Mexican who was nearly dead himself from fright, the Frio Kid had the deaths of eighteen men on his head. About half of these were killed in fair duels depending upon the quickness of the draw. The other half were men whom he assassinated from absolute wantonness and cruelty.

Many tales are told along the border of his impudent courage and daring. But he was not one of the breed of desperadoes who have seasons of generosity and even of softness. They say he never had mercy on the object of his anger. Yet at this and every Christmastide it is well to give each one credit, if it can be done, for whatever speck of good he may have possessed. If the Frio Kid ever did a kindly act or felt a throb of generosity in his heart it was once at such a time and season, and this is the way it happened.

One who has been crossed in love should never breathe the odor from the blossoms of the ratama tree. It stirs the memory to a dangerous degree.

One December in the Frio country there was a ratama tree in full bloom, for the winter had been as warm as springtime. That way rode the Frio Kid and his satellite co-murderer, Mexican Frank. The Kid reined in his mustang, and sat in his saddle, thoughtful and grim, with dangerously narrowing eyes. The rich, sweet scent touched him somewhere beneath his ice and iron.

"I don't know what I've been thinking about, Mex," he remarked in his usual mild drawl, "to have forgot all about a Christmas present I got to give. I'm going to ride over to-morrow night and shoot Madison Lane in his own house. He got my girl—Rosita would have had me if he hadn't cut into the game. I wonder why I happened to overlook it up to now?"

"Ah, shucks, Kid," said Mexican, "don't talk foolishness. You know you can't get within a mile of Mad Lane's house to-morrow night. I see old man Allen day before yesterday, and he says Mad is going to have Christmas doings at his house. You remember how you shot up the festivities when Mad was married, and about the threats you made? Don't you suppose Mad Lane'll kind of keep his eye open for a certain Mr. Kid? You plumb make me tired, Kid, with such remarks."

"I'm going," repeated the Frio Kid, without heat, "to go to Madison Lane's Christmas doings, and kill him. I ought to have done it a long time ago. Why, Mex, just two weeks ago I dreamed me and Rosita was married instead of her and him; and we was living in a house, and I could see her smiling at me, and—oh! h—l, Mex, he got her; and I'll get him—yes, sir, on Christmas Eve he got her, and then's when I'll get him."

"There's other ways of committing suicide," advised Mexican. "Why don't you go and surrender to the sheriff?"

"I'll get him," said the Kid.

Christmas Eve fell as balmy as April. Perhaps there was a hint of far-away frostiness in the air, but it tingled like seltzer, perfumed faintly with late prairie blossoms and the mesquite grass.

When night came the five or six rooms of the ranch-house were brightly lit. In one room was a Christmas tree, for the Lanes had a boy of three, and a dozen or more guests were expected from the nearer ranches.

At nightfall Madison Lane called aside Jim Belcher and three other cowboys employed on his ranch.

"Now, boys," said Lane, "keep your eyes open. Walk around the house and watch the road well. All of you know the 'Frio Kid,' as they call him now, and if you see him, open fire on him without asking any questions. I'm not afraid of his coming around, but Rosita is. She's been afraid he'd come in on us every Christmas since we were married."

The guests had arrived in buckboards and on horseback, and were making themselves comfortable inside.

The evening went along pleasantly. The guests enjoyed and praised Rosita's excellent supper, and afterward the men scattered in groups about the rooms or on the broad "gallery," smoking and chatting.

The Christmas tree, of course, delighted the youngsters, and above all were they pleased when Santa Claus himself in magnificent white beard and furs appeared and began to distribute the toys.

"It's my papa," announced Billy Sampson, aged six. "I've seen him wear 'em before."

Berkly, a sheepman, an old friend of Lane, stopped Rosita as she was passing by him on the gallery, where he was sitting smoking.

"Well, Mrs. Lane," said he, "I suppose by this Christmas you've gotten over being afraid of that fellow McRoy, haven't you? Madison and I have talked about it, you know."

"Very nearly," said Rosita, smiling, "but I am still nervous sometimes. I shall never forget that awful time when he came so near to killing us."

"He's the most cold-hearted villain in the world," said Berkly. "The citizens all along the border ought to turn out and hunt him down like a wolf."

"He has committed awful crimes," said Rosita, "but—I—don't—know. I think there is a spot of good somewhere in everybody. He was not always bad—that I know."

Rosita turned into the hallway between the rooms. Santa Claus, in muffling whiskers and furs, was just coming through.

"I heard what you said through the window, Mrs. Lane," he said. "I was just going down in my pocket for a Christmas present for your husband. But I've left one for you, instead. It's in the room to your right."

"Oh, thank you, kind Santa Claus," said Rosita, brightly.

Rosita went into the room, while Santa Claus stepped into the cooler air of the yard.

She found no one in the room but Madison.

"Where is my present that Santa said he left for me in here?" she asked.

"Haven't seen anything in the way of a present," said her husband, laughing, "unless he could have meant me."

The next day Gabriel Radd, the foreman of the X O Ranch, dropped into the post-office at Loma Alta.

"Well, the Frio Kid's got his dose of lead at last," he remarked to the postmaster.

"That so? How'd it happen?"

"One of old Sanchez's Mexican sheep herders did it!—think of it! the Frio Kid killed by a sheep herder! The Greaser saw him riding along past his camp about twelve o'clock last night, and was so skeered that he up with a Winchester and let him have it. Funniest part of it was that the Kid was dressed all up with white Angora-skin whiskers and a regular Santy Claus rig-out from head to foot. Think of the Frio Kid playing Santy!"

SANTA CLAUS

SONNY BOY WILLIAMSON

My baby went shoppin' yesterday,
said "I'm gonna buy what you need for Santa Claus"
My baby went shoppin' yesterday,
said "I'm gonna buy what you need for Santa Claus,
I'm gonna take mine with me,
but I'll leave yours in my dresser drawer"
So that started me to
ramblin'
lookin' in all of my baby's dresser drawers
Whoa, that started me to ramblin',
lookin' all in my baby's dresser drawers
Tryin' to find out,
what did she bought me for Santa Claus
When I pulled out the bottom dresser drawer,
the landlady got mad and called the law
When I pulled out the bottom dresser drawer,
the landlady got mad and called the law
I was just tryin' to find,
what did she bought me for Santa Claus
The police walked in and tapped me on the shoulder,
"What you doing with your hand in that woman's dresser drawer?"
I hand the police a letter my baby wrote me,
showin' where I should find my Santa Claus
I just kept on pullin' out all of my baby's dresser drawers

I walked out and left the police and the landlady arguin',
said, "Look at the man done pull out all the lady's dresser drawers"
Yes, I walked out and left the police and the landlady arguin',
said, "Look at the man done pull out all the lady's dresser drawers"
But he said, "I got the letter and show the judge
The boy just tryin' to find his Santa Claus"
Oh yeah

Saint Nicholas

MARIANNE MOORE

might I, if you can find it, be given
a chameleon with tail
that curls like a watch spring; and vertical
on the body—including the face—pale
    tiger-stripes, about seven
        (the melanin in the skin
    having been shaded from the sun by thin
        bars; the spinal dome
            beaded along the ridge
    as if it were platinum)?

If you can find no striped chameleon,
might I have a dress or suit—
I guess you have heard of it—of qiviut?
And, to wear with it, a taslon shirt, the drip-dry fruit
    of research second to none,
        sewn, I hope, by Excello,
        as for buttons to keep down the collar-points, no.
            The shirt could be white—
                and be "worn before six,"
        either in daylight or at night.

But don't give me, if I can't have the dress,
a trip to Greenland, or grim
trip to the moon. The moon should come here. Let him

make the trip down, spread on my dark floor some dim
    marvel, and if a success
        that I stoop to pick up and wear,
        I could ask nothing more. A thing yet more rare,
            though, and different,
                would be this: Hans von Marées'
        St. Hubert, kneeling with head bent,

    form erect—in velvet, tense with restraint—
hand hanging down; the horse, free.
Not the original, of course. Give me
a postcard of the scene—huntsman and divinity—
    hunt-mad Hubert startled into a saint
        by a stag with a Figure entined.
        But why tell you what you must have divined?
        Saint Nicholas, O Santa Claus,
            would it not be the most
        prized gift that ever was!

Saint Nicholas

from *The Christmas Encyclopedia*

WILLIAM D. CRUMP,

Editor

(?304–?345). ARCHBISHOP OF MYRA IN Asia Minor (now Demre, Turkey) and popularly accepted as the personage on whom the mythical Santa Claus is based.

With the exception of a few fairly certain factors, virtually everything written about St. Nicholas is based on legends. He is known to have lived during the fourth century and was present at the Council of Nicea in the year 325.

Tradition states that St. Nicholas was a native of Patara, a city in the district of Lycia. After serving as a monk in the monastery of Sion near Myra, he rapidly advanced to the office of bishop at a rather early age (for which he was dubbed the "Boy-Bishop") and finally achieved the rank of archbishop of Myra. He is said to have been quite wealthy, and his acts of secret charity and munificence became legendary to the point that, following his death, any gift received under mysterious circumstances was automatically attributed to the spirit of St. Nicholas.

Tradition also held that his death occurred on December 6, which subsequently became St. Nicholas's Day, and that his remains initially rested at the Church of St. Nicholas in Myra, with the exception that in the year 1000, that church transferred some of the relics to Kiev in Russia. In 1087, however, when Muslim occupation of Turkey allegedly threatened to desecrate Nicholas's tomb, sailors from Bari in southern Italy relocated the remains to the Church of St. Stephen in Bari. Today St. Nicholas's relics lie not only in Bari but at the Greek Orthodox Church in New York City, where some were transferred in 1972. This latter church subsequently transferred most of the relics to the Shrine of St. Nicholas in Flushing, New York.

St. Nicholas's various legendary miracles and acts of charity led a number of people and places to adopt him as their patron saint. After he supposedly compelled a group of thieves to return their stolen goods, thieves in general earned the title of "clerks of St. Nicholas" during the Middle Ages. In another story, St. Nicholas miraculously restored life back to three young boys whom an innkeeper in Myra had murdered, dismembered, and stuffed in a salting tub. . . . Another legend holds that on making a voyage to the Holy Land, St. Nicholas quieted a violent storm and later saved some sailors when they invoked his name. Finally, when his remains came to rest in Bari, it is said that 30 people were cured of distemper after calling upon his name. Thus, St. Nicholas has not only become the patron saint of thieves, children, and sailors, but also of Russia, Greece, Sicily, Liege, Lucerne, Freiburg, Laplanders, scholars, lawyers, and travelers.

The legend that firmly linked St. Nicholas with hanging up stockings and the spirit of giving at Christmastime centered around three dowerless maidens. A father in Myra was unable to give his three daughters in marriage because they lacked sufficient dowries. The desperate father was about to give his daughters up to lives of slavery or prostitution when Nicholas heard about their plight. On each of three successive nights, Nicholas secretly tossed a purse of gold through the father's window and supplied the dowries. . . . Instead of landing on the hearth, where he had aimed them, the purses landed in stockings hanging by the chimney to dry. Because of this legend, some portraits depict St. Nicholas holding three gold balls, which symbolize the purses of gold. When the Medici family of Florentine bankers adopted the three gold balls on their coat of arms in honor of St. Nicholas, the symbol eventually became that of lenders, especially pawnbrokers. From this, pawnbrokers also adopted Nicholas as their patron saint, as did virgins, in recognition of his act of compassion for the three young women. . . .

. . . [Some] assert that not only the fur-clad, American Santa Claus but also the host of antithetical demons that have accompanied the European St. Nicholas can be traced to a formidable, dark, hairy beast-god of primordial civilizations. Virtually omnipotent, this god commanded all elements of nature, including the cycles of reproduction and death, planting and harvesting; thus to renew the earth, at year's end he "recycled" himself by dying and was resurrected in the following spring. Ancient civilizations reenacted this death, which included sacrifices of people or animals in the god's name. A seer, healer, and god of fertility as well as storm and destruction, he became known as the so-called "Wild Man" of the Middle Ages. Because his pagan popularity vied with conversions to Christianity, the

Church branded him as evil and, in the seventh century, declared him to be the personification of Satan. Traces of the Wild Man figure are still seen in year-end celebrations throughout Europe and elsewhere, which almost always feature people dressed variously as masked animals or devils.

[They] conclude that Santa Claus is actually a more recent derivative of the Teutonic being "Pelz Nicholas" ("Furry Nicholas") and not St. Nicholas. Another alias for the Wild Man, Pelz Nicholas (also with numerous spellings such as Pelznickel, Pelznichol, Belznickel, Belsnichol, Bellsniggle) migrated to America with German immigrants, the so-called Pennsylvania Dutch, as the one who brought not only Christmas gifts but punishment to naughty children. In the perennial favorite poem "A Visit from St. Nicholas," [there can be seen] a number of characteristics that link Santa to the Wild Man–turned–Pelz Nicholas: dressing completely in sooty fur, shouting to reindeer whose names reflect those of the elements or mythical beings ("Dasher" resembling Thor's "Ghasher," "Vixen" the fox, the astronomical "Comet," the god "Cupid," the respective German-American "Donder" and "Blitzen" for "thunder" and "lightning"), erratic behavior such as disturbing the peace with a clatter on the lawn, and toting a sack of toys (the sack originally symbolized the article with which to kidnap children). And Santa's trademark phrase of "Ho Ho Ho" is identical to that of the "devil's bluster" of medieval mystery plays, the literary and folk prankster Robin Goodfellow (a god of vegetation), and those spirits who participated in the "Wild Hunt" during the 12 days of Christmas. . . .

[Over time, Santa came to live] at the North Pole, and traditions would add elves as his assistants, making Christmas toys for children. Although mythical elves originated in the rich Viking folklore of Scandinavia and northern Europe which long predated St. Nicholas and Santa Claus, they seemed to be ideal polar assistants. Denmark's *julnisse* and Sweden's *jultomte*, prototypical elves, are mischievous little beings who live in the attic, under floorboards, or out in the barn. Guardians of the home and livestock, these elves must receive a bowl of rice pudding on Christmas Eve; otherwise, the homeowner falls victim to their pranks, and harvests will be poor.

Another Scandinavian myth contributed to the concept of Santa's personal descent into chimneys on Christmas Eve to deliver gifts. During pre-Christmas

Germanic feasts at the winter solstice, families prepared altars of flat stones in their homes and laid fires of fir boughs. It was believed that these fires would invite Hertha, Norse goddess of the home, to descend through the fire and smoke to bring health and good fortune to all. Not only was Hertha another forerunner of Santa, but the flat stone altars became the modern hearths of today.

Santa's appearance changed somewhat again in the early twentieth century. Beginning in 1931, the Coca-Cola Company ran a series of commercial ads that featured a full-sized Santa as pitchman for the beverage. We find Santa's second evolution from small elf back to robust human size in the art of Haddon Sundblom, who enlarged the "standardized" Santa image for Coca-Cola.

Popular all through America, Santa Claus has not only crossed the Atlantic to a warm reception in Europe, but he has also influenced the celebration of Christmas the world over.

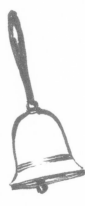

Six to Eight Black Men

DAVID SEDARIS

I'VE NEVER BEEN MUCH FOR GUIDEBOOKS, so when trying to get my bearings in some strange American city, I normally start by asking the cabdriver or hotel clerk some silly question regarding the latest census figures. I say "silly" because I don't really care how many people live in Olympia, Washington, or Columbus, Ohio. They're nice-enough places, but the numbers mean nothing to me. My second question might have to do with the average annual rainfall, which, again, doesn't tell me anything about the people who have chosen to call this place home.

What really interests me are the local gun laws. Can I carry a concealed weapon and, if so, under what circumstances? What's the waiting period for a tommy gun? Could I buy a Glock 17 if I were recently divorced or fired from my job? I've learned from experience that it's best to lead into this subject as delicately as possible, especially if you and the local citizen are alone and enclosed in a relatively small area. Bide your time, though, and you can walk away with some excellent stories. I've learned, for example, that the blind can legally hunt in both Texas and Michigan. In Texas they must be accompanied by a sighted companion, but I heard that in Michigan they're allowed to go it alone, which raises the question: How do they find whatever it is they just shot? In addition to that, how do they get it home? Are the Michigan blind allowed to drive as well? I ask about guns not because I want one of my own but because the answers vary so widely from state to state. In a country that's become increasingly homogeneous, I'm reassured by these last charming touches of regionalism.

Firearms aren't really an issue in Europe, so when traveling abroad, my first question usually relates to barnyard animals. "What do your roosters say?" is a good icebreaker, as every country has its own unique interpretation. In Germany, where dogs bark "vow vow" and both the frog and the duck say "quack," the rooster greets the dawn with a hearty "kik-a-riki." Greek roosters crow "kiri-a-kee," and in France they scream "coco-rico," which sounds like one of those horrible premixed cocktails with a pirate on the label. When told that an American rooster says "cock-a-doodle-doo," my hosts look at me with disbelief and pity.

"When do you open your Christmas presents?" is another good conversation starter, as I think it explains a lot about national character. People who traditionally open gifts on Christmas Eve seem a bit more pious and family-oriented than those who wait until Christmas morning. They go to Mass, open presents, eat a late meal, return to church the following morning, and devote the rest of the day to eating another big meal. Gifts are generally reserved for children, and the parents tend not to go overboard. It's nothing I'd want for myself, but I suppose it's fine for those who prefer food and family to things of real value.

In France and Germany gifts are exchanged on Christmas Eve, while in the Netherlands the children open their presents on December 5, in celebration of Saint Nicholas Day. It sounded sort of quaint until I spoke to a man named Oscar, who filled me in on a few of the details as we walked from my hotel to the Amsterdam train station.

Unlike the jolly, obese American Santa, Saint Nicholas is painfully thin and dresses not unlike the pope, topping his robes with a tall hat resembling an embroidered tea cozy. The outfit, I was told, is a carryover from his former career, when he served as the bishop of Turkey.

"I'm sorry," I said, "but could you repeat that?"

One doesn't want to be too much of a cultural chauvinist, but this seemed completely wrong to me. For starters, Santa didn't *used to do* anything. He's not retired and, more important, he has nothing to do with Turkey. It's too dangerous there, and the people wouldn't appreciate him. When asked how he got from Turkey to the North Pole, Oscar told me with complete conviction that Saint Nicholas currently resides in Spain, which again is simply not true. Though he could probably live wherever he wanted, Santa chose the North Pole specifically because it is harsh and isolated. No one can spy on him, and he doesn't have to worry about people coming to the door. Anyone can come to the door in Spain, and in that outfit he'd most certainly be recognized. On top of that, aside from a few pleasantries, Santa doesn't speak Spanish. "Hello. How are you? Can I get you some candy?" Fine. He knows enough to get by, but he's not fluent and he certainly doesn't eat tapas.

While our Santa flies in on a sled, the Dutch version arrives by boat and then transfers to a white horse. The event is televised, and great crowds gather at the waterfront to greet him. I'm not sure if there's a set date, but he generally docks in late November and spends a few weeks hanging out and asking people what they want.

"Is it just him alone?" I asked. "Or does he come with some backup?"

Oscar's English was close to perfect, but he seemed thrown by a term normally reserved for police reinforcement.

"Helpers," I said. "Does he have any elves?"

Maybe I'm overly sensitive, but I couldn't help but feel personally insulted when Oscar denounced the very idea as grotesque and unrealistic. "Elves," he said. "They are just so silly."

The words *silly* and *unrealistic* were redefined when I learned that Saint Nicholas travels with what was consistently described as "six to eight black men." I asked several Dutch people to narrow it down, but none of them could give me an exact number. It was always "six to eight," which seems strange, seeing as they've had hundreds of years to get an accurate head count.

The six to eight black men were characterized as personal slaves until the mid-1950s, when the political climate changed and it was decided that instead of being slaves they were just good friends. I think history has proved that something usually comes *between* slavery and friendship, a period of time marked not by cookies and quiet hours beside the fire but by bloodshed and mutual hostility. They have such violence in the Netherlands, but rather than duking it out amongst themselves, Santa and his former slaves decided to take it out on the public. In the early years if a child was naughty, Saint Nicholas and the six to eight black men would beat him with what Oscar described as "the small branch of a tree."

"A switch?"

"Yes," he said. "That's it. They'd kick him and beat him with a switch. Then if the youngster was really bad, they'd put him in a sack and take him back to Spain."

"Saint Nicholas would kick you?"

"Well, not anymore," Oscar said. "Now he just *pretends* to kick you."

He considered this to be progressive, but in a way I think it's almost more perverse than the original punishment. "I'm going to hurt you but not really." How many times have we fallen for that line? The fake slap invariably makes contact, adding the elements of shock and betrayal to what had previously been plain old-fashioned fear. What kind of a Santa spends his time pretending to kick people before stuffing them into a canvas sack? Then, of course, you've got the six to eight former slaves who could potentially go off at any moment. This, I think, is the greatest difference between us and the Dutch. While a certain segment of our population might be perfectly happy with the arrangement, if you told the average white American that six to eight nameless black men would be sneaking into his house in the middle of the night, he would barricade the doors and arm himself with whatever he could get his hands on.

"Six to eight, did you say?"

In the years before central heating, Dutch children would leave their shoes by the fireplace, the promise being that unless they planned to beat you, kick you, or stuff you into a sack, Saint Nicholas and the six to eight black men would fill your clogs with presents. Aside from the threats of violence and kidnapping, it's not much different than hanging your stockings from the mantel. Now that so few people actually have a working fireplace, Dutch children are instructed to leave their shoes beside the radiator, furnace, or space heater. Saint Nicholas and the six to eight black men arrive on horses, which jump from the yard onto the roof. At this point I guess they either jump back down and use the door or stay put and vaporize through the pipes and electrical cords. Oscar wasn't too clear about the particulars, but really, who can blame him? We have the same problem with our Santa. He's supposed to use the chimney, but if you don't have one, he still manages to get in. It's best not to think about it too hard.

While eight flying reindeer are a hard pill to swallow, our Christmas story remains relatively dull. Santa lives with his wife in a remote polar village and spends one night a year traveling around the world. If you're bad, he leaves you coal. If you're good and live in America, he'll give you just about anything you want. We tell our children to be good and send them off to bed, where they lie awake, anticipating their great bounty. A Dutch parent has a decidedly hairier story to relate, telling his children, "Listen, you might want to pack a few of your things together before going to bed. The former bishop of Turkey will be coming tonight along with six to eight black men. They might put some candy in your shoes, they might stuff you into a sack and take you to Spain, or they might just pretend to kick you. We don't know for sure, but we want you to be prepared."

This is the reward for living in the Netherlands. As a child you get to hear this story, and as an adult you get to turn around and repeat it. As an added bonus, the government has thrown in legalized drugs and prostitution—so what's not to love about being Dutch?

Oscar finished his story just as we arrived at the station. He was an amiable guy—very good company—but when he offered to wait until my train arrived I begged off, claiming I had some calls to make. Sitting alone in the vast, vibrant terminal, surrounded by thousands of polite, seemingly interesting Dutch people, I couldn't help but feel second-rate. Yes, the Netherlands was a small country, but it had six to eight black men and a really good bedtime story. Being a fairly competitive person, I felt jealous, then bitter. I was edging toward hostile when I remembered the blind hunter tramping off alone into the Michigan forest. He may bag a deer, or he may happily shoot a camper in the stomach. He may find his way back to the car, or he may wander around for a week or two before stumbling through your back door. We don't know for sure, but in pinning that license to his chest, he inspires the sort of narrative that ultimately makes me proud to be an American.

SANTALAND 2006

from *Santa Guide for the Macy's Santa*

. . . AS A MACY'S SANTA YOU HAVE now joined a long line of talented and hard-working professionals (Elves, Managers and Santas) who have, season after season, continued to maintain the Macy's Santa tradition. That tradition is long and the standards are high.

> Macy's Santa Claus is all things to all people.
> Macy's Santa is the "jolly old elf" of Clement C. Moore's poem.
> Macy's Santa "continues to make glad the hearts of childhood."
> Macy's Santa is the embodiment of every child's Christmas Eve dream.
> Macy's Santa is the only real Santa Claus.

Macy's Santa is always jolly. Be it with a hearty chuckle, a silent wink of his eye or a nod of his head. He is always glad to have his favorite children visit him. He is never moody, never out of sorts, never bad tempered. Santa never has a bad day. Santa is always happy, polite and filled with the Christmas Spirit.

Macy's Santa is always gentle. His movements are never sudden or threatening. He never forces a visitor, young or old, to sit with him, or even to talk to him—even when the parents insist. He lifts children carefully to and from his knee, and never grips them too tight for a photograph. Santa also gently helps visitors off his knee.

Macy's Santa is always patient. Santa has the patience of a saint (actually, he is a saint). He never loses his cool, no matter what the situation. He doesn't cut off shy children who have trouble talking to him, but gently reminds them that he has others waiting. He is as patient as time will allow with those who may not want to sit with him, but realizes that sometimes it's best to "wait until next year."

Macy's Santa loves all children. Even those who pull his beard or step on his foot. Santa knows that love is the greatest gift of all at Christmas, or at any time. Santa never forgets that the reason the child came to see him was to talk about Christmas, even though parents or guardians may be more concerned about the photo or shopping time. Every child gets a gift from Santa. Santa loves all children, even if they may not enjoy him.

Macy's Santa is always picture perfect. Santa's bright white beard is always shiny and curled and his brilliant red suit is always pressed and in order, right down to the harness. His hair is always in place, and his hat always on at the right angle. He is never untidy, unkempt, or dirty. Despite the often-oppressive conditions, he always does his best to appear comfortable and cool.

Macy's Santa is all knowing. He knows if you've been bad or good. He knows all the popular toys of the season, and most of the children's television shows.

Macy's Santa always remembers. He recalls your last visit, the cookies you left for him on Christmas Eve and your letter or list that he has just received. Sometimes he remembers with the help of parents, Elves or Managers.

Macy's Santa is a good listener. He pays close attention to what each child says, and to their parents, who may just pass on a helpful hint or two.

Macy's Santa can communicate with everyone. A gentle handshake, a wink, a nod, a laugh can reach anyone, no matter the language, no matter the handicap. All people understand a sincere "Merry Christmas," in spirit. Santa speaks a universal language.

Macy's Santa never promises. When presented with a list of Christmas requests, he always says that "he'll see" or "he'll do the best he can."

Macy's Santa never assumes. Santa realizes that not every child has parents who bring them to see him; sometimes other family members, or guardians, or teachers or friends bring the children to see Santa. Santa, in these cases, never questions about "Mom and Dad," as he knows that some children have no parents, or only one, or are separated from one or both parents for various reasons, some of which may be painful for the child to discuss. Santa also never assumes that his visitors always get a Christmas Eve visit (for many, the visit to Santa is their whole Christmas) or that an older child no longer believes in him.

Macy's Santa is always Santa. No matter the circumstance, with children, with teenagers, with adults, with press, even with personal friends, when Santa is in costume he is Santa. People, and especially Press, will ask you what job you do the rest of the year, or what it is like to play Santa. You are not an actor playing Santa. You ARE the real Santa Claus.

Macy's Santa is the only Santa. Many people will ask you how many Santas work at Macy's. There is only one Santa, and he is you.

With time and a few visits you will find your own individual interpretation of Santa Claus and it will be your own best judgment as to the handling of certain situations that will prevail. Toward that end, work within the perimeters of the tradition and within the guidelines above, study the procedures that follow and always remember that you are Santa Claus, the Ambassador of Good Will and Holiday Cheer.

WHAT MACY'S SANTA IS NOT

Macy's Santa is not a punishment. Some parents try to use Santa and his Christmas Eve visit as a threat. "Santa won't visit you unless you get an A in spelling," "Santa won't visit you unless you stop sucking your thumb," or "Santa's not going to bring you toys unless you smile for the picture." In these cases, remember: Santa loves all children and visits all the children on Christmas Eve (even if he only leaves them with the Christmas Spirit). The proper response in these cases is "Well, I'd certainly like it if you tried to get that A in spelling, but I know how good you've tried to be all year in everything, so tell me what you'd like for Christmas." Treat the rest of the visit as you would any other.

Macy's Santa is not a Biographer. Some Santas ask the children so many questions you wonder if they're writing an expose for <u>The National Enquirer.</u> "Do you get good grades on your report card?" "What's your teacher's name?" "What's the name of your goldfish?" "Do you have any Aunts or Uncles?" "What's your favorite game, television show, baseball team, dessert . . ." It really takes away from the idea that Santa is all knowing. It also adds time to the visit.

Macy's Santa is not The Veggie Police. Some Santas love to push eating vegetables as a prerequisite for being good. (For some reason, especially in school groups.) It is much more important that they be good to each other and listen to their parents or guardians. Forcing some child to eat broccoli to receive a Christmas gift is rather cruel.

Macy's Santa is not a Game Show Host. Asking the visitors questions like "Can you name my reindeer?" "Do you remember what I brought you last year?" "What color should you color Santa's coat in this picture?" or "Can you guess my favorite cookie?" not only can put a child on the spot and embarrass him or her if they don't know the answer, it also adds too much time to the visit.

Macy's Santa is not a photograph expert. The photo elf is. Let the photo elf be in charge of the picture. If there seems to be a problem that is persistent visit after visit, then call for the Santa Supervisor.

Macy's Santa is not a caroler. Sometimes school groups have prepared a song to sing to Santa. Santa should not join in as it will: A) Be heard throughout Santaland, thus confusing visitors to other houses and B) Encourage a second song or chorus. Santa should never suggest or start a sing-along. Santa does enjoy singing the songs of the season with Mrs. Claus and the Elves—but on their own time.

Macy's Santa is not the boss of the house. While Santa's name may be featured on the marquee, Santaland is an ensemble effort. The Elves have their duties and responsibilities, equally as important as yours. Because of their contact with the out-side of the houses, they also may have a better understanding of the situation in regards to pace and visit times than you do. They also, since they deal with the guest before you do, have a better sense of the immediate situation. For some reason, however, "Santa is not the boss of the house" is the most ignored statement made during training, and therefore will become the most enforced policy this year.

Q: What are the names of your reindeer?
A: Dasher, Dancer, Prancer, Vixen, Comet, Cupid, Donner, Blitzen & Rudolph.

Q: Whose child is Rudolph?
A: Donner's.

Q: How do the reindeer fly?
A: They are fed a magic mixture of corn and oats that only grows near the North Pole.

Q: Where are the reindeer now?
A: The ones that brought Santa here are sleeping, the rest are at the North Pole.

Q: Where do you live?
A: The North Pole.

Q: How many Elves do you have?
A: Hundreds and hundreds.

Q: What's your favorite color?
A: Red.

Q: What do the Elves do?
A: Make the toys and keep Santa's list of who is naughty and nice.

Q: Are you married?
A: Yes, to Mrs. Claus.

Q: Where is Mrs. Claus?
A: Sometimes she's at Macy's, sometimes the North Pole.

Q: What's your favorite kind of cookie?
A: Santa loves all kinds of cookies, but especially Christmas cookies.

Q: Are you lactose intolerant?

A: No, Santa likes all kinds of milk, except buttermilk, although he will use buttermilk in cakes and pancakes.

Q: What kind of snack can I leave for the reindeer?

A: The reindeer like cookies too, but they really love carrots, celery and lettuce.

Q: How do you fit down the chimney?

A: Magic.

Q: How do you get into a home that doesn't have a chimney?

A: Magic.

Q: What do you do the rest of the year?

A: Make toys, & keep naughty and nice lists.

Q: Do you use a computer?

A: Yes, a special one designed and built by the Elves.

Q: Do you read every letter that you get, and every wish list?

A: Every one, and the Elves help Santa remember the details.

Q: What if a child is visiting with relatives on Christmas Eve? Will you find that child?

A: Santa knows where all the good children are on Christmas Eve, and visits them all, no matter how far from home.

Q: How do you fly around the world in one night?

A: Through a combination of lots of practice and hard work, judicious use of time zones, and a little magic.

Q: How come Santa doesn't visit everyone on Christmas Eve?

A: He does, and always leaves the greatest gift of all—love.

Q: How come I don't always get everything on my list?

A: Thanks to the Elves and children's lists, Santa knows what presents every child wants to receive. However, sometimes Santa also knows that the child's family or guardians have other special things in mind. Also, Santa does not like to bring gifts that he knows parents, etc. would prefer the child not to have—such as a horse, or toys that they think the child should wait a year or so to get, or that might be inappropriate.

Q: Do you need snow to deliver the toys?
A: No, Santa delivers toys all around the world, including many places where it never snows.

Q: How do you know who has been naughty and who has been good?
A: Magic.

Q: How come I see you in so many places?
A: Santa can move very quickly, and he also has many helpers who dress like him at Christmas time to make sure he gets every child's wish list.

Q: Can I pull your beard?
A: Only if I can pull your hair just as hard. (Or ear or nose.)

Q: How old are you?
A: "As old as my tongue, and slightly older than my teeth."

Q: What do you want for Christmas?
A: Peace on Earth, goodwill towards all people.

Q: Are you the real Santa?
A: Of course.

. . .

CHILDREN OF THE WORLD V. SANTA CLAUS

ANDREW J. MCCLURG

THE COMPLAINT

Plaintiffs, consisting of the class of all children who on or about Dec. 24, 1999, were hanging stockings by the chimney with care in the reasonable belief that St. Nicholas soon would be there, sue defendant and allege:

1. This is an action for an accounting, damages and injunctive relief.

2. Upon information and belief, defendant is a citizen and resident of the North Pole, where he maintains his principal place of business. The court has subject matter jurisdiction of the action pursuant to 28 U.S.C. 1332.

Count I: Breach of Contract. Throughout the fall of 1999, plaintiffs met with agents of defendant at various shopping malls to negotiate the delivery of certain goods on the evening of Dec. 24, for which plaintiffs paid valuable consideration in the form of exorbitant tie-in charges for photographs of the negotiating sessions.

Plaintiffs repeatedly informed defendant, through his agents, that time was of the essence in completing such deliveries. As of this date, many of the contracted goods have not been delivered.

Other goods were noncomforming and lacked batteries, rendering them useless to plaintiffs.

Count II: Deceit. Defendant fraudulently induced plaintiffs to improve their conduct against their will by misrepresenting that defendant knows if plaintiffs have been bad or good, when, in fact, defendant lacks sufficient knowledge upon which to form a reasonable belief regarding such matters.

In justifiable reliance upon these representations, plaintiffs invested substantial labor in not shouting, pouting or crying, and at all times relevant hereto were good for goodness sake.

Count III: Infliction of Emotional Distress. On the relevant night, defendant knew or should have known that plaintiffs were snug in their beds with visions of hand-held video games and name-brand athletic apparel dancing in their heads.

Despite such knowledge, defendant willfully and maliciously concealed off-brand goods and inherently worthless property such as sweaters and umbrellas in packages that misrepresented their true contents. Plaintiffs suffered severe emotional shock and fright upon opening such packages.

Count IV: Trespass and Conversion. Defendant's implied license to enter plaintiffs' premises terminated upon his substantial breaches of contract. Once on the premises, defendant exercised substantial dominion and control over an estimated 200 tons of cookies and 44,000 gallons of milk, converting such property and depriving plaintiffs of its beneficial use.

WHEREFORE, plaintiffs demand judgment for damages, injunctive relief and an accounting.

The Deadweight Loss of Christmas

from *American Economic Review*

JOEL WALDFOGEL

WHEN ECONOMISTS COMMENT ON HOLIDAY GIFT-GIVING, it is usually to condone the healthy effect of spending on the macro-economy. However, an important feature of gift-giving is that consumption choices are made by someone other than the final consumer. A potentially important *micro*economic aspect of gift-giving is that gifts may be mismatched with the recipients' preferences. In the standard microeconomic framework of consumer choice, the best a gift-giver can do with, say, $10 is to duplicate the choice that the recipient would have made. While it is possible for a giver to choose a gift which the recipient ultimately values above its price—for example, if the recipient is not perfectly informed—it is more likely that the gift will leave the recipient worse off than if she had made her own consumption choice with an equal amount of cash. In short, gift-giving is a potential source of deadweight loss.

This paper gives estimates of the deadweight loss of holiday gift-giving based on surveys given to Yale undergraduates. I find that holiday gift-giving destroys between 10 percent and a third of the value of gifts. While these recipients may be unrepresentative of the U.S. population, their *gifts* are not necessarily unrepresentative. Holiday expenditures average $40 billion per year, implying that a conservative estimate of the deadweight loss of Christmas[*] is a tenth as large as estimates of the deadweight loss of income taxation. I also explore how deadweight loss and the tendency to give cash gifts vary with the relationship and age difference between

---

[*]References to the deadweight loss of Christmas should be understood to apply equally to Hanukkah and other holidays with gift-giving rituals.

giver and recipient. I find that gifts from friends and "significant others" are most efficient, while noncash gifts from members of the extended family are least efficient and destroy a third of their value. I develop a simple expected-utility model to explain the decision to give cash, as opposed to in-kind gifts. The data are consistent with the model: cash gifts are most common from the sorts of givers whose noncash gifts have the lowest expected value to recipients (given their cost) and high variability in recipient valuation.

I. THEORY

. . . Students are customarily taught in economics courses that unfettered consumer choice leads the consumer to higher utility than constrained choice. Thus, for example, government grants-in-kind are inefficient, unless the consumer would have chosen to consume at least the amount of the good granted, had the grant been cash. . . .

The size of the deadweight loss depends on both the giver's acquaintance with the recipient's preferences and the recipient's knowledge of her own preferences. If the recipient is perfectly informed about gift items, then the giver can do no better than to give cash; and the better the giver knows the recipient's preferences, the closer the giver can come to reproducing the recipient's choice. However, if recipients are imperfectly informed, the giver may be able to choose a gift that the recipient would not have chosen but which makes the recipient better off than a cash amount equal to the cost of the gift. In this case, it is possible for a gift to create, rather than destroy, value. The better the giver knows the recipient's preferences—including, possibly, preferences the recipient is unaware of—the more likely it is that the giver will choose a gift that the recipient values above its cost and will thereby create value through giving. . . .

II. DATA

In the first of the two surveys, completed voluntarily by 86 intermediate microeconomics students in January 1993, gift recipients were asked to estimate the total amounts paid (by the givers) for all of the holiday gifts the respondents received in 1992. Students were asked their gender and whether they exchanged any of their gifts. Finally, students were asked to place a value on their gifts, based on their willingness to pay for the gifts. The question was worded as follows:

If you made no exchanges, think of the gifts you received directly.

If you made exchanges, think of the gifts you did not exchange as well as the things you obtained in exchange for gifts you received directly.

Apart from any sentimental value of the items, if you did not have them, how much would you be willing to pay to obtain them?

The second survey, given in March 1993, gathered data on each respondent's individual gifts. Fifty-eight respondents gave usable information on 278 gifts. The survey asked respondents to describe each of their gifts, identify the givers' ages and relationships to the recipients (parent, aunt or uncle, sibling, grandparent, friend, or "significant other"), estimate the prices that the givers paid for the gifts, and indicate whether the gifts were exchanged. The gift description allows gifts to be divided into three categories: cash, gift certificates, and gifts. The respondents were asked to estimate the value of the gifts as the

> . . . amount of cash such that you are indifferent between the gift and the cash, not counting the sentimental value of the gift. If you exchanged the original gift, assess the value of the object you got in exchange for the original gift. If you exchanged the original gift for cash, put the cash amount you received here.

The survey also asked gender, age, family income, and the amount the recipient spent on holiday gifts for others in 1992. Note that valuations from both surveys take exchanges into account.

The difference between the two surveys' valuation methods may be described as follows: the first survey asks for the *maximum* the respondent would pay for her gifts, while the second survey asks for the *minimum* the respondent would accept in lieu of the gifts. As Jack L. Knetsch and J. A. Sinden (1984) demonstrate, experimental subjects require more in return than they are willing to pay for similar objects. Hence, we expect valuations to be higher—and deadweight losses to be lower—in the second survey. The true amount of deadweight loss lies in between.

III. EMPIRICAL ANALYSIS

. . . In survey I, respondents estimate that friends and family paid an average $438 for the recipients' total gifts, but respondents express a willingness to pay only $313, on average, for the same gifts. Because losses are approximately proportionate to receipts across receipt sizes, the ratio of average value to the average price (71.5 percent) is close to the average ratio of value to price, or average "yield," of 66.1 percent. A regression of log value on log price across recipients' total gift receipts confirms that the relationship between value and price is essentially proportional:

$$\log(\text{value}_i) = -0.314 + 0.964\log(\text{price}_i)$$
$$(0.44) \quad (0.08)$$

with standard errors in parentheses and an R^2 of 65.6 percent. Forming a deadweight-loss measure from average yield indicates that gift-giving destroys a third of gift value. . . . Hence, the average yield on noncash gifts is below 66.1 percent, and the deadweight loss among noncash gifts actually exceeds one-third. Putting aside the inclusion of cash, the valuation by willingness to pay in survey I makes one-third an upper-bound estimate of the deadweight-loss fraction.

TABLE I

Average Amounts Paid and Values of Gifts, by Recipient

VARIABLE	SURVEY 1	SURVEY 2
Amount paid ($)	438.2	508.9
Value ($)[a]	313.4	462.1
Percentage ratio of average value to average price paid[b]	71.5	90.8
Average percentage yield[c]	66.1	87.1
	(3.3)	(3.2)
Number of recipients	86	58

[a]In survey I, respondents valued their gifts by their willingness to pay for them. In survey 2, respondents valued their gifts as the money they would accept in lieu of the gifts (see text).
[b]Ratio of average value to average price paid.
[c]Average of ($\text{value}_i/\text{price}_i$). The standard error of average yield is given in parentheses.

The 58 respondents to the second survey estimate that $509 was paid for their gifts, but they value these gifts at only $462. The average yield across these recipients (87.1 percent) is quite similar to the ratio of the average value to the average price (90.8 percent). A regression of the log value of receipts on log prices across recipients again confirms that value is nearly proportional to price:

$$\log(\text{value}_i) = -0.618 + 1.075\log(\text{price}_i)$$
$$(0.23) \quad (0.04)$$

with standard errors in parentheses and an R^2 of 93.2 percent. As expected, the implied deadweight loss is less than the results of the first survey would suggest. For comparability with total receipt figures in survey I, cash is not excluded, so that the deadweight loss among noncash gifts is higher. Averaged across gifts, rather than recipients, the average yield on noncash gifts is 83.9 percent, suggesting a deadweight-loss fraction of 16.1 percent. This is a lower bound because of the survey-2 valuation method.

While the survey respondents' total gift receipts (averaging $400–500) and family incomes (averaging $143,000 for the 43 students reporting family income) are unrepresentative of the U.S. population, the fraction of the gifts' value destroyed through inefficent exchange need not be unrepresentative. First, among survey recipients the yield ratio does not vary with family income. Thus, while the general population has lower average income than the survey recipients, yield rates for survey recipients with income nearer to the population average do not differ from the survey average.

Second, deadweight losses are large and significant for gifts in all price ranges, thus including price ranges typical for gift recipients generally. . . . Over a third of the gifts in [another] survey are estimated to cost less than $25, a range with an average yield of 85.8 percent (with a standard error [SE] of 5.6 percent). Nearly an additional third of gifts are estimated to cost between $26 and $50; these gifts have an average yield of 74.4 percent (SE = 3.4 percent). Average yield is somewhat higher for larger gifts, about 89 percent for gifts estimated to cost over $50. The fraction of gift price that is wasted reaches a maximum of a quarter for gifts costing between $25 and $50 and is otherwise approximately constant at 10–15 percent. Recall that these figures are based on the conservative valuation method of survey 2. Whatever the average size of gifts in the general population, if their yields are similar to the yields on similar-sized gifts in this sample, then the deadweight loss will be at least 10 percent of the price of gifts. . . .

IV. CONCLUSION

Estimates in this paper indicate that between a tenth and a third of the value of holiday gifts is destroyed by gift-giving. Because average losses of at least 10 percent hold for all gift price ranges in the sample, the lower-bound proportionate loss estimates may be reasonably applied to other populations. While the generality of these results is not settled, the deadweight losses arising from holiday gift-giving may well be large: holiday gift expenditures in 1992 totaled $38 billion according to one estimate. If between a tenth and a third of this spending was wasted, then the deadweight loss of 1992 holiday gift-giving was between $4 billion and $13 billion. . . .

NORAD (NORTH AMERICAN AIR DEFENSE COMMAND) TRACKS SANTA

WWW.NORADSANTA.ORG

WHY TRACK HIM?

For more than 50 years, NORAD and its predecessor, the Continental Air Defense Command (CONAD) have tracked Santa. The tradition began after a Colorado Springs–based Sears Roebuck & Co. store advertisement for children to call Santa on a special "hotline" included an inadvertently misprinted telephone number. Instead of Santa, the phone number put kids through to the CONAD Commander-in-Chief's operations "hotline." The Director of Operations, Colonel Harry Shoup, received the first "Santa" call on Christmas Eve 1955. Realizing what had happened, Colonel Shoup had his staff check radar data to see if there was any indication of Santa making his way south from the North Pole. Indeed there were signs of Santa and children who called were given an update on Santa's position. Thus, the tradition was born. In 1958, the governments of Canada and the United States created a bi-national air defense command for the North American continent called the North American Air Defense Command, known as NORAD. Canada and the U.S. believed they could better defend North America together as a team instead of separately.

NORAD carried out its first Santa tracking in 1958 after inheriting the tradition from CONAD. Since that time, Canadian and American men and women who work at NORAD have responded to phone calls from children personally. Additionally, media from all over the world call NORAD on Christmas Eve for updates on Santa's location. Last year this Website was visited by millions of people who wanted to know Santa's whereabouts. This year, the information is provided in six languages.

NORAD relies on many volunteers to help make the Santa tracking possible. Hundreds of volunteers spend part of their Christmas Eve at the Santa Tracking Operations Center answering phones and e-mails to provide Santa updates to thousands of inquiring children worldwide.

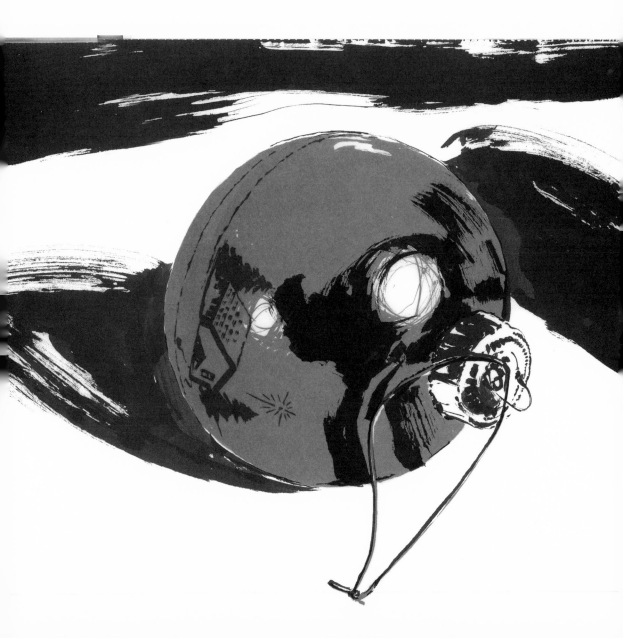

ABOUT NORAD

NORAD is the bi-national U.S.-Canadian military organization responsible for the aerospace defense of the United States and Canada. NORAD was created by a 1958 agreement between Canada and the United States. The agreement has been renewed nine times—most recently this year. NORAD provides warning of missile and air attack against both of its member nations, safeguards the air sovereignty of North America, and provides air defense forces for defense against an air attack.

NORAD's mission has evolved over the years to meet the aerospace defense needs of Canada and the United States. The most recent "evolution" in NORAD's mission came as a result of September 11, 2001. Because of that day, NORAD now monitors the airspace within Canada and the United States, too. In addition, the command also conducts maritime warning. There are men and women in NORAD constantly watching the skies and waterways to keep the United States and Canada safe.

HOW DOES NORAD TRACK SANTA?

NORAD uses four high-tech systems to track Santa—radar, satellites, Santa Cams and jet fighter aircraft.

Detecting Santa all starts with the NORAD radar system called the North Warning System. This powerful radar system has 47 installations strung across the northern border of North America. NORAD makes a point of checking the radar closely for indications of Santa Claus leaving the North Pole on Christmas Eve.

The moment our radar tells us that Santa has lifted off, we use our second mode of detection, the same satellites that we use in providing warning of possible missile launches aimed at North America. These satellites are located in a geo-synchronous orbit (that's a cool phrase meaning that the satellite is always fixed over the same spot on Earth) at 22,300 miles above the Earth. The satellites have infrared sensors, meaning they can detect heat. When a rocket or missile is launched, a tremendous amount of heat is produced—enough for the satellites to detect. Rudolph's nose gives off an infrared signature similar to a missile launch. The satellites can detect Rudolph's bright red nose with practically no problem.

With so many years of experience, NORAD has become good at tracking aircraft entering North America, detecting worldwide missile launches and tracking the progress of Santa, thanks to Rudolph.

The third detection system we use is the Santa Cam. We began using it in 1998—the year we put our Santa Tracking program on the Internet. NORAD Santa Cams are ultra-cool high-tech high-speed digital cameras that are pre-positioned at many places around the world. NORAD only uses these cameras once a year—Christmas Eve. The cameras capture images of Santa and the Reindeer as they make their journey around the world. We immediately download the images on to our Website for people around the world to see. Santa Cams produce both video and still images.

The fourth detection system we use is the NORAD jet fighter. Canadian NORAD fighter pilots, flying the CF-18, take off out of Newfoundland to intercept and welcome Santa to North America. Then at numerous locations in Canada other CF-18 fighter pilots escort Santa. While in the United States, American NORAD fighter pilots in either the F-15 or F-16 get the thrill of flying with Santa and the famous reindeer Dasher, Dancer, Prancer, Vixen, Comet, Cupid, Donner, Blitzen and Rudolph. About a dozen NORAD fighters in Canada and the United States are equipped with Santa Cams.

FATHER CHRISTMAS
EXECUTED

CLAUDE LÉVI-STRAUSS

CHRISTMAS OF 1951 IN FRANCE WAS marked by a controversy—of great interest to press and public alike—that gave the generally festive atmosphere an unusual note of bitterness. A number of the clergy had for several months expressed disapproval of the increasing importance given by both families and the business sector to the figure of Father Christmas. They denounced a disturbing "paganization" of the Nativity that was diverting public spirit from the true Christian meaning of Christmas to the profit of a myth devoid of religious value. Attacks spread just before Christmas; with more discretion, but just as much conviction, the Protestant Church chimed in with the Catholic Church. A number of articles and letters in the press bore witness to a keen public interest in the affair and showed general hostility to the Church's position. It came to a head on Christmas Eve with a demonstration that a reporter from *France-soir* described as follows:

SUNDAY SCHOOL CHILDREN WITNESS FATHER CHRISTMAS BURNT IN DIJON CATHEDRAL PRECINCT

Dijon, 24 December

Father Christmas was hanged yesterday afternoon from the railings of Dijon Cathedral and burnt publicly in the precinct. This spectacular execution took place in the presence of several hundred Sunday school children. It was a decision made with the agreement of the clergy who had condemned Father Christmas as a usurper and heretic. He was accused of "paganizing" the Christmas festival and installing himself like a cuckoo in the nest, claiming more and more space for himself. Above all he was blamed for infiltrating all the state schools from which the crib has been scrupulously banished.

On Sunday, at three o'clock in the afternoon, the unfortunate fellow with the white beard, scapegoated like so many innocents before him, was executed by his accusers. They set fire to his beard and he vanished into smoke.

At the time of the execution a communiqué was issued to the following effect:

"Representing all Christian homes of the parish keen to struggle against lies, 250 children assembled in front of the main door of Dijon Cathedral and burned Father Christmas.

"It wasn't intended as an attraction, but as a symbolic gesture. Father Christmas has been sacrificed. In truth, the lies about him cannot arouse religious feeling in a child and are in no way a means of education. Others may say and write what they want about Father Christmas, but the fact is he is only the counterweight of a modern-day Mr. Bogeyman.

"For Christians the festivity of Christmas must remain the annual celebration of the birth of the Saviour."

Father Christmas's execution in the Cathedral precinct got a mixed response from the public and provoked lively commentaries even from Catholics.

❋

THE AFFAIR HAS divided the town into two camps.

Dijon awaits the resurrection of Father Christmas, assassinated yesterday in the cathedral precinct. He will arise this evening at six o'clock in the Town Hall. An official communiqué announced that, as every year, the children of Dijon are invited to Liberation Square where Father Christmas will speak to them from the floodlit roof of the Town Hall.

Canon Kir, deputy-mayor of Dijon, will not take part in this delicate affair.

❋

THE SAME DAY, the torture of Father Christmas became front-page news. Not one newspaper missed an article on it, some—like *France-soir*, which has the highest circulation of all French papers—even went so far as to make it the subject of an editorial. There was general disapproval towards the attitude of the Dijon clergy. It would seem that the religious authorities were right to withdraw from the battle, or at least to keep silent. Yet they are apparently divided on the issue. The tone of most of the articles was one of tactful sentimentality: it's so nice to believe in Father Christmas, it doesn't harm anyone, the children get such satisfaction from it and store up such delicious memories for their adulthood, etc.

They are, in fact, begging the question. It is not a matter of rationalizing why children like Father Christmas, but rather, why adults invented him in the first place. Widespread reaction to the issue, however, clearly suggests a rift between public opinion and the Church. The incident is important, despite its apparent pettiness. . . . Father Christmas, symbol of irreligion—what a paradox! For in this case everything is happening as if it were the Church adopting an avidly critical attitude on honesty and truth, while the rationalists act as guardians of superstition. This apparent role reversal is enough to suggest that the whole naïve business is about something much more profound. . . . There is nothing specifically new in what might be called (no pun intended) the rebirth of Christmas. Then why does it arouse such emotion and why is Father Christmas the focus for hostility from some?

❅

FATHER CHRISTMAS IS dressed in scarlet: he is a king. His white beard, his furs and his boots, the sleigh in which he travels evoke winter. He is called "Father" and he is an old man, thus he incarnates the benevolent form of the authority of the ancients. That is quite clear, yet in what category can he be placed from the point of view of religious typology? He is not a mythic being, for there is no myth that accounts for his origin or his function. Nor is he a legendary figure, as there is no semi-historical account attached to him. In fact, this supernatural and immutable being, eternally fixed in form and defined by an exclusive function and a periodic return, belongs more properly to the family of the gods. Moreover, children pay him homage at certain times of the year with letters and prayers; he rewards the good and punishes the wicked. He is the deity of an age group of our society, an age group that is in fact defined by belief in Father Christmas. The only difference between Father Christmas and a true deity is that adults do not believe in him, although they encourage their children to do so and maintain this belief with a great number of tricks.

Father Christmas thus first of all expresses the difference in status between little children on the one hand, and adolescents and adults on the other. In this sense he is linked to a vast array of beliefs and practices which anthropologists have studied in many societies to try and understand rites of passage and initiation. There are, in fact, few societies where, in one way or another, children (and at times also women) are not excluded from the company of men through ignorance of certain mysteries or their belief—carefully fostered—in some illusion that the adults keep secret until an opportune moment, thus sanctioning the addition of the younger generation to the adult world.

. . . Initiation rites and myths have a practical function in human societies: they help the elders to keep the younger generation in order and disciplined. All through the year we tell children Father Christmas is coming, to remind them that his generosity is in proportion to their good behavior. Giving presents only at certain times is a useful way of disciplining children's demands, reducing to a brief period the time when they really have the *right* to demand presents. This simple explanation alone is enough to challenge the tenets of utilitarian explanations. For where do children get rights in the first place, and how is it these rights are imposed so imperiously on adults that they are obliged to work out an expensive and complex ritual in order to satisfy them? It can be seen straight away that belief in Father Christmas is not just a *hoax* imposed by adults on children for fun; it is, to a large extent, the result of a very onerous *transaction* between the two generations. He is part of a complete ritual, like the evergreens—pine, holly, ivy, mistletoe—with which we decorate our homes. Today a simple luxury, in some regions they were once the object of an *exchange* between two social groups. On Christmas Eve in England up until the end of the eighteenth century women used to go *gooding*, that is, begging from house to house and offering evergreen branches in return. We find children in the same bargaining position and it is worth noting here that when they beg on Saint Nicholas's Eve, children sometimes dress up as women—women, children: in both cases, the uninitiated.

. . . Without pushing the argument too much further, it should still be pointed out that, to the extent that rituals and beliefs linked to Father Christmas relate to a sociology of initiation (and that is beyond doubt), it reveals that beyond the conflict between children and adults lies a deeper dispute between the living and the dead.

❊

FOR HISTORIANS OF religion and folklorists both generally agree that the distant origin of Father Christmas is to be found in the Abbé de Liesse, *Abbas Stultorum*, Abbé de la Malgouverné, a replica of the English Lord of Misrule, all characters who rule for a set period as kings of Christmas and who are all heirs of the King of the Roman Saturnalia. Now the Saturnalia was the festival of the *larvae*, those who died a violent death or were left unburied. The aged Saturn, devourer of his children, is the prototype for a number of similar figures: Father Christmas, benefactor of children; the Scandinavian Julebok, horned demon from the underworld who brings presents to the children; Saint Nicholas, who revives them and inundates them with presents. It should be added that the ancient prototype of Saturn is a god of germination. In fact, the contemporary character of Santa Claus or Father Christmas is a result of a syncretic fusion of several different characters: Abbé de Liesse, child-bishop elected by Saint Nicholas; Saint Nicholas himself from whose festival beliefs in stockings, shoes, and chimneys originated. The Abbé de Liesse reigned on 25 December, Saint Nicholas on 6 December, the child-bishops were elected on Holy Innocents Day, i.e. 28 December. The Scandinavian Jul was celebrated in December. This leads us straight back to the *libertas decembris* of which Horace speaks and which [was] cited as early as the eighteenth century linking Christmas with the Saturnalia.

Explanations in terms of survivals are always inadequate. Customs neither disappear nor survive without a reason. When they do survive, the reason is less likely to be found in the vagaries of history than in the permanence of a function which analyzing the present allows us to discover.

. . . It is not surprising that non-Christian aspects of Christmas resemble the Saturnalia, as there are good reasons to suppose the Church fixed the date of the Nativity on 25 December (instead of March or January) to substitute its commemoration for the pagan festival that originally began on 17 December, but which at the end of the empire spread out over seven days, i.e. until the 24th. In fact, from antiquity up until the Middle Ages the "festivals of December" show similar characteristics. First, the decoration of buildings with evergreens; next, the exchange, or giving to children, of gifts; gaiety and feasting; and finally, fraternization between rich and poor, masters and servants.

Looking more closely at the facts, certain structural analogies become strikingly evident. Like the Roman Saturnalia, medieval Christmas had two syncretic and opposite traits. It was first of all a gathering and a communion: distinction between class and status was temporarily abolished. Slaves and servants sat next to masters, and these became their servants. Richly stocked tables were open to everybody. There was cross-dressing. Yet at the same time the social group split into two. Youth formed itself into an autonomous group, elected a sovereign, the Abbot of Youth or, as in Scotland, *Abbot of Unreason*, and, as the title suggests, they indulged in outlandish behavior taking the form of abuse directed at the rest of the population and which we know, up until the Renaissance, took extreme forms: blasphemy, theft, rape, and even murder. During both Christmas and the Saturnalia society functions according to a double rhythm of *heightened solidarity* and *exaggerated antagonism* and these two aspects act together in balanced opposition. The character of the Abbé de Liesse acts as a kind of mediator between the two extremes. He is recognized and even enthroned by the regular authorities. His mission is to demand excess while at the same time containing it within certain limits. What connection is there between this character and his function, and the character and function of Father Christmas, his distant descendant?

At this point it is important to distinguish between the historical and the structural points of view. Historically, as we have already seen, the Father Christmas of Western Europe, with his partiality for chimneys and stockings, is purely and simply a result of a recent shift from the festival of Saint Nicholas which has been assimilated to the celebration of Christmas, three weeks later. This explains how the young abbot has become an old man, though only in part, for the transformations are more systematic than historical accidents and calendar dates might suggest. A real person has become a mythical person. A figure of youth, symbolizing antagonism to adults, has changed into a symbol of maturity which is favorably disposed towards youth. The Lord of Misrule has taken charge of sanctioning good behavior. Instead of open adolescent aggression to parents, we now have parents hiding behind false beards to gratify their children with kindness. The imaginary mediator replaces the real mediator, while at the same time as he changes his nature he begins to function in the opposite way.

. . . In the Middle Ages children did not wait patiently for their toys to come down the chimney. Variously disguised they gathered in groups which were known as "guisarts" and went from house to house singing and offering their good wishes, in return for fruit and cakes. Significantly, they invoked death to back up their demands. Thus in eighteenth-century Scotland they sang this verse:

> Rise up, good wife, and be no' swier [lazy]
> To deal your bread as long's you're here;
> The time will come when you'll be dead,
> And neither want nor meal nor bread.

Even without this valuable piece of information and the no less significant one of disguises that change the actors into ghosts or spirits, there are still others concerning children's quests. It is known that these are not limited to Christmas. They go on during the whole critical time of autumn when night threatens day just as the dead menace the living. Christmas quests begin several weeks before the Nativity— usually three, thus establishing a link between the similar quests of Saint Nicholas (which also use disguises), when dead children come to life, and the even more clearly defined initial quest of the season, that of Hallow-Even, which was turned into All Saints' Eve by ecclesiastical decision. Even today in Anglo-Saxon countries, children dressed up as ghosts and skeletons hassle adults unless they reward them with small presents. The progress of autumn from its beginning until the solstice, which marks the salvation of light and of life, is accompanied, in terms of rituals, by a dialectical process of which the principal stages are as follows: the return of the dead; their threatening and persecuting behavior; the establishment of a *modus vivendi* with the living made up of an exchange of services and presents; finally, the triumph of life when, at Christmas, the dead laden with presents leave the living in peace until the next autumn. It is revealing that up until the last century the Latin Catholic countries put most emphasis on Saint Nicholas, in other words, the most *restrained* version, while the Anglo-Saxon countries willingly split it into the two extreme and antithetical forms of Halloween, when children play the part of the dead to make demands on adults, and Christmas, when adults indulge children in celebration of their vitality.

❄

AS A RESULT of this, apparently contradictory aspects of the Christmas rites become clear: for three months the visit of the dead among the living becomes more and more persistent and tyrannical. Thus on the day of their departure it becomes permissible to entertain them and give them a last chance *to raise hell*. But who can personify the dead in a society of the living if not those who, one way or another, are incompletely incorporated into the group, who, that is, share the *otherness* which symbolizes the supreme dualism: that of the dead and the living? Therefore it should come as no surprise that foreigners, slaves, and children become the main beneficiaries of the festival. Inferior political or social status becomes equated with age difference. There is in fact a great deal of evidence, especially from Scandinavia and the Slav countries, that the real essence of the Réveillon is a meal offered to the dead, where the guests play the part of the dead, as the children play that of the angels, and the angels themselves, the dead. It is thus not surprising that Christmas and New Year (its double) should be festivals for present-giving. The festival of the dead is basically the festival of the others, while the fact of being other is the nearest image we can get of death.

This brings us back to the two questions posed at the beginning of the essay. Why did the figure of Father Christmas develop, and why has the Church been worried about its development?

It has been shown that Father Christmas is the heir to, as well as the opposite of, the Abbé de Liesse. This transformation primarily indicates an improvement in our relationships with death. We no longer find it necessary to settle our debts with death and allow it periodic transgression of order and laws. The relationship is now dominated by a slightly disdainful spirit of goodwill. We can allow ourselves to be generous, because this now consists of nothing more than offering presents or toys—that is, symbols. Yet this weakening of the relationship between the living and the dead has not been made at the expense of the character who embodies it. On the contrary, it could even be said to have improved. This contradiction would be inexplicable if it were not that another attitude towards death seems to be gaining sway in our society. It is no longer the traditional fear of spirits and ghosts that prevails, but instead a dread of everything death represents, both in itself and in life: degeneration, desiccation, and deprivation. We should reflect on the tender care we take of Father Christmas, the precautions and sacrifices we make to keep his prestige intact for the children. Is it not that, deep within us, there is a small desire to believe in boundless generosity, kindness without ulterior motives, a brief interlude during which all fear, envy, and bitterness are suspended? No doubt we cannot fully share the illusion, but sharing with others at least gives us a chance to warm our hearts by the flame that burns in young souls. The belief that we help to perpetuate in our children that their toys come from "out there" gives us an alibi for our own secret desire to offer them to those "out there" under the pretext of giving them to the children. In this way, Christmas presents remain a true sacrifice to the sweetness of life, which consists first and foremost of not dying.

Salomon Reinach once wrote with much insight that the main difference between ancient and modern religions was that "pagans prayed to the dead, while Christians prayed for the dead." No doubt it is a long way from the prayer to the dead to this muddled prayer we increasingly offer each year to little children—traditional incarnations of the dead—in order that they consent, by believing in Father Christmas, to help us believe in life. We have disentangled the threads that testify to a continuity between these two manifestations of the same reality. The Church was certainly not wrong to denounce the belief in Father Christmas, one of the most solid bastions and active centers of paganism in modern humanity. It remains to be seen if modern humanity can defend its right to be pagan. One final remark: it is a long way from the King of the Saturnalia to Father Christmas. Along the way an essential trait—maybe the most ancient—of the first seems to have been definitely lost. For . . . the King of the Saturnalia was himself the heir of an ancient prototype who, having enjoyed a month of unbridled excess, was solemnly sacrificed on the altar of God. Thanks to the *auto-da-fé* of Dijon we have the reconstructed hero in full. The paradox of this unusual episode is that in wanting to put an end to Father Christmas, the clergymen of Dijon have only restored in all his glory, after an eclipse of several thousand years, a ritual figure they had intended to destroy.

CHRISTMAS IN HOLLIS

RUN-D.M.C.

[RUN]

It was December 24th on Hollis Ave in the dark

When I see a man chilling with his dog in the park

I approached very slowly with my heart full of fear

Looked at his dog oh my God an ill reindeer

But then I was illin because the man had a beard

And a bag full of goodies 12 o'clock had neared

So I turned my head a second and the man had gone

But he left his driver's wallet smack dead on the lawn

I picket the wallet up then I took a pause

Took out the license and it cold said "Santa Claus"

A million dollars in it, cold hundreds of G's

Enough to buy a boat and matching car with ease

But I'd never steal from Santa, cause that ain't right

So I'm going home to mail it back to him that night

But when I got home I bugged, cause under the tree

Was a letter from Santa and all the dough was for me

[D.M.C.]

It's Christmas time in Hollis Queens

Mom's cooking chicken and collard greens

Rice and stuffing, macaroni and cheese

And Santa put gifts under Christmas trees

Decorate the house with lights at night

Snow's on the ground, snow white so bright

In the fireplace is the yule log

Beneath the mistle toe as we drink egg nog

The rhymes you hear are the rhymes of Darryl's

But each and every year we bust Chrsitmas carols

(Christmas melodies)

[RUN-D.M.C.]

Rhymes so loud and prod you hear it

It's Christmas time and we got the spirit

Jack Frost chillin, the hawk is out

And that's what Christmas is all about

The time is now, the place is here

And the whole wide world is filled with cheer

[D.M.C.]

My name's D.M.C. with the mic in my hand

And I'm chilling and coolin just like a snowman

So open your eyes, lend us an ear

We want to say Merry Christmas and Happy New Year!

AWAY IN A MANGER

Away in a Manger

MUSIC BY WILLIAM JAMES KIRKPATRICK

WORDS: ANONYMOUS

Away in a manger,
No crib for a bed,
The little Lord Jesus
Laid down his sweet head.
The stars in the bright sky
Look'd down where he lay,
The little Lord Jesus
Asleep on the hay.

The cattle are lowing,
The baby awakes,
But little Lord Jesus
No crying he makes.
I love thee, Lord Jesus!
Look down from the sky,
And stay by my cradle
Till morning is nigh.

Be near me, Lord Jesus;
I ask thee to stay
Close by me forever,
And love me, I pray.
Bless all the dear children
In thy tender care,
And fit us for heaven,
To live with thee there.

ISAIAH 9: 2–6

The people that walked in darkness have seen a great light: they that dwell in the land of the shadow of death, upon them hath the light shined. . . .

For unto us a child is born, unto us a son is given: and the government shall be upon his shoulder: and his name shall be called Wonderful, Counsellor, The mighty God, The everlasting Father, The Prince of Peace.

LUKE 2: 1–20

And it came to pass in those days, that there went out a decree from Cæsar Augustus, that all the world should be taxed.

And this taxing was first made when Cyrenius was governor of Syria.

And all went to be taxed, every one into his own city.

And Joseph also went up from Galilee, out of the city of Nazareth, into Judæa, unto the city of David, which is called Bethlehem; (because he was of the house and lineage of David:)

To be taxed with Mary his espoused wife, being great with child.

And so it was, that, while they were there, the days were accomplished that she should be delivered.

And she brought forth her firstborn son, and wrapped him in swaddling clothes, and laid him in a manger; because there was no room for them in the inn.

And there were in the same country shepherds abiding in the field, keeping watch over their flock by night.

And, lo, the angel of the Lord came upon them, and the glory of the Lord shone round about them: and they were sore afraid.

And the angel said unto them, Fear not: for, behold, I bring you good tidings of great joy, which shall be to all people.

For unto you is born this day in the city of David a Saviour, which is Christ the Lord.

And this shall be a sign unto you: Ye shall find the babe wrapped in swaddling clothes, lying in a manger.

And suddenly there was with the angel a multitude of the heavenly host praising God, and saying,

Glory to God in the highest, and on earth peace, good will toward men.

And it came to pass, as the angels were gone away from them into heaven, the shepherds said one to another, Let us now go even unto Bethlehem, and see this thing which is come to pass, which the Lord hath made known unto us.

And they came with haste, and found Mary, and Joseph, and the babe lying in a manger.

And when they had seen it, they made known abroad the saying which was told them concerning this child.

And all they that heard it wondered at those things which were told them by the shepherds.

But Mary kept all these things, and pondered them in her heart.

And the shepherds returned, glorifying and praising God for all the things that they had heard and seen, as it was told unto them.

Pedida de la Posada

Asking for Lodging

FOR NINE DAYS LEADING UP TO Christmas, the *posadas* are celebrated, reenacting Joseph's search for an inn where Mary could give birth to the baby Jesus. There is a procession from house to house with candles and a manger scene, usually carried by children. Outside each house, the group sings Joseph's verses, begging for shelter, while inside, the host, who takes the part of the innkeeper, sings back his objections. When the door is opened at the end of the song, the group is invited in for refreshments—tamales, hot chocolate, and other treats. And there is often a piñata to break and sweets for the children.

SAN JOSE	SAINT JOSEPH
En nombre del cielo	*In the name of Heaven*
Os pido posada	*I beg you for lodging*
Pues no puede andar	*For my beloved wife*
Mi esposa amada	*Cannot walk.*

CASERO	INNKEEPER
Aquí no es mesón;	*This is not an inn here,*
Sigan adelante.	*So keep going.*
Yo no puedo abrir;	*I cannot open my door;*
No sea algún tunante.	*You might be lazy vagrants.*

SAN JOSE	SAINT JOSEPH
No seáis inhumano;	*Don't be inhuman;*
Tennos caridád.	*Have pity on us.*
Que el Dios de los cielos	*God in Heaven*
Te lo premiará.	*Will reward you for it.*

CASERO	INNKEEPER
Ya se pueden ir	*You had better go*
Y no molestar.	*And don't disturb us.*
Porque si me enfado	*Because if I get angry*
Los voy a apalear.	*I'll beat you up.*

SAN JOSE	SAINT JOSEPH
Venimos rendidos	*We are worn out,*
Desde Nazaret.	*Coming from Nazareth.*
Yo soy carpintero.	*I am a carpenter.*
De nombre José.	*My name is Joseph.*

CASERO	INNKEEPER
No me importa el nombre;	*I don't care what your name is;*
Déjenme dormir,	*Let me go back to sleep.*
Pues que ya les digo	*I already told you,*
Que no hemos de abrir.	*We're not opening the door.*

SAN JOSE	SAINT JOSEPH
Posada te pido,	*I ask you for lodging,*
Amado casero,	*Dear innkeeper,*
Por solo una noche,	*Only for one night,*
La Reina del Cielo.	*For the Queen of Heaven.*

CASERO	INNKEEPER
¿Pues si es una reina	*Well, if it's for a queen*
Quien lo solicita,	*You are asking,*
Cómo es que de noche	*Why does she travel at night,*
Anda tan solita?	*So alone?*

SAN JOSE	SAINT JOSEPH
Mi esposa es María	*My wife is Mary.*
Es Reina del Cielo,	*She's the Queen of Heaven*
Y madre va a ser	*And she's going to be mother*
Del Divino Verbo.	*Of the Divine Word.*

CASERO

¿Eres tú José?
¿Tu esposa es María?
Entren, peregrinos
No los conocía.

SAN JOSE

Dios pague, señores,
Vuestra caridad,
Y así os colme el cielo
De felicidad.

CASERO

Posada os damos
Con mucha alegría,
Entra, José justo,
Entra con María.

INNKEEPER

Are you Joseph?
Your wife is Mary?
Enter, pilgrims.
I didn't know who you were.

SAINT JOSEPH

May God repay
Your kindness, señores,
And the heavens
Heap happiness upon you.

INNKEEPER

Lodging I give you
with much joy.
Enter righteous Joseph.
Enter with Mary.

THE STABLE

GABRIELA MISTRAL

When midnight came
and the Child's first cry arose,
a hundred beasts awakened
and the stable became alive.

And drawing near they came
reaching out toward the Child
a hundred eager necks
like a forest swaying.

An ox whose eyes were as tender
as though filled with dew,
lowered its head to breathe
quietly in His face.

Against Him rubbed a lamb
with the softest of fleece,
and two baby goats squatted,
licking His hands.

The walls of the stable
unnoticed were covered
with pheasants and with geese
and cocks and with blackbirds.

The pheasants flew down
and swept over the Child
tails of many colors;
while the geese with wide bills
soothed His pallet of straw;
and a swarm of blackbirds
became a veil rising and falling
above the new born.

The Virgin, confused among such horns
and whiteness of breathing,
fluttered hither and yon
unable to pick up her Child.

And Joseph arrived laughing
to help her in her confusion,
and the upset stable was like
a forest in the wind.

THE BARN

ELIZABETH COATSWORTH

"I am tired of this barn!" said the colt.
"And every day it snows.
Outside there's no grass any more
And icicles grow on my nose.
I am tired of hearing the cows
Breathing and talking together.
I am sick of these clucking hens.
I hate stables and winter weather!"

"Hush, little colt," said the mare
"And a story I will tell
Of a barn like this one of ours
And the wonders that there befell.
It was weather much like this,
And the beasts stood as we stand now
In the warm good dark of the barn—
A horse and an ass and a cow."

"And sheep?" asked the colt. "Yes, sheep,
And a pig and a goat and a hen
All of the beasts of the barnyard,
The usual servants of men.
And into their midst came a lady
And she was cold as death,
But the animals leaned above her
and made her warm with their breath.

"There was her baby born
And laid to sleep in the hay,
While music flooded the rafters
And the barn was as light as day.
And angels and kings and shepherds
Came to worship the babe from afar,
But we looked at him first of all the creatures
By the bright strange light of a star!"

PRESEPIO

JOSEPH BRODSKY

Translated by Richard Wilbur

The wise men; Joseph; the tiny Infant; Mary;
the cows; the drovers, each with his dromedary;
the hulking shepherds in their sheepskins—they
have all become toy figures made of clay.

In the cotton-batting snow that's strewn with glints,
a fire is blazing. You'd like to touch that tinsel
star with a finger—or all five of them,
as the infant wished to do in Bethlehem.

All this, in Bethlehem, was of greater size.
Yet the clay, round which the drifted cotton lies,
with tinsel overhead, feels good to be
enacting what we can no longer see.

Now you are huge compared to them, and high
beyond their ken. Like a midnight passerby
who finds the pane of some small hut aglow,
you peer from the cosmos at this little show.

There life goes on, although the centuries
require that some diminish by degrees,
while others grow, like you. The small folk there
contend with granular snow and icy air,

and the smallest reaches for the breast, and you
half wish to clench your eyes, or step into
a different galaxy, in whose wastes there shine
more lights than there are sands in Palestine.

The Puppy Who Wanted a Boy

JANE THAYER

ONE DAY PETEY, WHO WAS A puppy, said to his mother, "I'd like a boy for Christmas."

His mother, who was a dog, said she guessed he could have a boy if he was a very good puppy.

So the day before Christmas, Petey's mother asked, "Have you been a very good puppy?"

"Oh, yes!" said Petey.

"I guess you've been good," said his mother. "Anyway, you're awfully little. I shall go out and get you a boy for Christmas."

But when Petey's mother came back, she looked very much worried.

"How would you like a soft, white rabbit with pink ears for Christmas?" she said to Petey.

"No thanks," said Petey.

"Don't you want a lovely canary?"

"No, I just wanted a boy."

"How about some guppy fish? They're nice," said Petey's mother.

"I don't like fish," said Petey. "I'd like a boy."

"Petey," said his mother, "there are no boys to be had."

"No boys?" exclaimed Petey in dismay.

"Not one could I find. They're terribly short of boys this year."

Petey felt as if he couldn't stand it if he didn't have a boy.

Finally his mother said, "There, now, there must be a boy somewhere. Perhaps you could find some dog who would be glad to give his boy away."

So Petey hopefully started off.

It wasn't long before he saw a collie racing with a boy on a bicycle. Petey trembled with joy.

He called out to the collie, "Excuse me. Do you want to give your boy away?"

But the collie said *no,* he definitely *didn't,* in a dreadful tone of voice.

Petey sat down. He watched the collie and his boy on a bicycle until they were out of his sight.

"I didn't really want a boy on a bicycle anyway," said Petey.

After a while, he saw a red setter playing ball with a boy. Petey was just delighted.

But he remembered how cross the collie had been. So he sat down on the sidewalk and called out politely, "Excuse me. Do you want to give your boy away?"

But the setter said *no,* he definitely *didn't,* in a terrifying tone of voice!

"Oh, well," said Petey, trotting off, "I don't think playing ball is much."

Soon Petey came to a bulldog, sitting in a car with a boy. Petey was pleased, for he was getting a little tired from so much walking.

So he called out loudly, but very politely, "Excuse me. Do you want to give your boy away?"

But the bulldog said *no,* he definitely *didn't,* and he growled in Petey's face.

"Oh, dear!" said Petey. He ran off behind a house and stayed there until the bulldog and his boy drove away.

"Well, who wants to go riding in a car? Pff! Not me!" said Petey.

After a while he met a Scotty, walking with his boy and carrying a package in his mouth.

"Now that is a good kind of boy!" said Petey. "If I had a boy to take walks with and carry packages for, there might be some dog biscuit or cookies in the package."

He stayed across the street and shouted at the top of his lungs, but polite as could be, "Excuse me. Do you want to give your boy away?"

The Scotty had his mouth full of package. But he managed to say *no*, he definitely *didn't*, and he showed his sharp teeth at Petey.

"I guess that wasn't the kind of boy I wanted either," said poor Petey. "But my goodness, where will I find a boy?"

Petey went on and on. He saw Irish terriers, Scotch terriers, Skye terriers. He saw foxhounds, greyhounds, wolfhounds. He saw pointers, setters, spaniels, beagles, chows.

He asked every dog politely. But he couldn't find a single dog who would give his boy away.

Petey's ears began to droop. His tail grew limp. His legs were so tired. "My mother was right," he thought. "There isn't a boy to be had."

As it was getting dark, he came to a large building on the very edge of town. Petey was going by, very slowly because his paws hurt, when he saw a sign over the door. The sign said:

ORPHANS' HOME

"I know what orphans are," Petey said to himself. "They're children who have no mother, and no dog to take care of them either. Maybe I could find a boy here!"

He padded slowly up the walk of the Orphans' Home. He was so tired he could hardly lift his paws.

Then Petey stopped. He listened. He could hear music. He looked. Through the window he could see a lighted Christmas tree, and children singing carols.

On the front step of the Orphans' Home, all by himself, sat a boy! He was not a very big boy. He looked lonely.

Petey gave a glad little cry. He forgot about being tired. He leaped up the walk and landed in the boy's lap.

Sniff, sniff went Petey's little nose. Wiggle, wag went Petey's tail. He licked the boy with his warm, wet tongue.

How glad the boy was to see Petey! He put both his arms around the little dog and hugged him tight.

Then the front door opened. "Goodness, Dickie," a lady said, "what are you doing out here? Come on in to the Christmas tree."

Petey sat very still.

The boy looked up at the lady. Then he looked down at Petey. Petey began to tremble. Would the boy go in and leave him?

But the boy said, "I've got a puppy. Can he come, too?"

"A puppy!" The lady came over and looked down at Petey. "Why," she said, "you're a nice dog. Wherever did you come from? Yes, bring him in."

"Come on, puppy," said the boy, and in they scampered.

A crowd of boys was playing around the Christmas tree. They all rushed at Petey. They all wanted to pick him up. They all wanted to pet him.

Petey wagged his tail. He wagged his fat little body. He frisked about and licked every boy who came near.

"Can he stay?" the boys asked.

"Yes," said the lady, "he may stay."

Petey wriggled away from the hands that petted him. Dickie was the one he loved best.

"But who ever would think," said Petey to himself, "that I'd get *fifty* boys for Christmas!"

CHRISTMAS SUPERSTITIONS

from *Christmas in the Mountains*

HUBERT J. DAVIS

. . . THE MOUNTAINEERS OF SOUTHWEST VIRGINIA celebrated Christmas on January 6, or *Old Christmas*. There are a number of beliefs that many trees and plants bloom on Christmas Eve. These are probably based on the English legends surrounding the Glastonbury Thorn which is supposed to bloom at this time. One of these shrubs is the elder bush.

. . . Another belief is that the bees hum a melody from dusk to dawn on Old Christmas Eve. There are some who say they hum the Hundredth Psalm. They are supposed to come out of the hive at exactly midnight and swarm just as they do in summer.

❋

. . . IT WAS BELIEVED that the crowing of a cock would drive away evil spirits, and that on Christmas Eve, cocks would crow all night long. This shows that he is trying to drive away all evil spirits before the birth of the Savior.

The mountain people believed that the angels were so busy celebrating the birth of Christ that the gates of Heaven were unattended for about an hour on Christmas Eve. Hence, it was thought that if anyone should die at this particular time, he would be able to sneak into Heaven without giving an account of himself.

All through the mountains people believed that on Christmas Eve animals can talk and that they kneel at midnight. This seems to have been widely believed everywhere. Even the American Indians believed that on the eve of their sacred days honoring the Great Spirit, the deer, elk, buffalo, and other animals kneel to Him. . . .

"There are some still living who can remember the time when people went out at midnight Christmas Eve to the cow-byre to see the *Owsen* kneeling in their stalls in adoration of the Heavenly Babe."

Many of the mountain people believed that water will turn to wine at midnight on Christmas Eve. It is also thought to be very dangerous to try to check on the truth of this belief. The story is told of an old man and his wife who sat up to see if this could happen. As it neared twelve o'clock, they began tasting the water, but it was only water until just before the clock struck twelve. Then the old man tasted it again, and yelled to his wife that it was turning to wine. But at that moment, a voice spoke and said, "Go with me." The old man suddenly vanished and was never heard from again.

It is generally believed that if one sits under a pine tree in the forest on Christmas Eve, he or she can hear the Angels sing. But beware! Anyone who does this will die before the next Christmas.

Those lucky enough to be born on Christmas Eve or Christmas Day will have the power to see spirits as well as perform other unusual feats. They are supposed to be able to control witches and ghosts, to heal the sick and to cast out devils.

To hear the chirp of a cricket on the hearth on Christmas Eve was a good luck omen. Good luck would follow the hearer through the coming year.

It is also lucky to eat an apple as the clock strikes twelve on Christmas Eve. This is a guarantee of good health during the coming year.

CHRISTMAS EVE— NOCHEBUENA

CÉSAR VALLEJO

As the orchestra stops playing, veiled
feminine shadows stroll beneath the branches
through whose dead leaves are filtered
icy chimeras of the moon, pale clouds.

Here are lips that weep forgotten arias,
ivory gowns that pretend to be great lilies.
Chatter and smiles in wild flocks
perfume the rude thickets with silk.

I hope you laugh in the light of your turn;
and the epiphany of your form, graceful and slender,
will sing the fiesta in the key of gold major.

My verses will bleat in your meadow then,
humming with all their mystical bronze
that the child-Jesus of your love has been born.

Al callar la orquesta, pasean veladas
sombras femeninas bajo los ramajes,
por cuya hojarasca se filtran heladas
quimeras de luna, pálidos celajes.

Hay labios que lloran arias olvidadas,
grandes lirios fingen los ebúrneos trajes.
Charlas y sonrisas en locas bandadas
perfuman de seda los rudos boscajes.

Espero que ría la luz de tu vuelta;
y la epifanía de tu forma esbelta,
cantará la fiesta en oro mayor.

Balarán mis versos en tu predio entonces,
canturreando en todos sus místicos bronces
que ha nacido el niño-Jesús de tu amor.

CAROL OF THE BIRDS—
EL CANT DELS OCELLS

OLD SPANISH CAROL FROM CATALONIA

A star rose in the sky
and glory from on high
did fill the night with splendor.
Came birds with joyful voice
to carol and rejoice with
songs so sweet and tender.

The eagle then did rise,
went flying through the skies,
to tell the wondrous story,
sang, Jesus, born is he,
from sin we are set free,
he brings us joy and glory.

The sparrow with delight
said, This is Christmas night,
our happiness revealing.
The sky with praises rang,
as finch and robin sang—
oh, what a happy feeling!

En veure despuntar
el major lluminar
en la nit més ditxosa,
els ocellets, cantant,
a festejar-lo van
amb sa veu melindrosa.

L'àliga imperial
va pels aires volant,
cantant amb melodia,
dient: -Jesús és nat
per treuren's del pecat
i dar-nos alegria.-

Respon-li lo pardal:
-Esta nit és Nadal,
és nit de gran contento.-
El verdum i el lluer
diuen cantant, també:
-Quina alegria sento!-

The lark upon the wing
said, Now it seems like spring,
no more is winter pressing;
for now a flower is born
whose fragrance on this morn
to earth brings heaven's blessing.

Sang magpie, thrush, and jay,
It seems the month of May
in answer to our yearning.
The trees again are green
and blossoms now are seen,
it is the spring returning!

L'estiverola diu:
-No és hivern ni és estiu,
sinó que és primavera;
perquè ha nat una flor
que pertot dóna olor,
en el cel i la terra.

La garsa, griva i gaig
diuen: -Ja ve lo maing.-
Respon la cadernera:
-Tot arbre reverdeix,
tota planta floreix
com si fos primavera.-

The cuckoo sang, Come, come,
And celebrate the dawn
this glorious aurora.
The raven from his throat
then trilled a festive note
to the unexcelled Señora.

The partridge then confessed,
I want to build my nest
beneath that very gable
where I may see the Child
and watch whene'er he smiles
with Mary in that stable.

Cantava el cotoliu:
-Ocells, veniu, veniu,
a festejar l'Aurora.-
I lo merlot, xiulant,
anava festejant
a la millor Senyora.

Cantava el perdiu:
-Me'n vaig a fer lo niu
dinsd'aquella establia,
per a veure l'Infant
com està tremolant
en braços de Maria.-

Silent Night

WORDS BY JOSEPH MOHR
MUSIC BY FRANZ GRÜBER

Silent night, holy night,
All is calm, all is bright
Round yon Virgin mother and child,
Holy infant so tender and mild,
Sleep in heavenly peace,
Sleep in heavenly peace.

Silent night, holy night,
Shepherds quake at the sight;
Glories stream from heaven afar,
Heav'nly hosts sing Alleluia;
Christ, the Savior, is born,
Christ, the Savior, is born.

Silent night, holy night,
Son of God, love's pure light
Radiant beams from thy holy face,
With the dawn of redeeming grace,
Jesus, Lord, at thy birth,
Jesus, Lord, at thy birth.

JOY TO THE WORLD

Joy to the World!

WORDS BY ISAAC WATTS

MUSIC BY GEORGE FREDERICK HANDEL

Joy to the world! the Lord is come:
Let earth receive her King;
Let ev'ry heart prepare him room,
And heav'n and nature sing,
And heav'n and nature sing,
And heav'n, and heav'n and nature sing.

Joy to the world! the Savior reigns:
Let men their songs employ,
While fields and floods, rocks, hills, and plains,
Repeat the sounding joy,
Repeat the sounding joy,
Repeat, repeat the sounding joy.

He rules the world with truth and grace,
And makes the nations prove
The glories of his righteousness,
And wonders of his love,
And wonders of his love,
And wonders, wonders of his love.

CHRISTMAS SPARROW

BILLY COLLINS

The first thing I heard this morning
was a rapid flapping sound, soft, insistent —

wings against glass as it turned out
downstairs when I saw the small bird
rioting in the frame of a high window,
trying to hurl itself through
the enigma of glass into the spacious light.

Then a noise in the throat of the cat
who was hunkered on the rug
told me how the bird had gotten inside,
carried in the cold night
through the flap of a basement door,
and later released from the soft grip of teeth.
On a chair, I trapped its pulsations
in a shirt and got it to the door,
so weightless it seemed
to have vanished into the nest of cloth.

But outside, when I uncupped my hands,
it burst into its element,
dipping over the dormant garden
in a spasm of wingbeats
then disappeared over a row of tall hemlocks.

For the rest of the day,
I could feel its wild thrumming
against my palms as I wondered about
the hours it must have spent
pent in the shadows of that room,
hidden in the spiky branches
of our decorated tree, breathing there
among the metallic angels, ceramic apples, stars of yarn,
its eyes open, like mine as I lie in bed tonight
picturing this rare, lucky sparrow
tucked into a holly bush now,
a light snow tumbling through the windless dark.

CHRISTMAS DAY IN THE MORNING

PEARL S. BUCK

HE WOKE SUDDENLY AND COMPLETELY. IT was four o'clock, the hour at which his father had always called him to get up and help with the milking. Strange how the habits of his youth clung to him still! That was fifty years ago, and his father had been dead for thirty, yet he waked at four o'clock every morning. Over the years, he had trained himself to turn over and go to sleep, but this morning it was Christmas.

Why did he feel so awake tonight? He slipped back in time, as he did so easily nowadays. He was fifteen years old and still on his father's farm. He loved his father. He had not known it until one day a few days before Christmas, when he had overheard his father talking to his mother.

"Mary, I hate to wake Rob in the mornings. He's growing so fast and he needs his sleep. If you could see how hard he's sleeping when I go in to wake him up! I wish I could manage alone."

"Well, you can't, Adam." His mother's voice was brisk. "Besides, he isn't a child anymore. It's time he took his turn."

"Yes," his father said slowly. "But I sure do hate to wake him."

When he heard his father's words, something in him spoke: His father loved him! He had never thought of that before, simply taking for granted the tie of their blood. Neither his father nor his mother talked about loving their children—they had no time for such things. There was always so much to do on the farm.

Now that he knew his father loved him, there would be no loitering in the mornings and having to be called again. He always got up immediately after that. He stumbled blindly in his sleep and pulled on his clothes with his eyes shut, but he got up.

And then on the night before Christmas, that year when he was fifteen, he lay

for a few minutes thinking about the next day. They were poor, and most of the excitement about Christmas was in the turkey they had raised themselves and the mince pies his mother had made. His sister sewed presents for everyone and his mother and father always bought him something he needed, like a warm jacket, but usually something more too, such as a book. And he saved and bought them each something, too.

He wished, that Christmas when he was fifteen, he had a better present for his father. As usual he had gone to the ten-cent store and bought a tie. It had seemed nice enough until he lay thinking the night before Christmas. As he gazed out of his attic window, the stars were bright.

"Dad," he had once asked when he was a little boy, "what is a stable?"

"It's just a barn," his father had replied, "like ours."

Then Jesus had been born in a barn, and to a barn the shepherds had come.

The thought struck him like a silver dagger. Why couldn't he give his father a special gift too, out there in the barn? He could get up early, earlier than four o'clock, and he could creep into the barn and do all the milking before his father even got out of bed. He'd do it all alone, milk the cows and clean up, and then when his father went in to start the milking he'd see it all was done. And he would know who had done it. He laughed to himself as he looked at the stars. It was what he would do! He mustn't sleep too sound and forget to get up early.

He must have waked twenty times, scratching a match each time to look at his old watch—midnight, half past one, then two o'clock.

At a quarter to three he got up and put on his clothes. He crept downstairs, careful to avoid the creaky boards, and let himself out. The cows looked at him, sleepy and surprised. It was early for them too.

He had never milked all alone before, but it seemed almost easy. He kept thinking about his father's surprise. His father would come in to get him, saying that he would get things started while Rob was getting dressed. He'd go to the barn, open the door, and then he'd go get the two big empty milk cans waiting to be filled. But they wouldn't be waiting or empty, they'd be standing in the milk house, filled.

"What on earth!" he could hear his father exclaiming.

He smiled and milked steadily, two strong streams rushing into the pail frothing and fragrant.

The task went more easily than he had ever known it to go before. For once, milking was not a chore. It was something else, a gift to his father who loved him. He finished, the two milk cans were full, and he covered them and closed the milk house door carefully, making sure to close the latch.

Back in his room he had only a minute to pull off his clothes in the darkness and jump into bed, for he heard his father up and moving around. He put the covers over his head to silence his quick breathing. The door opened.

"Rob," his father called. "We have to get up, son, even if it is Christmas."

"Aw-right," he said sleepily.

His father closed the door and he lay still, laughing to himself. In just a few minutes his father would know. His dancing heart was ready to jump from his body.

The minutes were endless—ten, fifteen, he did not know how many, it seemed like hours—and he heard his father's footsteps again. When his father opened the door he lay perfectly still.

"Rob!"

"Yes, Dad?"

His father was laughing, a strange sobbing sort of laugh.

"Thought you'd fool me, did you?" His father was standing by his bed, feeling for him, pulling away the covers.

"Merry Christmas, Dad!"

He found his father and clutched him in a great hug. He felt his father's arms wrap around him. It was dark and they could not see each other's faces.

"Son, I thank you. Nobody ever did a nicer thing . . ."

"Oh, Dad, I want you to know—I do want to be good!" The words broke from him of their own will. He did not know what to say. His heart was bursting with love.

He got up and pulled on his clothes again and they went down to the Christmas tree. Oh, what a Christmas, and how his heart had nearly burst again with shyness and pride as his father told his mother and sister about how he, Rob, had got up all by himself and finished all the milking.

"The best Christmas gift I ever had, and I'll remember it, son, every year on Christmas morning, so long as I live."

They had both remembered it every year, and now that his father was dead, he remembered it alone: that blessed Christmas dawn when, alone with the cows in the barn, he had made his first gift of true love.

This Christmas he wanted to write a card to his wife and tell her how much he loved her. It had been a long time since he had really told her, although he loved her in a very special way, much more than he ever had when they were young. He had been fortunate that she had loved him. Ah, that was the true joy of life, the ability to love. Love was still alive in him, it still was.

It occurred to him suddenly that it was alive because long ago it had been born in him when he knew his father loved him. That was it: Love alone could awaken love. And he could give the gift again and again. This morning, this blessed Christmas morning, he would give it to his beloved wife. He would write it down in a letter for her to read and keep forever. He went to his desk and began to write: My dearest love . . .

Such a happy, happy, Christmas!

CHRISTMAS DAY AT SEA

JOSEPH CONRAD

THEOLOGICALLY CHRISTMAS DAY IS THE GREATEST occasion for rejoicing offered to sinful mankind; but this aspect of it is so august and so great that the human mind refuses to contemplate it steadily, perhaps because of its own little-ness, for which, of course, it is in no way to blame. It prefers to concentrate its attention on ceremonial observances, expressive generally of goodwill and festivity, such, for instance, as giving presents and eating plum-puddings. It may be said at once here that from that conventional point of view the spirit of Christmas Day at sea appears distinctly weak. The opportunities, the materials too, are lacking. Of course, the ship's company get a plum-pudding of some sort, and when the captain appears on deck for the first time the officer of the morning watch greets him with a "Merry Christmas, sir," in a tone only moderately effusive. Anything more would be, owing to the difference in station, not correct. Normally he may expect a return for this in the shape of a "the same to you" of a nicely graduated heartiness. He does not get it always, however.

On Christmas morning, many years ago (I was young then and anxious to do the correct thing), my conventional greeting was met by a grimly scathing "Looks like it, doesn't it?" from my captain. Nothing more. A three days' more or less thick weather had turned frankly into a dense fog, and I had him called according to orders. We were in the chops of the Channel, with the Scilly Islands on a vague bearing within thirty miles of us, and not a breath of wind anywhere. There the ship remained wrapped up in a damp blanket and as motionless as a post stuck right in the way of the wretched steamboats groping blindly in and out of the Channel. I felt I had behaved tactlessly; yet how rude it would have been to have withheld the season's greetings from my captain!

It is very difficult to know what is the right thing to do when one is young. I suffered exceedingly from my gaucherie; but imagine my disgust when in less than half an hour we had the narrowest possible escape from a collision with a steamer which, without the slightest warning sound, appeared like a vague dark blot in the fog on our bow. She only took on the shape of a ship as she passed within twenty yards of the end of our jib-boom, terrifying us with the furious screeching of her whistle. Her form melted into nothing, long before the end of the beastly noise, but I hope that her people heard the simultaneous yell of execration from thirty-six throats which we sent after her by way of a Christmas greeting. Nothing more at variance with the spirit of peace and goodwill could be imagined; and I must add that I never saw a whole ship's company get so much affected by one of the "close calls" of the sea. We remained jumpy all the morning and consumed our Christmas puddings at noon with restless eyes and straining ears as if under the shadow of some impending marine calamity or other.

On shore, of course, a calamity at Christmastime would hardly take any other shape than that of an avalanche—avalanche of unpaid bills. I think that it is the absence of that kind of danger which makes Christmas at sea rather agreeable on the whole. An additional charm consists in there being no worry about presents. Presents ought to be unexpected things. The giving and receiving of presents at appointed times seems to me a hypocritical ceremony, like exchanging gifts of Dead Sea fruit in proof of sham of good-fellowship. But the sea of which I write here is a live sea; the fruits one chances to gather on it may be salt as tears or bitter as death, but they never taste like ashes in the mouth.

In all my twenty years of wandering over the restless waters of the globe I can only remember one Christmas Day celebrated by a present given or received. It was, in my view, a proper live sea transaction, no offering of Dead Sea fruit; and in its unexpectedness perhaps worth recording. Let me tell you first that it happened in the year 1879, long before there was any thought of wireless messages, and when an inspired person trying to prophesy broadcasting would have been regarded as a particularly offensive nuisance and probably sent to a rest-cure home. We used to call them madhouses then, in our rude, cave-man way.

The daybreak of Christmas Day in the year 1879 was fine. The sun began to shine some time about four o'clock over the somber expanse of the Southern Ocean in latitude 51; and shortly afterwards a sail was sighted ahead. The wind was light, but a heavy swell was running. Presently I wished a "Merry Christmas" to my captain. He looked still sleepy, but amiable. I reported the distant sail to him and ventured the opinion that there was something wrong with her. He said, "Wrong?" in an incredulous tone. I pointed out that she had all her upper sails furled and that she was brought to the wind, which, in that region of the world, could not be accounted for on any other theory. He took the glasses from me, directed them towards her stripped masts resembling three Swedish safety matches, flying up and down and waggling to and fro ridiculously in that heaving and austere wilderness of countless water-hills, and returned them to me without a word. He only yawned. This marked display of callousness gave me a shock. In those days I was generally inexperienced and still a comparative stranger in that particular region of the world of waters.

The captain, as is a captain's way, disappeared from the deck; and after a time our carpenter came up the poop-ladder carrying an empty small wooden keg, of the sort in which certain ship's provisions are packed. I said, surprised, "What do you mean by lugging this thing up here, Chips?"—"Captain's orders, sir," he explained shortly.

I did not like to question him further, and so we only exchanged Christmas greetings and he went away. The next person to speak to me was the steward. He came running up the companion-stairs: "Have you any old newspapers in your room, sir?"

We had left Sydney, N. S. W., eighteen days before. There were several old Sydney *Heralds, Telegraphs* and *Bulletins* in my cabin, besides a few home papers received by the last mail. "Why do you ask, steward?" I inquired naturally. "The captain would like to have them," he said.

And even then I did not understand the inwardness of these eccentricities. I was only lost in astonishment at them. It was eight o'clock before we had closed with that ship, which, under her short canvas and heading nowhere in particular, seemed to be loafing aimlessly on the very threshold of the gloomy home of storms. But long before that hour I had learned from the number of the boats she carried that this nonchalant ship was a whaler. She was the first whaler I had ever seen. She had hoisted the Stars and Stripes at her peak, and her signal flags had told us already that her name was: "*Alaska*—two years out from New York—east from Honolulu—two hundred and fifteen days on the cruising-ground."

We passed, sailing slowly, within a hundred yards of her; and just as our steward started ringing the breakfast-bell, the captain and I held aloft, in good view of the figures watching us over her stern, the keg, properly headed up and containing, besides an enormous bundle of old newspapers, two boxes of figs in honor of the day. We flung it far out over the rail. Instantly our ship, sliding down the slope of a high swell, left it far behind in our wake. On board the *Alaska* a man in a fur cap flourished an arm; another, a much be-whiskered person, ran forward suddenly. I never saw anything so ready and so smart as the way that whaler, rolling desperately all the time, lowered one of her boats. The Southern Ocean went on tossing the two ships like a juggler his gilt balls, and the microscopic white speck of the boat seemed to come into the game instantly, as if shot out from a catapult on the enormous and lonely stage. That Yankee whaler lost not a moment in picking up her Christmas present from the English wool-clipper.

Before we had increased the distance very much she dipped her ensign in thanks, and asked to be reported "All well, with a catch of three fish." I suppose it paid them for two hundred and fifteen days of risk and toil, away from the sounds and sights of the inhabited world, like outcasts devoted, beyond the confines of mankind's life, to some enchanted and lonely penance.

Christmas Days at sea are a varied character, fair to middling and down to plainly atrocious. In this statement I do not include Christmas Days on board passenger ships. A passenger is, of course, a brother (or sister), and quite a nice person in a way, but his Christmas Days are, I suppose, what he wants them to be: the conventional festivities of an expensive hotel included in the price of his ticket.

CHRISTMAS

VLADIMIR NABOKOV

I

AFTER WALKING BACK FROM THE VILLAGE to his manor across the dimming snows, Sleptsov sat down in a corner, on a plush-covered chair which he never remembered using before. It was the kind of thing that happens after some great calamity. Not your brother but a chance acquaintance, a vague country neighbor to whom you never paid much attention, with whom in normal times you exchange scarcely a word, is the one who comforts you wisely and gently, and hands you your dropped hat after the funeral service is over, and you are reeling from grief, your teeth chattering, your eyes blinded by tears. The same can be said of inanimate objects. Any room, even the coziest and the most absurdly small, in the little-used wing of a great country house, has an unlived-in corner. And it was such a corner in which Sleptsov sat.

The wing was connected by a wooden gallery, now encumbered with our huge north Russian snowdrifts, to the master house, used only in summer. There was no need to awaken it, to heat it: the master had come from Petersburg for only a couple of days and had settled in the annex, where it was a simple matter to get the stoves of white Dutch tile going.

The master sat in his corner, on that plush chair, as in a doctor's waiting room. The room floated in darkness; the dense blue of early evening filtered through the crystal feathers of frost on the windowpane. Ivan, the quiet, portly valet, who had recently shaved off his moustache and now looked like his late father, the family butler, brought in a kerosene lamp, all trimmed and brimming with light. He set it on a small table, and noiselessly caged it within its pink silk shade. For an instant a tilted mirror reflected his lit ear and cropped grey hair. Then he withdrew and the door gave a subdued creak.

Sleptsov raised his hand from his knee and slowly examined it. A drop of candle wax had stuck and hardened in the thin fold of skin between two fingers. He spread his fingers and the little white scale cracked.

2

THE FOLLOWING MORNING, AFTER A NIGHT SPENT in nonsensical, fragmentary dreams totally unrelated to his grief, as Sleptsov stepped out into the cold veranda, a floorboard emitted a merry pistol crack underfoot, and the reflections of the many-coloured panes formed paradisal lozenges on the white-washed cushionless window seats. The outer door resisted at first, then opened with a luscious crunch, and the dazzling frost hit his face. The reddish sand providently sprinkled on the ice coating the porch steps resembled cinnamon, and thick icicles shot with greenish blue hung from the eaves. The snowdrifts reached all the way to the windows of the annex, tightly gripping the snug little wooden structure in their frosty clutches. The creamy white mounds of what were flower beds in summer swelled slightly above the level of snow in front of the porch, and farther off loomed the radiance of the park, where every black branchlet was rimmed with silver, and the firs seemed to draw in their green paws under their bright plump load.

Wearing high felt boots and a short fur-lined coat with a karakul collar, Sleptsov strode off slowly along a straight path, the only one cleared of snow, into that blinding distant landscape. He was amazed to be still alive, and able to perceive the brilliance of the snow and feel his front teeth ache from the cold. He even noticed that a snow-covered bush resembled a fountain and that a dog had left a series of saffron marks on the slope of a snowdrift, which had burned through its crust. A little farther, the supports of a foot-bridge stuck out of the snow, and there Sleptsov stopped. Bitterly, angrily, he pushed the thick, fluffy covering off the parapet. He vividly recalled how this bridge looked in summer. There was his son walking along the slippery planks, flecked with aments, and deftly plucking off with his net a butterfly that had settled on the railing. Now the boy sees his father. Forever-lost laughter plays on his face, under the turned-down brim of a straw hat burned dark by the sun; his hand toys with the chainlet of the leather purse attached to his belt, his dear, smooth, suntanned legs in their serge shorts and soaked sandals assume their usual cheerful widespread stance. Just recently, in Petersburg, after having babbled in his delirium about school, about his bicycle, about some great Oriental moth, he died, and yesterday Sleptsov had taken the coffin—weighed down, it seemed, with an entire lifetime—to the country, into the family vault near the village church.

It was quiet as it can be on a bright, frosty day. Sleptsov raised his leg high, stepped off the path and, leaving blue pits behind him in the snow, made his way among the trunks of amazingly white trees to the spot where the park dropped off toward the river. Far below, ice blocks sparkled near a hole cut in the smooth expanse of white and, on the opposite bank, very straight columns of pink smoke stood above the snowy roofs of log cabins. Sleptsov took off his karakul cap and leaned against a tree trunk. Somewhere far away peasants were chopping wood— every blow bounced resonantly skyward—and beyond the light silver mist of trees, high above the squat isbas, the sun caught the equanimous radiance of the cross on the church.

3

THAT WAS WHERE HE HEADED AFTER lunch, in an old sleigh with a high straight back. The cod of the black stallion clacked strongly in the frosty air, the white plumes of low branches glided overhead, and the ruts in front gave off a silvery blue sheen. When he arrived he sat for an hour or so by the grave, resting a heavy, woolen-gloved hand on the iron of the railing that burned his hand through the wool. He came home with a slight sense of disappointment, as if there, in the burial vault, he had been even further removed from his son than here, where the countless summer tracks of his rapid sandals were preserved beneath the snow.

In the evening, overcome by a fit of intense sadness, he had the main house unlocked. When the door swung open with a weighty wail, and a whiff of special, unwintery coolness came from the sonorous iron-barred vestibule, Sleptsov took the lamp with its tin reflector from the watchman's hand and entered the house alone. The parquet floors crackled eerily under his step. Room after room filled with yellow light, and the shrouded furniture seemed unfamiliar; instead of a tinkling chandelier, a soundless bag hung from the ceiling; and Sleptsov's enormous shadow, slowly extending one arm, floated across the wall and over the grey squares of curtained paintings.

He went into the room which had been his son's study in summer, set the lamp on the window ledge, and, breaking his fingernails as he did so, opened the folding shutters, even though all was darkness outside. In the blue glass the yellow flame of the slightly smoky lamp appeared, and his large, bearded face showed momentarily.

He sat down at the bare desk and sternly, from under bent brows, examined the pale wallpaper with its garlands of bluish roses; a narrow officelike cabinet, with sliding drawers from top to bottom; the couch and armchairs under slipcovers; and suddenly, dropping his head onto the desk, he started to shake, passionately, noisily, pressing first his lips, then his wet cheek, to the cold, dusty wood and clutching at its far corners.

In the desk he found a notebook, spreading boards, supplies of black pins, and an English biscuit tin that contained a large exotic cocoon which had cost three rubles. It was papery to the touch and seemed made of a brown folded leaf. His son had remembered it during his sickness, regretting that he had left it behind, but consoling himself with the thought that the chrysalid inside was probably dead. He also found a torn net: a tarlatan bag on a collapsible hoop (and the muslin still smelled of sumer and sun-hot grass).

Then, bending lower and lower and sobbing with his whole body, he began pulling out one by one the glass-topped drawers of the cabinet. In the dim lamplight the even files of specimens shone silklike under the glass. Here, in this room, on that very desk, his son had spread the wings of his captures. He would first pin the carefully killed insect in the cork-bottomed groove of the setting board, between the adjustable strips of wood, and fasten down flat with pinned strips of paper the still fresh, soft wings. They had now dried long ago and had been transferred to the cabinet—those spectacular Swallowtails, those dazzling Coppers and Blues, and the various Fritillaries, some mounted in a supine position to display the mother-of-pearl undersides. His son used to pronounce their Latin names with a moan of triumph or in an arch aside of disdain. And the moths, the moths, the first Aspen Hawk of five summers ago!

4

THE NIGHT WAS SMOKE-BLUE AND moonlit; thin clouds were scattered about the sky but did not touch the delicate, icy moon. The trees, masses of grey frost, cast dark shadows on the drifts, which scintillated here and there with metallic sparks. In the plush-upholstered, well-heated room of the annex Ivan had placed a two-foot fir tree in a clay pot on the table, and was just attaching a candle to its cruciform top when Sleptsov returned from the main house, chilled, red-eyed, with grey dust smears on his cheek, carrying a wooden case under his arm. Seeing the Christmas tree on the table, he asked absently: "What's that?"

Relieving him of the case, Ivan answered in a low, mellow voice:

"There's a holiday coming up tomorrow."

"No, take it away," said Sleptsov with a frown, while thinking, Can this be Christmas Eve? How could I have forgotten?

Ivan gently insisted: "It's nice and green. Let it stand for a while."

"Please take it away," repeated Sleptsov, and bent over the case he had brought. In it he had gathered his son's belongings—the folding butterfly net, the biscuit tin with the pear-shaped cocoon, the spreading board, the pins in their lacquered box, the blue notebook. Half of the first page had been torn out, and its remaining fragment contained part of a French dictation. There followed daily entries, names of captured butterflies, and other notes:

"*Walked across the bog as far as Borovichi, . . .*"

"*Raining today. Played checkers with Father, then read Goncharov's* Frigate, *a deadly bore.*"

"*Marvellous hot day. Rode my bike in the evening. A midge got in my eye. Deliberately rode by her dacha twice, but didn't see her . . .*"

Sleptsov raised his head, swallowed something hot and huge. Of whom was his son writing?

"*Rode my bike as usual,*" he read on. "*Our eyes nearly met. My darling, my love. . .*"

"This is unthinkable," whispered Sleptsov. "I'll never know. . . ."

He bent over again, avidly deciphering the childish handwriting that slanted up then curved down in the margin.

"Saw a fresh specimen of the Camberwell Beauty today. That means autumn is here. Rain in the evening. She has probably left, and we didn't even get acquainted. Farewell, my darling. I feel terribly sad. . . ."

"He never said anything to me. . . ." Sleptsov tried to remember, rubbing his forehead with his palm.

On the last page there was an ink drawing: the hind view of an elephant—two thick pillars, the corners of two ears, and a tiny tail.

Sleptsov got up. He shook his head, restraining yet another onrush of hideous sobs.

"I-can't-bear-it-any-longer," he drawled between groans, repeating even more slowly, "I—can't—bear—it—any—longer. . . ."

"It's Christmas tomorrow," came the abrupt reminder, "and I'm going to die. Of course. It's so simple. This very night . . ."

He pulled out a handkerchief and dried his eyes, his beard, his cheeks. Dark streaks remained on the handkerchief.

". . . death," Sleptsov said softly, as if concluding a long sentence.

The clock ticked. Frost patterns overlapped on the blue glass of the window. The open notebook shone radiantly on the table; next to it the light went through the muslin of the butterfly net, and glistened on a corner of the open tin. Sleptsov pressed his eyes shut, and had a fleeting sensation that earthly life lay before him, totally bared and comprehensible—and ghastly in its sadness, humiliatingly pointless, sterile, devoid of miracles. . . .

At that instant there was a suden snap—a thin sound like that of an overstretched rubber band breaking. Sleptsov opened his eyes. The cocoon in the biscuit tin had burst at its tip, and a black, wrinkled creature the size of a mouse was crawling up the wall above the table. It stopped, holding on to the surface with six black furry feet, and started palpitating strangely. It had emerged from the chrysalid because a man overcome with grief had transferred a tin box to his warm room, and the warmth had penetrated its taut leaf-and-silk envelope; it had awaited this moment so long, had collected its strength so tensely, and now, having broken out, it was slowly and miraculously expanding. Gradually the wrinkled tissues, the velvety fringes, unfurled; the fan-pleated veins grew firmer as they filled with air. It became a winged thing imperceptibly, as a maturing face imperceptibly becomes beautiful. And its wings—still feeble, still moist—kept growing and unfolding, and now they were developed to the limit set for them by God, and there, on the wall, instead of a little lump of life, instead of a dark mouse, was a great *Attacus* moth like those that fly, birdlike, around lamps in the Indian dusk.

And then those thick black wings, with a glazy eyespot on each and a purplish bloom dusting their hooked foretips, took a full breath under the impulse of tender, ravishing, almost human happiness.

A CHRISTMAS MEMORY

IMAGINE A MORNING IN LATE NOVEMBER. A coming of winter morning more than twenty years ago. Consider the kitchen of a spreading old house in a country town. A great black stove is its main feature; but there is also a big round table and a fireplace with two rocking chairs placed in front of it. Just today the fireplace commenced its seasonal roar.

A woman with shorn white hair is standing at the kitchen window. She is wearing tennis shoes and a shapeless gray sweater over a summery calico dress. She is small and sprightly, like a bantam hen; but, due to a long youthful illness, her shoulders are pitifully hunched. Her face is remarkable—not unlike Lincoln's, craggy like that, and tinted by sun and wind; but it is delicate too, finely boned, and her eyes are sherry-colored and timid. "Oh my," she exclaims, her breath smoking the windowpane, "it's fruitcake weather!"

The person to whom she is speaking is myself. I am seven; she is sixty-something. We are cousins, very distant ones, and we have lived together—well, as long as I can remember. Other people inhabit the house, relatives; and though they have power over us, and frequently make us cry, we are not, on the whole, too much aware of them. We are each other's best friend. She calls me Buddy, in memory of a boy who was formerly her best friend. The other Buddy died in the 1880's, when she was still a child. She is still a child.

"I knew it before I got out of bed," she says, turning away from the window with a purposeful excitement in her eyes. "The courthouse bell sounded so cold and clear. And there were no birds singing; they've gone to warmer country, yes indeed. Oh, Buddy, stop stuffing biscuit and fetch our buggy. Help me find my hat. We've thirty cakes to bake."

It's always the same: a morning arrives in November, and my friend, as though officially inaugurating the Christmas time of year that exhilarates her imagination and fuels the blaze of her heart, announces: "It's fruitcake weather! Fetch our buggy. Help me find my hat."

The hat is found, a straw cartwheel corsaged with velvet roses out-of-doors has faded: it once belonged to a more fashionable relative. Together, we guide our buggy, a dilapidated baby carriage, out to the garden and into a grove of pecan trees. The buggy is mine; that is, it was bought for me when I was born. It is made of wicker, rather unraveled, and the wheels wobble like a drunkard's legs. But it is a faithful object; springtimes, we take it to the woods and fill it with flowers, herbs, wild fern for our porch pots; in the summer, we pile it with picnic paraphernalia and sugar-cane fishing poles and roll it down to the edge of a creek; it has its winter uses, too: as a truck for hauling firewood from the yard to the kitchen, as a warm bed for Queenie, our tough little orange and white rat terrier who has survived distemper and two rattlesnake bites. Queenie is trotting beside it now.

Three hours later we are back in the kitchen hulling a heaping buggyload of windfall pecans. Our backs hurt from gathering them: how hard they were to find (the main crop having been shaken off the trees and sold by the orchard's owners, who are not us) among the concealing leaves, the frosted, deceiving grass. Caarackle! A cheery crunch, scraps of miniature thunder sound as the shells collapse and the golden mound of sweet oily ivory meat mounts in the milk-glass bowl. Queenie begs to taste, and now and again my friend sneaks her a mite, though insisting we deprive ourselves. "We mustn't, Buddy. If we start, we won't stop. And there's scarcely enough as there is. For thirty cakes." The kitchen is growing dark. Dusk turns the window into a mirror: our reflections mingle with the rising moon as we work by the fireside in the firelight. At last, when the moon is quite high, we toss the final hull into the fire and, with joined sighs, watch it catch flame. The buggy is empty, the bowl is brimful.

We eat our supper (cold biscuits, bacon, blackberry jam) and discuss tomorrow. Tomorrow the kind of work I like best begins: buying. Cherries and citron, ginger and vanilla and canned Hawaiian pineapple, rinds and raisins and walnuts and whiskey and oh, so much flour, butter, so many eggs, spices, flavorings: why, we'll need a pony to pull the buggy home.

But before these purchases can be made, there is the question of money. Neither of us has any. Except for skinflint sums persons in the house occasionally provide (a dime is considered very big money); or what we earn ourselves from various activities: holding rummage sales, selling buckets of hand-picked blackberries, jars of homemade jam and apple jelly and peach preserves, rounding up flowers for funerals and weddings. Once we won seventy-ninth prize, five dollars, in a national football contest. Not that we know a fool thing about football. It's just that we enter any contest we hear about: at the moment our hopes are centered on the fifty-thousand-dollar Grand Prize being offered to name a new brand of coffee (we suggested "A.M."; and, after some hesitation, for my friend thought it perhaps sacrilegious, the slogan "A.M.! Amen!"). To tell the truth, our only *really* profitable enterprise was the Fun and Freak Museum we conducted in a back-yard woodshed two summers ago. The Fun was a stereopticon with slide views of Washington and New York lent us by a relative who had been to those places (she was furious when she discovered why we'd borrowed it); the Freak was a three-legged biddy chicken hatched by one of our own hens. Everybody hereabouts wanted to see that biddy: we charged grownups a nickel, kids two cents. And took in a good twenty dollars before the museum shut down due to the decease of the main attraction.

But one way and another we do each year accumulate Christmas savings, a Fruitcake Fund. These moneys we keep hidden in an ancient bead purse under a loose board under the floor under a chamber pot under my friend's bed. The purse is seldom removed from this safe location except to make a deposit, or, as happens every Saturday, a withdrawal; for on Saturdays I am allowed ten cents to go to the picture show. My friend has never been to a picture show, nor does she intend to: "I'd rather hear you tell the story, Buddy. That way I can imagine it more. Besides, a person my age shouldn't squander their eyes. When the Lord comes, let me see him clear." In addition to never having seen a movie, she has never: eaten in a restaurant, traveled more than five miles from home, received or sent a telegram, read anything except funny papers and the Bible, worn cosmetics, cursed, wished someone harm, told a lie on purpose, let a hungry dog go hungry. Here are a few things she has done, does do: killed with a hoe the biggest rattlesnake ever seen in this county (sixteen rattles), dip snuff (secretly), tame hummingbirds (just try it) till they balance on her finger, tell ghost stories (we both believe in ghosts) so tingling they chill you in July, talk to herself, take walks in the rain, grow the prettiest japonicas in town, know the recipe for every sort of old-time Indian cure, including a magical wart-remover.

Now, with supper finished, we retire to the room in a faraway part of the house where my friend sleeps in a scrap-quilt-covered iron bed painted rose pink, her favorite color. Silently, wallowing in the pleasures of conspiracy, we take the bead purse from its secret place and spill its contents on the scrap quilt. Dollar bills, tightly rolled and green as May buds. Somber fifty-cent pieces, heavy enough to weight a dead man's eyes. Lovely dimes, the liveliest coin, the one that really jingles. Nickels and quarters, worn smooth as creek pebbles. But mostly a hateful heap of bitter-odored pennies. Last summer others in the house contracted to pay us a penny for every twenty-five flies we killed. Oh, the carnage of August: the flies that flew to heaven! Yet it was not work in which we took pride. And, as we sit counting pennies, it is as though we were back tabulating dead flies. Neither of us had a head for figures; we count slowly, lose track, start again. According to her calculations, we have $12.73. According to mine, exactly $13. "I do hope you're wrong, Buddy. We can't mess around with thirteen. The cakes will fall. Or put somebody in the cemetery. Why, I wouldn't dream of getting out of bed on the thirteenth."

This is true: she always spends thirteenths in bed. So, to be on the safe side, we subtract a penny and toss it out the window.

❉

OF THE INGREDIENTS that go into our fruitcakes, whiskey is the most expensive, as well as the hardest to obtain: State laws forbid its sale. But everybody knows you can buy a bottle from Mr. Haha Jones. And the next day, having completed our more prosaic shopping, we set out for Mr. Haha's business address, a "sinful" (to quote public opinion) fish-fry and dancing café down by the river. We've been there before, and on the same errand; but in previous years our dealings have been with Haha's wife, an iodine-dark Indian woman with brassy peroxided hair and a dead-tired disposition. Actually, we've never laid eyes on her husband, though we've heard that he's an Indian too. A giant with razor scars across his cheeks. They call him Haha because he's so gloomy, a man who never laughs. As we approach his café (a large log cabin festooned inside and out with chains of garish-gay naked light bulbs and standing by the river's muddy edge under the shade of river trees where moss drifts through the branches like gray mist) our steps slow down. Even Queenie stops prancing and sticks close by. People have been murdered in Haha's café. Cut to pieces. Hit on the head. There's a case coming up in court next month. Naturally these goings-on happen at night when the colored lights cast crazy patterns and the victrola wails. In the daytime Haha's is shabby and deserted. I knock at the door, Queenie barks, my friend calls: "Mrs. Haha, ma'am? Anyone to home?"

Footsteps. The door opens. Our hearts overturn. It's Mr. Haha Jones himself! And he *is* a giant; he *does* have scars; he *doesn't* smile. No, he glowers at us through Satan-tilted eyes and demands to know: "What you want with Haha?"

For a moment we are too paralyzed to tell. Presently my friend half-finds her voice, a whispery voice at best: "If you please, Mr. Haha, we'd like a quart of your finest whiskey."

His eyes tilt more. Would you believe it? Haha is smiling! Laughing, too. "Which one of you is a drinkin' man?"

"It's for making fruitcakes, Mr. Haha. Cooking."

This sobers him. He frowns. "That's no way to waste good whiskey." Nevertheless, he retreats into the shadowed café and seconds later appears carrying a bottle of daisy yellow unlabeled liquor. He demonstrates its sparkle in the sunlight and says: "Two dollars."

We pay him with nickels and dimes and pennies. Suddenly, jangling the coins in his hand like a fistful of dice, his face softens. "Tell you what," he proposes, pouring the money back into our bead purse, "just send me one of them fruitcakes instead."

"Well," my friend remarks on our way home, "there's a lovely man. We'll put an extra cup of raisins in *his* cake."

The black stove, stoked with coal and firewood, glows like a lighted pumpkin. Eggbeaters whirl, spoons spin round in bowls of butter and sugar, vanilla sweetens the air, ginger spices it; melting, nose-tingling odors saturate the kitchen, suffuse the house, drift out to the world on puffs of chimney smoke. In four days our work is done. Thirty-one cakes, dampened with whiskey, bask on window sills and shelves.

Who are they for?

Friends. Not necessarily neighbor friends: indeed, the larger share are intended for persons we've met maybe once, perhaps not at all. People who've struck our fancy. Like President Roosevelt. Like the Reverend and Mrs. J. C. Lucey, Baptist missionaries to Borneo who lectured here last winter. Or the little knife grinder who comes through town twice a year. Or Abner Packer, the driver of the six o'clock bus from Mobile, who exchanges waves with us every day as he passes in a dust-cloud whoosh. Or the young Wistons, a California couple whose car one afternoon broke down outside the house and who spent a pleasant hour chatting with us on the porch (young Mr. Wiston snapped our picture, the only one we've ever had taken). Is it because my friend is shy with everyone *except* strangers that these strangers, and merest acquaintances, seem to us our truest friends? I think yes. Also, the scrapbooks we keep of thank-you's on White House stationery, time-to-time communications from California and Borneo, the knife grinder's penny post cards, make us feel connected to eventful worlds beyond the kitchen with its view of a sky that stops.

Now a nude December fig branch grates against the window. The kitchen is empty, the cakes are gone; yesterday we carted the last of them to the post office, where the cost of stamps turned our purse inside out. We're broke. That rather depresses me, but my friend insists on celebrating—with two inches of whiskey left in Haha's bottle. Queenie has a spoonful in a bowl of coffee (she likes her coffee chicory-flavored and strong). The rest we divide between a pair of jelly glasses. We're both quite awed at the prospect of drinking straight whiskey; the taste of it brings screwed-up expressions and sour shudders. But by and by we begin to sing, the two of us singing different songs simultaneously. I don't know the words to mine, just: *Come on along, come on along, to the dark-town strutters' ball.* But I can dance: that's what I mean to be, a tap dancer in the movies. My dancing shadow rollicks on the walls; our voices rock the chinaware; we giggle: as if unseen hands were tickling us. Queenie rolls on her back, her paws plow the air, something like a grin stretches her black lips. Inside myself, I feel warm and sparky as those crumbling logs, carefree as the wind in the chimney. My friend waltzes round the stove, the hem of her poor calico skirt pinched between her fingers as though it were a party dress: *Show me the way to go home,* she sings, her tennis shoes squeaking on the floor. *Show me the way to go home.*

Enter: two relatives. Very angry. Potent with eyes that scold, tongues that scald. Listen to what they have to say, the words tumbling together into a wrathful tune: "A child of seven! whiskey on his breath! are you out of your mind? feeding a child of seven! must be loony! road to ruination! remember Cousin Kate? Uncle Charlie? Uncle Charlie's brother-in-law? shame! scandal! humiliation! kneel, pray, beg the Lord!"

Queenie sneaks under the stove. My friend gazes at her shoes, her chin quivers, she lifts her skirt and blows her nose and runs to her room. Long after the town has gone to sleep and the house is silent except for the chimings of clocks and the sputter of fading fires, she is weeping into a pillow already as wet as a widow's handkerchief.

"Don't cry," I say, sitting at the bottom of her bed and shivering despite my flannel nightgown that smells of last winter's cough syrup, "don't cry," I beg, teasing her toes, tickling her feet, "you're too old for that."

"It's because," she hiccups, "I *am* too old. Old and funny."

"Not funny. Fun. More fun than anybody. Listen. If you don't stop crying you'll be so tired tomorrow we can't go cut a tree."

She straightens up. Queenie jumps on the bed (where Queenie is not allowed) to lick her cheeks. "I know where we'll find real pretty trees, Buddy. And holly, too. With berries big as your eyes. It's way off in the woods. Farther than we've ever been. Papa used to bring us Christmas trees from there: carry them on his shoulder. That's fifty years ago. Well, now: I can't wait for morning."

Morning. Frozen rime lusters the grass; the sun, round as an orange and orange as hot-weather moons, balances on the horizon, burnishes the silvered winter woods. A wild turkey calls. A renegade hog grunts in the undergrowth. Soon, by the edge of knee-deep, rapid-running water, we have to abandon the buggy. Queenie wades the stream first, paddles across barking complaints at the swiftness of the current, the pneumonia-making coldness of it. We follow, holding our shoes and equipment (a hatchet, a burlap sack) above our heads. A mile more: of chastising thorns, burs and briers that catch at our clothes; of rusty pine needles brilliant with gaudy fungus and molted feathers. Here, there, a flash, a flutter, an ecstasy of shrillings remind us that not all the birds have flown south. Always, the path unwinds through lemony sun pools and pitch vine tunnels. Another creek to cross: a disturbed armada of speckled trout froths the water round us, and frogs the size of plates practice belly flops; beaver workmen are building a dam. On the farther shore, Queenie shakes herself and trembles. My friend shivers, too: not with cold but enthusiasm. One of her hat's ragged roses sheds a petal as she lifts her head and inhales the pine-heavy air. "We're almost there, can you smell it, Buddy?" she says, as though we were approaching an ocean.

And, indeed, it is a kind of ocean. Scented acres of holiday trees, prickly-leafed holly. Red berries shiny as Chinese bells: black crows swoop upon them screaming. Having stuffed our burlap sacks with enough greenery and crimson to garland a dozen windows, we set about choosing a tree. "It should be," muses my friend, "twice as tall as a boy. So a boy can't steal the star." The one we pick is twice as tall as me. A brave handsome brute that survives thirty hatchet strokes before it keels with a creaking rending cry. Lugging it like a kill, we commence the long trek out. Every few yards we abandon the struggle, sit down and pant. But we have the strength of triumphant huntsmen; that and the tree's virile, icy perfume revive us, goad us on. Many compliments accompany our sunset return along the red clay road to town; but my friend is sly and noncommittal when passers-by praise the treasure perched in our buggy: what a fine tree and where did it come from?

"Yonderways," she murmurs vaguely. Once a car stops and the rich mill owner's lazy wife leans out and whines, "Giveya twobits cash for that ol tree." Ordinarily my friend is afraid of saying no; but on this occasion she promptly shakes her head: "We wouldn't take a dollar." The mill owner's wife persists. "A dollar, my foot! Fifty cents. That's my last offer. Goodness, woman, you can get another one." In answer, my friend gently reflects: "I doubt it. There's never two of anything."

Home: Queenie slumps by the fire and sleeps till tomorrow, snoring loud as a human.

⁂

A TRUNK IN the attic contains: a shoebox of ermine tails (off the opera cape of a curious lady who once rented a room in the house), coils of frazzled tinsel gone gold with age, one silver star, a brief rope of dilapidated, undoubtedly dangerous candy-like light bulbs. Excellent decorations, as far as they go, which isn't far enough: my friend wants our tree to blaze "like a Baptist window," droop with weighty snows of ornament. But we can't afford the made-in-Japan splendors at the five-and-dime. So we do what we've always done: sit for days at the kitchen table with scissors and crayons and stacks of colored paper. I make sketches and my friend cuts them out: lots of cats, fish too (because they're easy to draw), some apples, some watermelons, a few winged angels devised from saved-up sheets of Hershey-bar tin foil. We use safety pins to attach these creations to the tree; as a final touch, we sprinkle the branches with shredded cotton (picked in August for this purpose). My friend, surveying the effect, clasps her hands together. "Now honest, Buddy. Doesn't it look good enough to eat?" Queenie tries to eat an angel.

After weaving and ribboning holly wreaths for all the front windows, our next project is the fashioning of family gifts. Tie-dye scarves for the ladies, for the men a home-brewed lemon and licorice and aspirin syrup to be taken "at the first Symptons of a Cold and after Hunting." But when it comes time for making each other's gift, my friend and I separate to work secretly. I would like to buy her a pearl-handled knife, a radio, a whole pound of chocolate-covered cherries (we tasted some once and she always swears: "I could live on them, Buddy, Lord yes I could—and that's not taking His name in vain"). Instead, I am building her a kite.

She would like to give me a bicycle (she's said so on several million occasions: "If only I could, Buddy. It's bad enough in life to do without something *you* want; but confound it, what gets my goat is not being able to give somebody something you want *them* to have. Only one of these days I will, Buddy. Locate you a bike. Don't ask how. Steal it, maybe"). Instead, I'm fairly certain that she is building me a kite—the same as last year, and the year before: the year before that we exchanged slingshots. All of which is fine by me. For we are champion kite-flyers who study the wind like sailors; my friend, more accomplished than I, can get a kite aloft when there isn't enough breeze to carry clouds.

Christmas Eve afternoon we scrape together a nickel and go to the butcher's to buy Queenie's traditional gift, a good gnawable beef bone. The bone, wrapped in funny paper, is placed high in the tree near the silver star. Queenie knows it's there. She squats at the foot of the tree staring up in a trance of greed: when bedtime arrives she refuses to budge. Her excitement is equaled by my own. I kick the covers and turn my pillow as though it were a scorching summer's night. Somewhere a rooster crows: falsely, for the sun is still on the other side of the world.

"Buddy, are you awake?" It is my friend, calling from her room, which is next to mine; and an instant later she is sitting on my bed holding a candle. "Well, I can't sleep a hoot," she declares. "My mind's jumping like a jack rabbit. Buddy, do you think Mrs. Roosevelt will serve our cake at dinner?" We huddle in the bed, and she squeezes my hand I-love-you. "Seems like your hand used to be so much smaller. I guess I hate to see you grow up. When you're grown up, will we still be friends?" I say always. "But I feel so bad, Buddy. I wanted so bad to give you a bike. I tried to sell my cameo Papa gave me. Buddy—" she hesitates, as though embarrassed—"I made you another kite." Then I confess that I made her one, too; and we laugh. The candle burns too short to hold. Out it goes, exposing the starlight, the stars spinning at the window like a visible caroling that slowly, slowly daybreak silences. Possibly we doze; but the beginnings of dawn splash us like cold water: we're up, wide-eyed and wandering while we wait for others to waken. Quite deliberately my friend drops a kettle on the kitchen floor. I tap-dance in front of closed doors. One by one the household emerges, looking as though they'd like to kill us both; but it's Christmas, so they can't. First, a gorgeous breakfast: just everything you can imagine—from flapjacks and fried squirrel to hominy grits and honey-in-the-comb. Which puts everyone in a good humor except my friend and I. Frankly, we're so impatient to get at the presents we can't eat a mouthful.

Well, I'm disappointed. Who wouldn't be? With socks, a Sunday school shirt, some handkerchiefs, a hand-me-down sweater and a year's subscription to a religious magazine for children. *The Little Shepherd*. It makes me boil. It really does.

My friend has a better haul. A sack of Satsumas, that's her best present. She is proudest, however, of a white wool shawl knitted by her married sister. But she *says* her favorite gift is the kite I built her. And it *is* very beautiful, though not as beautiful as the one she made me, which is blue and scattered with gold and green Good Conduct stars; moreover, my name is painted on it, "Buddy."

"Buddy, the wind is blowing."

The wind is blowing, and nothing will do till we've run to a pasture below the house where Queenie has scooted to bury her bone (and where, a winter hence, Queenie will be buried, too). There, plunging through the healthy waist-high grass, we unreel our kites, feel them twitching at the string like sky fish as they swim into the wind. Satisfied, sun-warmed, we sprawl in the grass and peel Satsumas and watch our kites cavort. Soon I forget the socks and hand-me-down sweater. I'm as happy as if we'd already won the fifty-thousand-dollar Grand Prize in that coffee-naming contest.

"My, how foolish I am!" my friend cries, suddenly alert, like a woman remembering too late she has biscuits in the oven. "You know what I've always thought?" she asks in a tone of discovery, and not smiling at me but a point beyond. "I've always thought a body would have to be sick and dying before they saw the Lord. And I imagined that when He came it would be like looking at the Baptist window: pretty as colored glass with the sun pouring through, such a shine you don't know it's getting dark. And it's been a comfort: to think of that shine taking away all the spooky feeling. But I'll wager it never happens. I'll wager at the very end a body realizes the Lord has already shown Himself. That things as they are"—her hand circles in a gesture that gathers clouds and kites and grass and Queenie pawing earth over her bone—"just what they've always seen, was seeing Him. As for me, I could leave the world with today in my eyes."

＊

THIS IS OUR last Christmas together.

Life separates us. Those who Know Best decide that I belong in a military school. And so follows a miserable succession of bugle-blowing prisons, grim reveille-ridden summer camps. I have a new home too. But it doesn't count. Home is where my friend is, and there I never go.

And there she remains, puttering around the kitchen. Alone with Queenie. Then alone. ("Buddy dear," she writes in her wild hard-to-read script, "yesterday Jim Macy's horse kicked Queenie bad. Be thankful she didn't feel much. I wrapped her in a Fine Linen sheet and rode her in the buggy down to Simpson's pasture where she can be with all her Bones . . ."). For a few Novembers she continues to bake her fruitcakes single-handed; not as many, but some: and, of course, she always sends me "the best of the batch." Also, in every letter she encloses a dime wadded in toilet paper: "See a picture show and write me the story." But gradually in her letters she tends to confuse me with her other friend, the Buddy who died in the 1880's; more and more thirteenths are not the only days she stays in bed: a morning arrives in November, a leafless birdless coming of winter morning, when she cannot rouse herself to exclaim: "Oh my, it's fruitcake weather!"

And when that happens, I know it. A message saying so merely confirms a piece of news some secret vein had already received, severing from me an irreplaceable part of myself, letting it loose like a kite on a broken string. That is why, walking across a school campus on this particular December morning, I keep searching the sky. As if I expected to see, rather like hearts, a lost pair of kites hurrying toward heaven.

BLOND

NATASHA TRETHEWEY

Certainly it was possible—somewhere
in my parents' genes the recessive traits
that might have given me a different look:
not attached earlobes or my father's green eyes,
but another hair color—gentleman-preferred,
have-more-fun blond. And with my skin color,
like a good tan—an even mix of my parents'—
I could have passed for white.

When on Christmas day I woke to find
a blond wig, a pink sequined tutu,
and a blond ballerina doll, nearly as tall as me,
I didn't know to ask, nor that it mattered,
if there'd been a brown version. This was years before
my grandmother nestled the dark baby
into our crèche, years before I'd understand it
as primer for a Mississippi childhood.

Instead, I pranced around our living room
in a whirl of possibility, my parents looking on
at their suddenly strange child. In the photograph
my mother took, my father—almost
out of the frame—looks on as Joseph must have
at the miraculous birth: I'm in the foreground—
my blond wig a shining halo, a newborn likeness
to the child that chance, the long odds,
might have brought.

All I Want for Christmas Is You

MARIAH CAREY
AND WALTER AFANASIEFF

I don't want a lot for Christmas
There's just one thing I need
I don't care about the presents
Underneath the Christmas tree
I just want you for my own
More than you could ever know
Make my wish come true
All I want for Christmas is . . .
You

I don't want a lot for Christmas
There's just one thing I need
I don't care about the presents
Underneath the Christmas tree
I don't need to hang my stocking
There upon the fireplace
Santa Claus won't make me happy
With a toy on Christmas day
I just want you for my own
More than you could ever know
Make my wish come true
All I want for Christmas is you
You baby

I won't ask for much this Christmas
I don't even wish for snow
I'm just gonna keep on waiting
Underneath the mistletoe
I won't make a list and send it
To the North Pole for Saint Nick
I won't even stay awake to
Hear those magic reindeers click
'Cause I just want you here tonight
Holding on to me so tight
What more can I do
Baby all I want for Christmas is you . . .

Oh I don't want a lot for Christmas
This is all I'm asking for
I just want to see my baby
Standing right outside my door
Oh I just want you for my own
More than you could ever know
Make my wish come true
Baby all I want for Christmas is . . .
You

HARK!
THE HERALD
ANGELS
SING—

HAIL THE
HEAV'N BORN
PRINCE OF
PEACE

CHRISTMAS
IN WARTIME

Hark! The Herald Angels Sing

WORDS BY CHARLES WESLEY,
GEORGE WHITEFIELD & MARTIN MADAN
MUSIC BY FELIX MENDELSSOHN

Hark! the herald angels sing,
Glory to the newborn King!
Peace on earth and mercy mild,
God and sinners reconciled.
Joyful, all ye nations, rise,
Join the triumph of the skies,
With th' angelic host proclaim,
Christ is born in Bethlehem.
Hark! the herald angels sing,
Glory to the newborn King!

Christ, by highest heav'n adored,
Christ the everlasting Lord,
Late in time behold him come,
Offspring of the Virgin's womb.
Veiled in flesh the Godhead see,
Hail th' incarnate deity!
Pleas'd as man with man to dwell,
Jesus, our Emmanuel.
Hark! the herald angels sing,
Glory to the newborn King!

Mild he lays his glory by,
Born that man no more may die,
Born to raise the sons of earth,
Born to give them second birth.
Ris'n with healing in his wings,
Light and life to all he brings,
Hail, the Son of righteousness!
Hail, the heav'n born Prince of Peace!
Hark! the herald angels sing
Glory to the newborn King!

PEACE

HENRY VAUGHAN

My Soul, there is a Countrie
  Far beyond the stars,
Where stands a winged Centrie
  All skilfull in the wars,
There above noise, and danger
  Sweet peace sits crown'd with smiles,
And one born in a Manger
  Commands the Beauteous files,
He is thy gracious friend,
  And (O my Soul awake!)
Did in pure love descend
  To die here for thy sake,
If thou canst get but thither,
  There growes the flowre of peace,
The Rose that cannot wither,
  Thy fortresse, and thy ease;
Leave then thy foolish ranges;
  For none can thee secure,
But one, who never changes,
  Thy God, thy life, thy Cure.

Letter to John Hancock, President of the Second Continental Congress

GEORGE WASHINGTON

George Washington describes crossing the Delaware River on Christmas.

December 27, 1776

Sir,

I have the pleasure of congratulating you upon the success of an enterprise which I had formed against a detachment of the enemy lying in Trenton, and which was executed yesterday morning.

The evening of the twenty-fifth I ordered the troops intended for this service to parade back of McKonkey's ferry, that they might begin to pass as soon as it grew dark, imagining we should be able to throw them all over, with the necessary artillery, by twelve o'clock, and that we might easily arrive at Trenton by five in the morning, the distance being about nine miles. But the quantity of ice, made that night, impeded the passage of the boats so much, that it was three o'clock before the artillery could all be got over; and near four, before the troops took up their line of march.

This made me despair of surprising the town, as I well knew we could not reach it before the day was fairly broke. But as I was certain there was no making a retreat without being discovered, and harrassed on repassing the river, I determined to push on at all events. I formed my detachment into two divisions, one to march by the lower or river road, the other by the upper or Pennington road. As the divisions had nearly the same distance to march, I ordered each of them, immediately upon forcing the out-guards, to push directly into the town, that they might charge the enemy before they had time to form.

The upper division arrived at the enemy's advanced post exactly at eight o'clock; and in three minutes after, I found, from the fire on the lower road, that that division had also got up. The out-guards made for small opposition, though, for their numbers, they behaved very well, keeping up a constant retreating fire from behind houses. We presently saw their main body formed: but, from their motions, they seemed undetermined how to act.

Being hard pressed by our troops who had already got possession of their artillery, they attempted to file off by a road on their right, leading to Princeton. But, perceiving their intention, I threw a body of troops in their way; which immediately checked them. Finding from our disposition, that they were surrounded, and that they must inevitably be cut to pieces if they made any further resistance, they agreed to lay down their arms. The number that submitted in this manner was twenty-three officers and eight hundred and eighty-six men. Colonel Rahl the commanding officer, and seven others, were found wounded in the town. I do not exactly know how many they had killed; but I fancy, not above twenty or thirty, as they never made any regular stand. Our loss is very trifling indeed,—only two officers and one or two privates wounded.

I find that the detachment of the enemy consisted of the three Hessian regiments of Lanspach, Kniphausen, and Rahl, amounting to about fifteen hundred men, and a troop of British light-horse: but, immediately upon the beginning of the attack, all those who were not killed or taken pushed directly down the road towards Bordentown. These would likewise have fallen into our hands, could my plan have been completely carried into execution. General Ewing was to have crossed before day at Trenton ferry, and taken possession of the bridge leading out of town: but the quantity of ice was so great, that, though he did every thing in his power to effect it, he could not get over. This difficulty also hindered General Cadwallader from crossing with the Pennsylvania militia from Bristol. He got part of his foot over: but finding it impossible to embark his artillery, he was obliged to desist.

I am fully confident, that, could the troops under Generals Ewing and Cadwallader have passed the river, I should have been able with their assistance to have driven the enemy from all their posts below Trenton. But the numbers I had with me being inferior to theirs below me, and a strong batallion of light infantry being at Princeton above me, I thought it most prudent to return the same evening with the prisoners and the artillery we had taken. We found no stores of any consequence in the town.

In justice to the officers and men, I must add that their behavior upon this occasion reflects the highest honor upon them. The difficulty of passing the river in a very severe night, and their march through a violent storm of snow and hail, did not in the least abate their ardor: but, when they came to the charge, each seemed to vie with the other in pressing forward: and were I to give a preference to any particular corps, I should do great injustice to the others. . . .

I have the honor to be, &c.

G. W.

CHRISTMAS BELLS

HENRY WADSWORTH LONGFELLOW

I heard the bells on Christmas Day
Their old, familiar carols play,
    And wild and sweet
    The words repeat
Of peace on earth, good-will to men!

And thought how, as the day had come,
The belfries of all Christendom
    Had rolled along
    The unbroken song
Of peace on earth, good-will to men!

Till ringing, singing on its way,
The world revolved from night to day,
    A voice, a chime,
    A chant sublime
Of peace on earth, good-will to men!

Then from each black, accursed mouth
The cannon thundered in the South,
    And with the sound
    The carols drowned
Of peace on earth, good-will to men!

It was as if an earthquake rent
The hearth-stones of a continent,
    And made forlorn
    The households born
Of peace on earth, good-will to men!

And in despair I bowed my head;
"There is no peace on earth," I said;
    "For hate is strong,
    And mocks the song
Of peace on earth, good-will to men!"

Then pealed the bells more loud and deep:
"God is not dead, nor doth He sleep;
    The Wrong shall fail,
    The Right prevail,
With peace on earth, good-will to men."

THE CHRISTMAS TRUCE, WORLD WAR I

from *The London Times*

January 2, 1915

AN OFFICER IN A HIGHLAND REGIMENT writes on December 28:—

You need not have pitied us on Christmas Day: I have seldom spent a more entertaining one, despite the curious conditions. We were in the trenches, and the Germans began to make merry on Christmas Eve, shouting at us to come out and meet them. They sang songs (very well); our men answered by singing "Who were you with last night?" and of course "Tipperary" (very badly). I was horrified at discovering some of our men actually had gone out, imbued more with the idea of seeing the German trenches than anything else; they met half-way, and there ensured the giving of cigarettes and receiving of cigars, and they arranged (the private soldiers of one army and the private soldiers of the other) a 48 hours' armistice. It was all most irregular, but the Peninsular and other wars will furnish many such examples; eventually both sides were induced to return to their respective trenches, but the enemy sang all night, and during my watch they played "Home, Sweet Home," and "God Save the King," at 2.30 a.m.! It was rather wonderful; the night was clear, cold, and frosty, and across to our lines at this usually miserable hour of night came the sound of such tunes very well played, especially by a man with a cornet, who is probably well known.

Christmas Day was very misty, and out came those Germans to wish us "A Happy Day"; we went out, told them we were at war with them, and that really they must play the game and pretend to fight; they went back, but again attempted to come towards us, so we fired over their heads, they fired a shot back to show they understood, and the rest of the day passed quietly in this part of the line, but in others a deal of fraternizing went on. So there you are; all this talk of hate, all this fury at each other that has raged since the beginning of the war, quelled and stayed by the magic of Christmas. Indeed, one German said, "But you are of the same religion as me, and to-day is the Day of Peace!" It is really a great triumph for the Church. It is a great hope for future peace when two great nations, hating each other as foes have seldom hated, one side vowing eternal hate and vengeance and setting their venom to music, should on Christmas Day, and for all that the word implies, lay down their arms, exchange smokes, and wish each other *happiness!* Beyond all this, the day itself was rendered impossible for war by mist. So altogether I expect, we had a better time than all you poor things at home, who were probably bothering your heads thinking of the chances of war and the discomfort of trenches. Next year, pray God, we will all be round the fire and at peace.

MUSICAL HONOURS.

An officer in the North Staffordshire Regiment writes on Christmas Eve:—

We had been calling to one another for some time Christmas wishes and other things. I went out and they shouted "No shooting," and then somehow the scene became a peaceful one. All our men got out of their trenches and sat on the parapet, the Germans did the same, and they talked to one another in English and in broken English. I got on top of the trench and talked German, and asked them to sing a German Volkslied, which they did; then our men sang quite well, and each side clapped and encored the other. I asked one German who sang a solo to sing one of Schumann's songs, so he sang "The Two Grenadiers" splendidly. Our men were a good audience and really enjoyed his singing. Then I walked across and held a conversation with the German officer in command. One of his men introduced us properly, he asked my name and then presented me to his officer. I gave the latter permission to bury some German dead who were lying in between us, and we agreed to have no shooting until 15 midnight to-morrow. We talked together 10 or more minutes—Germans gathered round, I was almost in their lines within a yard or so. We saluted each other, and he thanked me for permission to bury his dead, and we fixed up how many men were to do it, and that otherwise both sides must remain in their trenches.

Then we wished one another good night, a good night's rest, and a happy Christmas, and parted with a salute. I got back to the trench. The Germans sang "Die Wacht am Rhein." It sounded well. Then our men sang quite well "Christians Awake" and with a good night we all got back into our trenches. At times we heard the guns in the distance and an occasional rifle shot. I can hear them now, but about us is absolute quiet. I allowed one or two men to go out to meet a German or two halfway. They exchanged cigars or smokes and talked. The officer I spoke to hopes we shall do the same on New Year's Day. I said "Yes, if I am here." Of course no precautions are relaxed, but I think they mean to play the game. All the same, I think I shall be awake all night so as to be on the safe side. It is weird to think that to-morrow night we shall be at it again hard. If one gets through this show it will be a Christmastime to live in our memory. Am just off for a walk round the trenches to see all is well. . . . We had an absolutely quiet night in front of us, though just to our right and left there was some firing going on. In my trenches and in those of the enemy opposite to us were only nice big fires blazing and occasional songs and conversation.

This morning after réveillé the Germans sent out parties to bury their dead. Our men went out and in groups began to talk and exchange gifts of tobacco, food, &c. All the morning we have been fraternizing, singing songs, I have been within a yard, in fact, on to their trenches, and have spoken to and exchanged greetings with a colonel, staff officers, and various company officers. All were very nice, and we fixed up that the men should not go near their opponents' trenches, but remain about midway between the lines. The whole thing is extraordinary. The men were all so natural and friendly. Several photos were taken, a group of German officers, a German officer and myself, and a group of British and German soldiers. The Germans are Saxons, a good-looking lot, only wishing for peace, in a manly way, and they seem in no way at their last gasp. I was astonished at the easy way in which our men and theirs got on with each other. We have just knocked off for dinner and have arranged to meet again afterwards until dark, when we go in again and have songs until 9 p.m., when "war" begins again. I wonder who will start the shooting. They say, "Fire in the air and we will," and such things, but of course it will start, and to-morrow we shall be at it hard, killing one another.

LETTER TO TOMMY, WORLD WAR II

LT. COL. RALPH NOONAN,

Solomon Islands

December 25, 1943

Dear Tommy:-

This is the second Christmas that I have had to be away from you and mother and I don't like it, Tommy. More than anything else in the world I would like to be with you and mother today. But I know that it is impossible. Let's hope that there will be lots of other Christmas Days when we can be together, when we can decorate your Christmas tree and set up a nice, big electric train right in the middle of the living room floor. Mother won't approve of the idea at first, but wait and see! In a short time she will be playing with our trains, too. Christmas this year will be celebrated in many strange lands by men who only a few years ago were little boys like you playing with trains and jeeps. In the fog-bound mountains of the Aleutians and under the palm trees of the Solomons, American boys will be celebrating Christmas. . . .

It is a strange background for an American Christmas; yet it is no stranger than the background of the very first Christmas. . . . Sometimes I think that one of the reasons why we are fighting this war is because we want to save Christmas; because we want to play on the floor with electric trains; because we want to be free to live as we want to. But Christmas should be more than just external things, Tommy. Christmas should be something that guides your life just like the Star of Bethlehem guided the shepherds that first Christmas morning. If you always make mother happy, if you help other people whenever you can, if you live so that you are always a credit to mother, your country and your god, then you can be part of the real Christmas every day of the year. Anybody who keeps the real Christmas inside of him every day can't help but be a good boy, Tommy. And good boys make good American men. Give mother a big kiss for me. Tell her that you and I love her lots. Let's all of us pray hard that we can be together again for next Christmas.

Bye, Tommy
Daddy

TELEGRAM TO THE U.S. AMBASSADOR, MOSCOW

W. AVERELL HARRIMAN

December 15, 1968

Charge: *Classification* Control: 25363
Date: 12/15/68
ACTION: Amembassy MOSCOW 2240 PRIORITY
PARIS 25363
FOR AMBASSADOR FROM HARRIMAN
REF: Moscow 6832.

    1. I hope you will give personal attention to the forwarding of Christmas packages to our pilots in North Viet Nam by the Soviet mail. Our Post Office people say it is the direct route. Soviets can despatch them in sealed bags for transshipment to Hanoi.

    2. This is the break we have been looking for. As this subject is my personal responsibility, I would be grateful if you and all hands at the Embassy would see to it that packages are not delayed in transshipment. It is most important to get them there by Christmas. If the Russians need any further authority from Hanoi, let me know at once.

HARRIMAN

Drafted by:
USDEL; WAHARRIMAN: hbs
Concurrence:

Approving Officer:
W. Averell Harriman

S/S—Mr. McNamara
Classification
OFFICIAL FILE COPY

A Christmas Sermon on Peace

MARTIN LUTHER KING, JR.

PEACE ON EARTH. . . .

This Christmas season finds us a rather bewildered human race. We have neither peace within nor peace without. Everywhere paralyzing fears harrow people by day and haunt them by night. Our world is sick with war; everywhere we turn we see its ominous possibilities. And yet, my friends, the Christmas hope for peace and good will toward all men can no longer be dismissed as a kind of pious dream of some utopian. If we don't have good will toward men in this world, we will destroy ourselves by the misuse of our own instruments and our own power. Wisdom born of experience should tell us that war is obsolete. There may have been a time when war served as a negative good by preventing the spread and growth of an evil force, but the very destructive power of modern weapons of warfare eliminates even the possibility that war may any longer serve as a negative good. And so, if we assume that life is worth living, if we assume that mankind has a right to survive, then we must find an alternative to war—and so let us this morning explore the conditions for peace. Let us this morning think anew on the meaning of that Christmas hope: "Peace on Earth, Good Will toward Men." And as we explore these conditions, I would like to suggest that modern man really go all out to study the meaning of nonviolence, its philosophy and its strategy.

We have experimented with the meaning of nonviolence in our struggle for racial justice in the United States, but now the time has come for man to experiment with nonviolence in all areas of human conflict, and that means nonviolence on an international scale.

Now let me suggest first that if we are to have peace on earth, our loyalties must become ecumenical rather than sectional. Our loyalties must transcend our race, our tribe, our class, and our nation; and this means we must develop a world perspective. No individual can live alone; no nation can live alone, and as long as we try, the more we are going to have war in this world. Now the judgment of God is upon us, and we must either learn to live together as brothers or we are all going to perish together as fools.

Yes, as nations and individuals, we are interdependent. I have spoken to you before of our visit to India some years ago. It was a marvelous experience; but I say to you this morning that there were those depressing moments. How can one avoid being depressed when one sees with one's own eyes evidences of millions of people going to bed hungry at night? How can one avoid being depressed when one sees with one's own eyes thousands of people sleeping on the sidewalks at night? More than a million people sleep on the sidewalks of Bombay every night; more than half a million sleep on the sidewalks of Calcutta every night. They have no houses to go into. They have no beds to sleep in. As I beheld these conditions, something within me cried out: "Can we in America stand idly by and not be concerned?" And an answer came: "Oh, no!" And I started thinking about the fact that right here in our country we spend millions of dollars every day to store surplus food; and I said to myself: "I know where we can store that food free of charge—in the wrinkled stomachs of the millions of God's children in Asia, Africa, Latin America, and even in our own nation, who go to bed hungry at night."

It really boils down to this: that all life is interrelated. We are all caught in an inescapable network of mutuality, tied into a single garment of destiny. Whatever affects one directly, affects all indirectly. We are made to live together because of the interrelated structure of reality. Did you ever stop to think that you can't leave for your job in the morning without being dependent on most of the world? You get up in the morning and go to the bathroom and reach over for the sponge, and that's handed to you by a Pacific islander. You reach for a bar of soap, and that's given to you at the hands of a Frenchman. And then you go into the kitchen to drink your coffee for the morning, and that's poured into your cup by a South American. And maybe you want tea: that's poured into your cup by a Chinese. Or maybe you're desirous of having cocoa for breakfast, and that's poured into your cup by a West African. And then you reach over for your toast, and that's given to you at the hands of an English-speaking farmer, not to mention the baker. And before you finish eating breakfast in the morning, you've depended on more than half of the world. This is the way our universe is structured, this is its interrelated quality. We aren't going to have peace on earth until we recognize this basic fact of the interrelated structure of all reality.

Now let me say, secondly, that if we are to have peace in the world, men and nations must embrace the nonviolent affirmation that ends and means must cohere. One of the great philosophical debates of history has been over the whole question of means and ends. And there have always been those who argued that the end justifies the means, that the means really aren't important. The important thing is to get to the end, you see.

So, if you're seeking to develop a just society, they say, the important thing is to get there, and the means are really unimportant; any means will do so long as they get you there—they may be violent, they may be untruthful means; they may even be unjust means to a just end. There have been those who have argued this throughout history. But we will never have peace in the world until men everywhere recognize that ends are not cut off from means, because the means represent the ideal in the making, and the end in process, and ultimately you can't reach good ends through evil means, because the means represent the seed and the end represents the tree.

It's one of the strangest things that all the great military geniuses of the world have talked about peace. The conquerors of old who came killing in pursuit of peace, Alexander, Julius Caesar, Charlemagne, and Napoleon, were akin in seeking a peaceful world order. If you will read *Mein Kampf* closely enough, you will discover that Hitler contended that everything he did in Germany was for peace. And the leaders of the world today talk eloquently about peace. Every time we drop our bombs in North Vietnam, President Johnson talks eloquently about peace. What is the problem? They are talking about peace as a distant goal, as an end we seek, but one day we must come to see that peace is not merely a distant goal we seek, but that it is a means by which we arrive at that goal. We must pursue peaceful ends through peaceful means. All of this is saying that, in the final analysis, means and ends must cohere because the end is preexistent in the means, and ultimately destructive means cannot bring about constructive ends.

Now let me say that the next thing we must be concerned about if we are to have peace on earth and good will toward men is the nonviolent affirmation of the sacredness of all human life. Every man is somebody because he is a child of God. And so when we say "Thou shalt not kill," we're really saying that human life is too sacred to be taken on the battlefields of the world. Man is more than a tiny vagary of whirling electrons or a wisp of smoke from a limitless smoldering. Man is a child of God, made in His image, and therefore must be respected as such. Until men see this everywhere, until nations see this everywhere, we will be fighting wars. One day somebody should remind us that, even though there may be political and ideological differences between us, the Vietnamese are our brothers, the Russians are our brothers, the Chinese are our brothers; and one day we've got to sit down together at the table of brotherhood. But in Christ there is neither Jew nor Gentile. In Christ there is neither male nor female. In Christ there is neither Communist nor capitalist. In Christ, somehow, there is neither bound nor free. We are all one in Christ Jesus. And when we truly believe in the sacredness of human personality, we won't exploit people, we won't trample over people with the iron feet of oppression, we won't kill anybody.

There are three words for "love" in the Greek New Testament; one is the word *"eros." Eros* is a sort of esthetic, romantic love. Plato used to talk about it a great deal in his dialogues, the yearning of the soul for the realm of the divine. And there is and can always be something beautiful about *eros,* even in its expressions of romance. Some of the most beautiful love in all of the world has been expressed this way.

Then the Greek language talks about *"philia,"* which is another word for love, and *philia* is a kind of intimate love between personal friends. This is the kind of love you have for those people you get along with well, and those whom you like on this level you love because you are loved.

Then the Greek language has another word for love, and that is the word *"agape." Agape* is more than romantic love, it is more than friendship. *Agape* is understanding, creative, redemptive good will toward all men. *Agape* is an overflowing love which seeks nothing in return. Theologians would say that it is the love of God operating in the human heart. When you rise to love on this level, you love all men not because you like them, not because their ways appeal to you, but you love them because God loves them. This is what Jesus meant when he said, "Love your enemies." And I'm happy that he didn't say, "Like your enemies" because there are some people that I find it pretty difficult to like. Liking is an affectionate emotion, and I can't like anybody who would bomb my home. I can't like anybody who would exploit me. I can't like anybody who would trample over me with injustices. I can't like them. I can't like anybody who threatens to kill me day in and day out. But Jesus reminds us that love is greater than liking. Love is understanding, creative, redemptive good will toward all men. And I think this is where we are, as a people, in our struggle for racial justice. We can't ever give up. We must work passionately and unrelentingly for first-class citizenship. We must never let up in our determination to remove every vestige of segregation and discrimination from our nation, but we shall not in the process relinquish our privilege to love.

I've seen too much hate to want to hate, myself, and I've seen hate on the faces of too many sheriffs, too many white citizens' councilors, and too many Klansmen of the South to want to hate, myself; and every time I see it, I say to myself, hate is too great a burden to bear. Somehow we must be able to stand up before our most bitter opponents and say: "We shall match your capacity to inflict suffering by our capacity to endure suffering. We will meet your physical force with soul force. Do to us what you will and we will still love you. We cannot in all good conscience obey your unjust laws and abide by the unjust system, because non-cooperation with evil is as much a moral obligation as is cooperation with good, and so throw us in jail and we will still love you. Bomb our homes and threaten our children, and, as difficult as it is, we will still love you. Send your hooded perpetrators of violence into our communities at the midnight hour and drag us out on some wayside road and leave us half-dead as you beat us, and we will still love you. Send your propaganda agents around the country, and make it appear that we are not fit, culturally and otherwise, for integration, and we'll still love you. But be assured that we'll wear you down by our capacity to suffer, and one day we will win our freedom. We will not only win freedom for ourselves; we will so appeal to your heart and conscience that we will win you in the process, and our victory will be a double victory."

If there is to be peace on earth and good will toward men, we must finally believe in the ultimate morality of the universe, and believe that all reality hinges on moral foundations. Something must remind us of this as we once again stand in the Christmas season and think of the Easter season simultaneously, for the two somehow go together. Christ came to show us the way. Men love darkness rather than the light, and they crucified him, and there on Good Friday on the cross it was still dark, but then Easter came, and Easter is an eternal reminder of the fact that the truth-crushed earth will rise again. Easter justifies Carlyle in saying, "No lie can live forever." And so this is our faith, as we continue to hope for peace on earth and good will toward men: let us know that in the process we have cosmic companionship.

In 1963, on a sweltering August afternoon, we stood in Washington, D.C., and talked to the nation about many things. Toward the end of that afternoon, I tried to talk to the nation about a dream that I had had, and I must confess to you today that not long after talking about that dream I started seeing it turn into a nightmare. I remember the first time I saw that dream turn into a nightmare, just a few weeks after I had talked about it. It was when four beautiful, unoffending, innocent Negro girls were murdered in a church in Birmingham, Alabama. I watched that dream turn into a nightmare as I moved through the ghettos of the nation and saw my black brothers and sisters perishing on a lonely island of poverty in the midst of a vast ocean of material prosperity, and saw the nation doing nothing to grapple with the Negroes' problem of poverty. I saw that dream turn into a nightmare as I watched my black brothers and sisters in the midst of anger and understandable outrage, in the midst of their hurt, in the midst of their disappointment, turn to misguided riots to try to solve that problem. I saw that dream turn into a nightmare as I watched the war in Vietnam escalating, and as I saw so-called military advisors, sixteen thousand strong, turn into fighting soldiers until today over five hundred thousand American boys are fighting on Asian soil. Yes, I am personally the victim of deferred dreams, of blasted hopes, but in spite of that I close today by saying I still have a dream, because, you know, you can't give up in life. If you lose hope, somehow you lose that vitality that keeps life moving, you lose that courage to be, that quality that helps you go on in spite of all. And so today I still have a dream.

I have a dream that one day men will rise up and come to see that they are made to live together as brothers. I still have a dream this morning that one day every Negro in this country, every colored person in the world, will be judged on the basis of the content of his character rather than the color of his skin, and every man will respect the dignity and worth of human personality. I still have a dream that one day the idle industries of Appalachia will be revitalized, and the empty stomachs of Mississippi will be filled, and brotherhood will be more than a few words at the end of a prayer, but rather the first order of business on every legislative agenda. I still have a dream today that one day justice will roll down like water, and righteousness like a mighty stream. I still have a dream today that in all of our state houses and city halls men will be elected to go there who will do justly and love mercy and walk humbly with their God. I still have a dream today that one day war will come to an end, that men will beat their swords into plowshares and their spears into pruning hooks, that nations will no longer rise up against nations; neither will they study war any more. I still have a dream today, that one day the lamb and the lion will lie down together and every man will sit under his own vine and fig tree and none shall be afraid. I still have a dream today that one day every valley shall be exalted and every mountain and hill will be made low, the rough places will be made smooth and the crooked places straight, and the glory of the Lord shall be revealed, and all flesh shall see it together. I still have a dream that with this faith we will be able to adjourn the councils of despair and bring new light into the dark chambers of pessimism. With this faith we will be able to speed up the day when there will be peace on earth and good will toward men. It will be a glorious day, the morning stars will sing together, and the sons of God will shout for joy.

CHRISTMAS E-MAILS FROM IRAQ

from Capt. Trent Weston

Date: Sun, 25 Dec 2005 11:59:45 +0300
Subject: Christmas Greetings

All,

I want to wish you all a very merry christmas. I am
for sure having a very merry christmas given the
circumstances. For the past week I have been volunteer-
ing at the Hospital in the Emergency Ward. It has been
quite an experience and makes me feel both guilty and
opens my eyes a lot. I say guilty because I feel that I
should be doing so much more and not riding a desk for
the entire time I am here in Iraq.

As, I still do think of myself as both a warrior and an
Infantryman. It gives me an eye opener because, I look
at what is going on as everyone is complaining about
being in Iraq for the holidays, and about everything
else when they never leave the base. Last night when I
was at the hospital, there was one Marine that sustained
shrapnel wounds to his legs, and back. He was doing very
well and it was not life threatening. There was also an
EPW (enemy prisoner of war) that was complaining of

stomach pains (turned out he was constipated) by the time he got to the hospital, he was fine. There were two Marines that sustained third degree burns to their hands, both were doing very well. However, another Marine was not so lucky as he sustained third degree burns over 30% of his body. All three Marines were hit by IEDs. The last marine was rushed into surgery after he was stabilized. I am sure that I will remember where I was on Christmas Eve 2005. . . . I know that these Marines will always remember where they were.

As for everything else. Things are going well as I count down the days as to when I get back to Germany. Beth is back in Maine celebrating Christmas with her family and is doing very well. I am looking forward to eating dinner tonight as they were roasting pigs last night and it smelled really great.

I hope you all have a great Christmas and an even better New Years.
Trent

CPT Weston's Unit: A Co. 1st MI BN (AE) Iraq

from Sgt. Mike Mira

Sent: Tuesday, December 23, 2003 1:52:05 PM
Subject: Merry Christmas mia bella moglie

Hey Beautiful!

. . . Time isn't passing very fast for me these days. I
can't seem to get into any of the books I've got so I'm
mostly bored. . . .

Got everything ready for christmas yet?

I love you and miss you very much.

I still want to take you out on the town in Nashville
and possibly stay the night. When we do this I'll buy
you a completely new outfit. Whatever you want from
wherever you want to go. Of course we'll go to a nice
restaurant to eat probably inside the opryland hotel,
then go out dancing or to a show of some kind.

Speaking of how you look. I'm proud of you that you
have lost the weight you wanted to lose. I'm also proud
of you for the way you've handled the household manage-
ment and problems that have come up since I've been
gone. I really appreciate you and want you to know that.
I know I don't tell you enough how much you mean to me.
That's part of why I want to take out and buy you
clothes and show you a fun night on the town is to
thank you for all you've done and show how much I care.

How are the kids doing? Did Sienna and Auburn get to
play in the snow while you were up north? Did they do

christmas while you were up there? If so did the kids get anything they really liked? . . .

Anyways. Merry Christmas I miss you and the girls very much. I can't wait to see you. I know it's less than 25 days now.

I love you
M&M

SGT Mira's Unit: A Co. 3/187th INF 101st ABN Div. Iraq

HAPPY XMAS (WAR IS OVER)

JOHN LENNON AND YOKO ONO

So this is Christmas
And what have you done
Another year over
And a new one just begun
And so this is Christmas
I hope you have fun
The near and the dear one
The old and the young

A very Merry Christmas
And a happy New Year
Let's hope it's a good one
Without any fear

And so this is Christmas
For weak and for strong
For rich and the poor ones

The world is so wrong
And so happy Christmas
For black and for white
For yellow and red ones
Let's stop all the fight

A very Merry Christmas
And a happy New Year
Let's hope it's a good one
Without any fear

War is over, if you want it
War is over now
Happy Christmas

WE WISH YOU A MERRY CHRISTMAS

THE CHRISTMAS FEAST

WE WISH YOU A MERRY CHRISTMAS

TRADITIONAL

We wish you a Merry Christmas,
We wish you a Merry Christmas,
We wish you a Merry Christmas
and a Happy New Year!
Good tidings we bring to you and your kin.
Good tidings for Christmas
and a Happy New Year!

Oh, bring us a figgy pudding,
Oh, bring us a figgy pudding,
Oh, bring us a figgy pudding,
And a cup of good cheer.

We won't go until we've got some,
We won't go until we've got some,
We won't go until we've got some,
So bring some out here.

ALL YOU THAT TO FEASTING AND MIRTH ARE INCLINED

ANONYMOUS ENGLISH (MEDIEVAL)

All you that to feasting and mirth are inclined,
Come here is good news for to pleasure your mind,
Old Christmas is come for to keep open house,
He scorns to be guilty of starving a mouse:
Then come, boys, and welcome for diet the chief,
Plum-pudding, goose, capon, minced pies, and roast beef.
The holly and ivy about the walls wind
And show that we ought to our neighbors be kind,
Inviting each other for pastime and sport,
And where we best fare, there we most do resort;
We fail not of victuals, and that of the chief,
Plum-pudding, goose, capon, minced pies, and roast beef.
All travellers, as they do pass on their way,
At gentlemen's halls are invited to stay,
Themselves to refresh, and their horses to rest,
Since that he must be Old Christmas's guest;
Nay, the poor shall not want, but have for relief,
Plum-pudding, goose, capon, minced pies, and roast beef.

"Amos 'n' Andy" Christmas Show Fails Test of Time

from *The New York Times*

HENRY LOUIS GATES, JR.

December 25, 1994

THE CHRISTMAS SEASON—THAT PERILOUS TIME between Thanksgiving indigestion and midnight Mass on Christmas Eve—is an emotional gauntlet for me.

It's a month of almost irresistible appeal for "essential" items that I can't afford and could easily have done without—followed by the sticker shock of credit card statements after New Year's.

Besides, I find relentless holiday cheer inexpressibly depressing.

It wasn't always so.

Last year, determined to recapture the warm glow of childhood memories, I decided to spend Christmas back home in Piedmont, the West Virginia village in the Allegheny Mountains where I spent my first 18 Christmases.

It was a hard sell with my two daughters, who are 12 and 14 years old. No manual for parenting ever prepares you for the battle of wills when you try to persuade adolescents to spend a vacation away from their friends.

Reason soon fails, leaving only the recourse of the desperate: "Because I say so, that's why."

One of the cruelest features of parenthood is the gradual discovery that your children have lives—their own lives.

"Going back to Piedmont is like traveling in a time machine," Liza, the younger child, remarked tartly. "A time machine to nowhere." The cruelty of youth!

Walking with my wife, Sharon Adams, and daughters down the main drag, Ashfield Street, which resembles those frontier sets you see in bad Westerns, I sorted through my abundant reserves of nostalgia to find my happiest Christmas memory.

As we passed what used to be the five-and-10-cent store—it's now a warehouse—I remembered Christmas 1956, when I was 6 years old.

That year, my father invited me to "ring the bell" for the Salvation Army sidewalk appeal, installed between the two double doors of the five-and-dime. Although it meant standing in the snow, half-frozen, I enjoyed myself—more because my father kept me supplied with hot cocoa than because shoppers were tossing money into the red kettle.

I was gulping my umpteenth cup of cocoa when an old black man walked by. His name was Mr. Smoke Clagett.

"Evenin', Mr. Smoke," my father said. "How's it going today?"

"White man still in the lead," Mr. Smoke mumbled as he tossed a quarter into the kettle, then shuffled off through the snow.

"What's that mean, Daddy?" I blurted. My father laughed.

"He always says that," he replied. "I'll explain later."

I don't know that he ever did. He must have realized I was bound to figure it out on my own one day. We had other things on our mind just then.

Back home, while I was still shivering and about drowned in all that hot chocolate, my parents consoled me by letting me and my older brother open one present early. We picked a big box, ripped open the wrapping paper to find a record player and a package of 45s that came with it.

While my brother sang "The Great Pretender" along with the Platters, his arms spread wide and his eyes closed, I tried to puzzle out what kind of thrill Fats Domino had found up on Blueberry Hill.

But the big event of Christmas Eve was always the "Amos 'n' Andy" Christmas TV episode, "Andy Plays Santa Claus." We watched it on a 12-inch set, which seemed mammoth in those days.

The episode opens with the miserly Kingfish visiting his friends' homes, pulling out a Christmas card, reading it out loud, then leaving.

"I just bought one," he explains, proud of his thrift, "and I goin' around readin' it."

But what really captivated me was that in the all-black world of Amos 'n' Andy's Harlem, there was an all-black department store, owned and operated by black attendants for a black clientele, whose children could sit on the lap of a black Santa Claus—even if that Santa was a red-robed and white-bearded Andy—that's Andrew H. Brown to you.

Andy had taken the job late on Christmas Eve just so he could buy a present for Amos' daughter, Arbadella: an expensive talking doll, which Amos "just couldn't afford this year."

And then I saw it. As the camera panned across an easel and paint set—marked $5.95—and a $14.95 perambulator set, there in the heart of Santa Claus Land, perched high on the display shelf, was Arbadella's talking doll.

She was wearing a starched, white fluffy dress, made all the brighter by contrast with the doll baby's gleaming black skin. A black doll! The first I'd ever seen.

How fortunate those people in Harlem are, I thought. Not only do they have their own department stores. Those department stores sell black dolls! My cousins had about a zillion dolls, but none of them black, brown or even yellow.

You could bet your bottom dollar that Piedmont's five-and-dime would stock no such item. That Arbadella was one lucky little girl. And Andy Brown was not as dumb as he looked.

Last Christmas, in Piedmont, I found myself struggling against the gravitational force of family and time, feeling drawn into the same old family roles, helplessly watching the re-emergence of "little Skippy" Gates as we assembled for dinner with so many aunts, uncles and cousins that our children needed a scorecard to tell the players.

Somehow childhood anxieties were easier to tap than childhood merriment.

"Have you washed your hands?" Uncle Harry asked me as we sat down, as if I were still 6. I realized that to him I would always be stuck in a time zone of ancient Christmases.

Then I remembered our collection of "Amos 'n' Andy" videotapes and decided to show it to the girls.

While the dishes drip-dried in the kitchen, I set up the VCR and told Liza and

Maggie to take off their CD headphones and discover that marvelous world of warmth and solidarity that makes the "Amos 'n' Andy" Christmas show such a rare and poignant memory.

I found myself laughing so hard at Kingfish's malapropisms and Andy's gullibility that it took me a while to realize that I was laughing alone.

They'll get it—eventually—I thought. Just wait until they see Arbadella's doll and the scene when Amos tucks his daughter in bed and teaches her the Lord's Prayer while the kindhearted Andy sneaks the doll under the Christmas tree.

So how did these two post-modernists, reared on "A Very Brady Christmas," Kwanzaa festivals, multicultural Barbies and a basement full of black dolls with names like Kenya and Kianja, respond to my desperate effort to drag them down my memory lane?

"It was garbage," Liza pronounced, to my disbelief.

Maggie volunteered, "Fake, pathetic and stupid."

Liza added: "No 8-year-old's gonna lay there while their father recites them the Lord's Prayer. Yeah, Amos, cut the prayer stuff."

Then Maggie demanded, "Why can't we watch 'Ernest Saves Christmas'?"—a 6-year-old movie for children about a goofy white Florida cabdriver who helps to find Santa's successor.

My father, who had entered the room near the end of the program, listened quietly to this aftermath.

"Looks like the white man's still in the lead," he said.

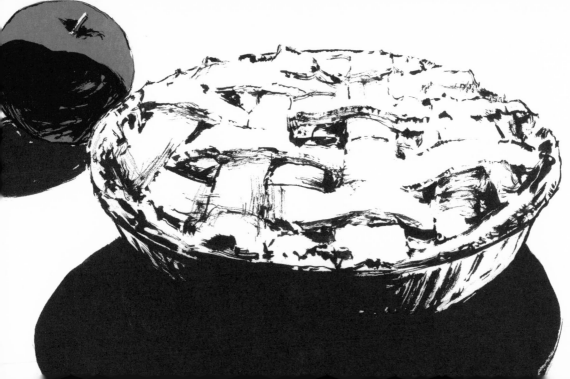

CHRISTMAS IN QATAR

CALVIN TRILLIN

(A new holiday classic, for those tiring of
"White Christmas" and "Jingle Bells")

VERSE:

The shopping starts, and every store's a zoo.
I'm frantic, too: I haven't got a clue
Of what to get for Dad, who's got no hobby,
Or why Aunt Jane, who's shaped like a kohlrabi,
Wants frilly sweater sets, or where I'll find
A tie my loudmouthed Uncle Jack won't mind.
A shopper's told it's vital he prevails:
Prosperity depends on Christmas sales.
"Can't stop to talk," I say. "No time. can't halt.
Economy could fail. Would be my fault."

CHORUS:

I'd like to spend next Christmas in Qatar,
Or someplace else that Santa won't find handy.
Qatar will do, although, Lord knows, it's sandy.
I need to get to someplace pretty far.
I'd like to spend next Christmas in Qatar.

VERSE:

Young Cousin Ned, his presents on his knees,
Says Christmas wrappings are a waste of trees.
Dad's staring, vaguely puzzled, at his gift.
And Uncle Jack, to give us all a lift,
Now tells a Polish joke he heard at work.

So Ned calls Jack a bigot and a jerk.
Aunt Jane, who knows that's true, breaks down and cries.
Then Mom comes out to help, and burns the pies.
Of course, Jack hates the tie. He'll take it back.
That's fair, because I hate my Uncle Jack.

CHORUS:

I'd like to spend next Christmas in Tibet,
Or any place where folks cannot remember
That there is something special in December.
Tibet's about as far as you can get.
I'd like to spend next Christmas in Tibet.

VERSE:

Mom's turkey is a patriotic riddle:
It's red and white, plus bluish in the middle.
The blue's because the oven heat's not stable.
The red's from ketchup Dad snuck to the table.
Dad says he loves the eyeglass stand from me—
Unless a sock rack's what it's meant to be.
"A free-range turkey's best," Ned says. "It's pure."
"This hippie stuff," Jack says, "I can't endure."
They say goodbye, thank God. It's been a strain.
At least Jack's tie has got a ketchup stain.

CHORUS:

I'd like to spend next Christmas in Rangoon,
Or any place where Christmas is as noisy
As Buddhist holidays might be in Boise.
I long to hear Der Bingle smoothly croon,
"I'm dreaming of a Christmas in Rangoon"—
Or someplace you won't hear the Christmas story,
And reindeer's something eaten cacciatore.
I know things can't go on the way they are.
I'd like to spend next Christmas in Qatar.

CHRISTMAS LAUGHTER

NIKKI GIOVANNI

My family is very small
Eleven of us
Three are over 80
Three are over 60
Three are over 50
Two of us are sons

Come Labor Day the quilts
are taken from the clean white sheets
in which they summered

We seldom have reason
and need no excuse
to polish the good silver
wash the tall stemmed glasses
and invite one another
into our homes

We win at Bid Whist
and lose at Canasta
and eat the lightest miniature Parker House rolls
and the world's best
five cheese macaroni and cheese

I grill the meat
Mommy boils the beans

Come first snow the apple cider
with nutmeg . . . cloves . . . cinnamon . . .
and just a hint of ginger
brews every game day and night

We have no problem
luring
Santa Claus
down
our chimney

He can't resist
The laughter

Penalty for Keeping Christmas

Records of the Governor and Company of
the Massachusetts Bay in New England

FOR PREVENTING DISORDERS ARISING IN SEVERALL places within this jurisdiction, by reason of some still observing such festivalls as were superstitiously kept in other countrys, to the great dishonnor of God and offence of others, it is therefore ordered by this Court and the authority thereof, that whosoever shall be found observing any such day as Christmas or the like, either by forbearing of labour, feasting, or any other way, upon any such accounts as aforesaid, every such person so offending shall pay for every such offence five shillings, as a fine to the county. And whereas, not only at such times, but at severall other times also, it is a custome too frequent in many places to expend time in unlawfull games, as cards, dice, &c, it is therefore further ordered, and by this Court declared, that, after publication hereof, whosoever shall be found in any place within this jurisdiction playing either at cards or dice, contrary to this order, shall pay as a fine to the county the some of five shillings for every such offence.

GRACE DEFENDED

COTTON MATHER, D.D.

A Censure on the Ungodliness, By which the Glorious GRACE of GOD, is too commonly Abused. A SERMON Preached on the Twenty fifth Day of December, 1712.

Containing Some SEASONABLE Admonitions of Piety.

. . . . I HAVE ONE WORD MORE TO speak; and I may the more freely speak it, inasmuch as the Cause of *Godliness* is Evidently Concerned in it. It is this, 'Tis an Evident Affront unto the *Grace of God*, for Men to make the *Birth* of our *Holy Saviour*, an Encouragement and an Occasion for very *Unholy Enormities*. The *Grace of God* never Shone out more Gloriously, than in that occurrence upon which an *Angel* flew from Heaven to tell us, *Behold I bring you good Tidings of Great Joy; That unto you there is born this Day a Saviour*. But if such an *Angel* were *this day* to Preach among you, do you think, He would not Thunder and Lighten Wonderfully against the Vicious practices, in which this *Grace of God*, and that Holy Saviour, is this Day Affronted by multitudes of *Ungodly Men* in the World! . . . *That the Feast of Christs Nativity is spent in Revelling, Dicing, Carding, Masking, and in all Licentious Liberty, for the most part, as tho' it were some Heathen Feast, of* Ceres, *or* Bacchus. Yea, the zealous Martyr *Latymer* complained, *That Men dishonour Christ more in the Twelve Days of Christmas, than in all the twelve Months of the Year beside*s. . . . My Concern is now, with our own Children; and for such as we must faithfully Admonish in our Ministry, as we shall answer the same unto GOD. Children, We lay the Charges of God upon you; That if any People take *this Time*, for any thing of a *Riotous Tendency*, you do not associate with them, in such Ungodliness. No, but let your Answer to those Children of Folly be, *The Grace of God in Sending us a Great Saviour calls for more Pious Acknowledgments*. Let your Own *Conscience* be appeal'd unto; the Preacher which every one of you has in his own bosome, hearken'd to ! Can you in your *Conscience* think, that our *Holy Saviour* is honoured, by *Mad Mirth*, by long *Eating*, by hard *Drinking*, by lewd *Gaming*, by rude *Reveling*; . . . You cannot possibly think so! . . . I must faithfully tell you, This way of honouring the Blessed JESUS, who came to *Redeem us from a Vain Conversation, received by Tradition from our Fathers*, 'tis a practical *Blasphemy* upon Him; an High-handed *Blasphemy* upon Him! It is to outrage the Holy Son of God! . . . If you will yet go on, and will do Such Things, I forewarn you, That the Burning Wrath of God, will break forth among you. . . .

From Martha Washington's Kitchen

A Yorkshire Christmas-Pye

First make a good Standing Crust, let the Wall and Bottom be very thick, bone a Turkey, a Goose, a Fowl, a Partridge, and a Pigeon, season them all very well, take half an Ounce of Mace, half an Ounce of Nutmegs, a quarter of an Ounce of Cloves, half an Ounce of black Pepper, all beat fine together, two large Spoonfuls of Salt, mix them together. Open the Fowls all down the Back, and bone them; first the Pigeon, then the Partridge, cover them; then the Fowl, then the Goose, and then the Turkey, which must be large; season them all well first, and lay them in the Crust, so as it will look only like a whole Turkey; then have a Hare ready cased, and wiped with a clean Cloth. Cut it to Pieces, that is jointed; season it, and lay it as close as you can on one Side; on the other Side Woodcock, more Game, and what Sort of wild Fowl you can get. Season them well, and lay them close; put at least four Pounds of Butter into the Pye, then lay on your Lid, which must be a very thick one, and let it be well baked. It must have a very hot Oven, and will take at least four Hours.

This Pye will take a Bushel of Flour; in the Chapter, you will see how to make it. These Pies are often sent to *London* in a Box as Presents; therefore the Walls must be well built.

A GREAT CAKE

The Original Recipe

Martha Washington's great cake recipe results in the type of cake traditionally served for Twelfth Night (January 6), also known as Epiphany, which was the last of the twelve days of Christmas. The original recipe was copied by hand by Martha's niece, and is in the manuscript collection at Mount Vernon.

"Take 40 eggs and divide the whites from the yolks & beat them to a froth then work 4 pounds of butter to a cream & put the whites of eggs to it a Spoon full at a time till it is well work'd then put 4 pounds of sugar finely powdered to it in the same manner then put in the Youlks [sic] of eggs & 5 pounds of flower [sic] & 5 pounds of fruit. 2 hours will bake it add to it half an ounce of mace & nutmeg half a pint of wine & some frensh [sic] brandy."

Icing Recipe from One of
Martha Washington's Cookbooks

"Take two Pound of double refin'd Sugar, beat and sift it very fine, and likewise beat and sift a little Starch and mix with it, then beat six Whites of Eggs to Froth, and put to it some Gum-Water, the Gum must be steep'd in Orange-flower-water, then mix and beat all these together two Hours, and put it on your Cake: when it is baked, set it in the Oven again to harden a quarter of a Hour, take great Care it is not discolour'd. When it is drawn, ice it over the Top and Sides, take two Pound of double refin'd Sugar beat and sifted, and the Whites of three Eggs beat to a Froth, with three or four Spoonfuls of Orange-flower-water, and three Grains of Musk and Amber-grease together: put all these in a Shore Mortar, and beat these till it is as white as Snow, and with a Brush or Bundle of Feathers, spread it all over the Cake, and put it in the Oven to dry; but take Care the Oven does not discolor it. When it is cold paper it, and it will keep good five or six Weeks."

Incidents in the Life of a Slave Girl

WRITTEN BY HERSELF—HARRIET A. JACOBS

CHRISTMAS FESTIVITIES

Christmas was approaching. Grandmother brought me materials, and I busied myself making some new garments and little playthings for my children. Were it not that hiring day is near at hand, and many families are fearfully looking forward to the probability of separation in a few days, Christmas might be a happy season for the poor slaves. Even slave mothers try to gladden the hearts of their little ones on that occasion. Benny and Ellen had their Christmas stockings filled. Their imprisoned mother could not have the privilege of witnessing their surprise and joy. But I had the pleasure of peeping at them as they went into the street with their new suits on. I heard Benny ask a little playmate whether Santa Claus brought him anything. "Yes," replied the boy; "but Santa Claus ain't a real man. It's the children's mothers that put things into the stockings." "No, that can't be," replied Benny, "for Santa Claus brought Ellen and me these new clothes, and my mother has been gone this long time."

How I longed to tell him that his mother made those garments, and that many a tear fell on them while she worked!

Every child rises early on Christmas morning to see the Johnkannaus. Without them, Christmas would be shorn of its greatest attraction. They consist of companies of slaves from the plantations, generally of the lower class. Two athletic men, in calico wrappers, have a net thrown over them, covered with all manner of bright-colored stripes. Cows' tails are fastened to their backs, and their heads are decorated with horns. A box, covered with sheepskin, is called the gumbo box. A dozen beat on this, while others strike triangles and jawbones, to which bands of dancers keep time. For a month previous they are composing songs, which are sung on this occasion. These companies, of a hundred each, turn out early in the morning, and are allowed to go round till twelve o'clock, begging for contributions. Not a door is left unvisited where there is the least chance of obtaining a penny or a glass of rum. They do not drink while they are out, but carry the rum home in jugs, to have a carousal. These Christmas donations frequently amount to twenty or thirty dollars. It is seldom that any white man or child refuses to give them a trifle. If he does, they regale his ears with the following song:—

"Poor massa, so dey say;
Doen in de heel, so dey say;
Got no money, so dey say;
Not one shillin, so dey say;
God A'mighty bress you, so dey say."

Christmas is a day of feasting, both with white and colored people. Slaves, who are lucky enough to have a few shillings, are sure to spend them for good eating; and many a turkey and pig is captured, without saying, "By your leave, sir." Those who cannot obtain these, cook a 'possum, or a raccoon, from which savory dishes can be made. My grandmother raised poultry and pigs for sale; and it was her established custom to have both a turkey and a pig roasted for Christmas dinner. . . .

THE SLAVES' NEW YEAR'S DAY

. . . Hiring-day at the south takes place on the 1st of January. On the 2d, the slaves are expected to go to their new masters. On a farm, they work until the corn and cotton are laid. They then have two holidays. Some masters give them a good dinner under the trees. This over, they work until Christmas eve. If no heavy charges are meantime brought against them, they are given four or five holidays, whichever the master or overseer may think proper. Then comes New Year's eve; and they gather together their little alls, or more properly speaking, their little nothings, and wait anxiously for the dawning of day. At the appointed hour the grounds are thronged with men, women, and children, waiting, like criminals, to hear their doom pronounced. The slave is sure to know who is the most humane, or cruel master, within forty miles of him.

It is easy to find out, on that day, who clothes and feeds his slaves well; for he is surrounded by a crowd, begging, "Please, massa, hire me this year. I will work *very* hard, massa."

If a slave is unwilling to go with his new master, he is whipped, or locked up in jail, until he consents to go, and promises not to run away during the year. Should he chance to change his mind, thinking it justifiable to violate an extorted promise, woe unto him if he is caught! The whip is used till the blood flows at his feet; and his stiffened limbs are put in chains, to be dragged in the field for days and days!

If he lives until the next year, perhaps the same man will hire him again, without even giving him an opportunity of going to the hiring-ground. After those for hire are disposed of, those for sale are called up.

O, you happy free women, contrast *your* New Year's day with that of the poor bond-woman! With you it is a pleasant season, and the light of the day is blessed. Friendly wishes meet you everywhere, and gifts are showered upon you. Even hearts that have been estranged from you soften at this season, and lips that have been silent echo back, "I wish you a happy New Year." Children bring their little offerings, and raise their rosy lips for a caress. They are your own, and no hand but that of death can take them from you.

But to the slave mother New Year's day comes laden with peculiar sorrows. She sits on her cold cabin floor, watching the children who may all be torn from her the next morning; and often does she wish that she and they might die before the day dawns. She may be an ignorant creature, degraded by the system that has brutalized her from childhood; but she has a mother's instincts, and is capable of feeling a mother's agonies.

On one of these sale days, I saw a mother lead seven children to the auction-block. She knew that some of them would be taken from her; but they took *all.* The children were sold to a slave-trader, and their mother was bought by a man in her own town. Before night her children were all far away. She begged the trader to tell her where he intended to take them; this he refused to do. How could he, when he knew he would sell them, one by one, wherever he could command the highest price? I met that mother in the street, and her wild, haggard face lives to-day in my mind. She wrung her hands in anguish, and exclaimed, "Gone! All gone! Why don't God kill me?" I had no words wherewith to comfort her. Instances of this kind are of daily, yea, of hourly occurrence.

Slaveholders have a method, peculiar to their institution, of getting rid of *old* slaves, whose lives have been worn out in their service. I knew an old woman, who for seventy years faithfully served her master. She had become almost helpless, from hard labor and disease. Her owners moved to Alabama, and the old black woman was left to be sold to any body who would give twenty dollars for her.

CHRISTMAS IN THE OLDEN TIME

SIR WALTER SCOTT

On Christmas-eve the bells were rung;
The damsel donned her kirtle sheen;
The hall was dressed with holly green;
Forth to the wood did merry men go,
To gather in the mistletoe.
Thus opened wide the baron hall
To vassal, tenant, serf and all;
Power laid his rod of rule aside
And ceremony doffed his pride.
The heir, with roses in his shoes,
That night might village partner choose;
The lord, underogating, share
The vulgar game of "Post and Pair."
All hailed, with uncontrolled delight,
And general voice, the happy night
That to the cottage, as the crown,
Brought tidings of salvation down.

The fire, with well-dried logs supplied,
Went roaring up the chimney wide;
The huge hall-table's oaken face,
Scrubbed till it shone, the day to grace,
Bore then upon its massive board
No mark to part the squire and lord.
Then was brought in the lusty brawn

By old blue-coated serving man;
Then the grim boar's head frowned on high,
Crested with bays and rosemary.
Well can the green-garbed ranger tell
How, when and where the monster fell;
What dogs before his death he tore,
And all the baitings of the boar.
The wassail round, in good brown bowls,
Garnished with ribbons, blithely trowls.
There the huge sirloin reeked: hard by
Plum-porridge stood, and Christmas pye;
Nor failed old Scotland to produce,
At such high-tide, her savory goose.

Then came the merry maskers in,
And carols roared with blithesome din.
If unmelodious was the song,
It was a hearty note, and strong;
Who lists may in their murmuring see
Traces of ancient mystery;
White shirts supplied the masquerade,
And smutted cheeks the visors made;
But O, what maskers richly dight,
Can boast of bosoms half so light!

THE SECOND OF THE THREE SPIRITS

from *A Christmas Carol*

CHARLES DICKENS

AWAKING IN THE MIDDLE OF A prodigiously tough snore, and sitting up in bed to get his thoughts together, Scrooge had no occasion to be told that the bell was again upon the stroke of One. He felt that he was restored to consciousness in the right nick of time, for the especial purpose of holding a conference with the second messenger despatched to him through Jacob Marley's intervention. But finding that he turned uncomfortably cold when he began to wonder which of his curtains this new spectre would draw back, he put them every one aside with his own hands, and, lying down again, established a sharp look-out all round the bed. For he wished to challenge the Spirit on the moment of its appearance, and did not wish to be taken by surprise and made nervous.

Gentlemen of the free-and-easy sort, who plume themselves on being acquainted with a move or two, and being usually equal to the time of day, express the wide range of their capacity for adventure by observing that they are good for anything from pitch-and-toss to manslaughter; between which opposite extremes, no doubt, there lies a tolerably wide and comprehensive range of subjects. Without venturing for Scrooge quite as hardily as this, I don't mind calling on you to believe that he was ready for a good broad field of strange appearances, and that nothing between a baby and a rhinoceros would have astonished him very much.

Now, being prepared for almost anything, he was not by any means prepared for nothing; and consequently, when the bell struck One, and no shape appeared, he was taken with a violent fit of trembling. Five minutes, ten minutes, a quarter of an hour went by, yet nothing came. All this time he lay upon his bed, the very core and centre of a blaze of ruddy light, which streamed upon it when the clock pro-claimed the hour; and which, being only light, was more alarming than a dozen ghosts, as he was powerless to make out what it meant, or would be at; and was sometimes apprehensive that he might be at that very moment an interesting case of spontaneous combustion, without having the consolation of knowing it. At last, however, he began to think—as you or I would have thought at first; for it is always the person not in the predicament who knows what ought to have been done in it, and would unquestionably have done it too—at last, I say, he began to think that the source and secret of this ghostly light might be in the adjoining room, from whence, on further tracing it, it seemed to shine. This idea taking full possession of his mind, he got up softly, and shuffled in his slippers to the door.

The moment Scrooge's hand was on the lock, a strange voice called him by his name, and bade him enter. He obeyed.

It was his own room. There was no doubt about that. But it had undergone a surprising transformation. The walls and ceiling were so hung with living green, that it looked a perfect grove; from every part of which bright gleaming berries glis-tened. The crisp leaves of holly, mistletoe, and ivy reflected back the light, as if so many little mirrors had been scattered there; and such a mighty blaze went roaring up the chimney as that dull petrification of a hearth had never known in Scrooge's time, or Marley's, or for many and many a winter season gone. Heaped up on the floor, to form a kind of throne, were turkeys, geese, game, poultry, brawn, great joints of meat, sucking-pigs, long wreaths of sausages, mince-pies, plum-puddings, barrels of oysters, red-hot chestnuts, cherry-cheeked apples, juicy oranges, luscious pears, immense twelfth-cakes, and seething bowls of punch, that made the cham-ber dim with their delicious steam. In easy state upon this couch there sat a jolly Giant, glorious to see; who bore a glowing torch, in shape not unlike Plenty's horn, and held it up, high up, to shed its light on Scrooge as he came peeping round the door.

"Come in!" exclaimed the Ghost. "Come in! and know me better, man!"

Scrooge entered timidly, and hung his head before this Spirit. He was not the dogged Scrooge he had been; and though the Spirit's eyes were clear and kind, he did not like to meet them.

"I am the Ghost of Christmas Present," said the Spirit. "Look upon me!"

Scrooge reverently did so. It was clothed in one simple deep green robe, or mantle, bordered with white fur. This garment hung so loosely on the figure, that its capacious breast was bare, as if disdaining to be warded or concealed by any artifice. Its feet, observable beneath the ample folds of the garment, were also bare; and on its head it wore no other covering than a holly wreath, set here and there with shining icicles. Its dark-brown curls were long and free; free as its genial face, its sparkling eye, its open hand, its cheery voice, its unconstrained demeanour, and its joyful air. Girded round its middle was an antique scabbard; but no sword was in it, and the ancient sheath was eaten up with rust.

"You have never seen the like of me before!" exclaimed the Spirit.

"Never," Scrooge made answer to it.

"Have never walked forth with the younger members of my family; meaning (for I am very young) my elder brothers born in these later years?" pursued the Phantom.

"I don't think I have," said Scrooge. "I am afraid I have not. Have you had many brothers, Spirit?"

"More than eighteen hundred," said the Ghost.

"A tremendous family to provide for," muttered Scrooge.

The Ghost of Christmas Present rose.

"Spirit," said Scrooge submissively, "conduct me where you will. I went forth last night on compulsion, and I learned a lesson which is working now. Tonight if you have aught to teach me, let me profit by it."

"Touch my robe!"

Scrooge did as he was told, and held it fast.

Holly, mistletoe, red berries, ivy, turkeys, geese, game, poultry, brawn, meat, pigs, sausages, oysters, pies, puddings, fruit, and punch, all vanished instantly. So did the room, the fire, the ruddy glow, the hour of night, and they stood in the city streets on Christmas morning, where (for the weather was severe) the people made a rough, but brisk and not unpleasant kind of music, in scraping the snow from the pavement in front of their dwellings, and from the tops of their houses, whence it was mad delight to the boys to see it come plumping down into the road below, and splitting into artificial little snowstorms.

The house-fronts looked black enough, and the windows blacker, contrasting with the smooth white sheet of snow upon the roofs, and with the dirtier snow upon the ground; which last deposit had been ploughed up in deep furrows by the heavy wheels of carts and wagons: furrows that crossed and recrossed each other hundreds of times where the great streets branched off; and made intricate channels, hard to trace in the thick yellow mud and icy water. The sky was gloomy, and the shortest streets were choked up with a dingy mist, half thawed, half frozen, whose heavier particles descended in a shower of sooty atoms, as if all the chimneys in Great Britain had, by one consent, caught fire, and were blazing away to their dear heart's content. There was nothing very cheerful in the climate or the town, and yet was there an air of cheerfulness abroad that the clearest summer air and brightest summer sun might have endeavored to diffuse in vain.

For the people who were shoveling away on the house-tops were jovial and full of glee; calling out to one another from the parapets, and now and then exchanging a facetious snowball—better-natured missile far than many a wordy jest— laughing heartily if it went right, and not less heartily if it went wrong. The poulterers' shops were still half open, and the fruiterers' were radiant in their glory. There were great, round, pot-bellied baskets of chestnuts, shaped like the waist- coats of jolly old gentlemen, lolling at the doors, and tumbling out into the street in their apoplectic opulence. There were ruddy, brown-faced, broad-girthed Spanish onions, shining in the fatness of their growth like Spanish friars, and wink- ing from their shelves in wanton slyness at the girls as they went by, and glanced demurely at the hung-up mistletoe. There were pears and apples clustered high in blooming pyramids; there were bunches of grapes, made, in the shopkeepers' benevolence, to dangle from conspicuous hooks that people's mouths might water gratis as they passed; there were piles of filberts, mossy and brown, recalling, in their fragrance, ancient walks among the woods, and pleasant shufflings ankle deep through withered leaves; there were Norfolk Biffins, squab and swarthy, setting off the yellow of the oranges and lemons, and, in the great compactness of their juicy persons, urgently entreating and beseeching to be carried home in paper bags and eaten after dinner. The very gold and silver fish, set forth among these choice fruits in a bowl, though members of a dull and stagnant-blooded race, appeared to know that there was something going on; and, to a fish, went gasping round and round their little world in slow and passionless excitement.

The Grocers'! oh, the Grocers'! nearly closed, with perhaps two shutters down, or one; but through those gaps such glimpses! It was not alone that the scales descending on the counter made a merry sound, or that the twine and roller parted company so briskly, or that the canisters were rattled up and down like juggling tricks, or even that the blended scents of tea and coffee were so grateful to the nose, or even that the raisins were so plentiful and rare, the almonds so extremely white, the sticks of cinnamon so long and straight, the other spices so delicious, the candied fruits so caked and spotted with molten sugar as to make the coldest lookers-on feel faint, and subsequently bilious. Nor was it that the figs were moist and pulpy, or that the French plums blushed in modest tartness from their highly-decorated boxes, or that everything was good to eat and in its Christmas dress; but the customers were all so hurried and so eager in the hopeful promise of the day, that they tumbled up against each other at the door, crashing their wicker baskets wildly, and left their purchases upon the counter, and came running back to fetch them, and committed hundreds of the like mistakes, in the best humour possible; while the grocer and his people were so frank and fresh, that the polished hearts with which they fastened their aprons behind might have been their own, worn outside for general inspection, and for Christmas daws to peck at if they chose.

But soon the steeples called good people all to church and chapel, and away they came, flocking through the streets in their best clothes and with their gayest faces. And at the same time there emerged, from scores of by-streets, lanes, and nameless turnings, innumerable people, carrying their dinners to the bakers' shops. The sight of these poor revelers appeared to interest the Spirit very much, for he stood with Scrooge beside him in a baker's doorway, and, taking off the covers as their bearers passed, sprinkled incense on their dinners from his torch. And it was a very uncommon kind of torch, for once or twice, when there were angry words between some dinner-carriers who had jostled each other, he shed a few drops of water on them from it, and their good-humor was restored directly. For they said, it was a shame to quarrel upon Christmas Day. And so it was! God love it, so it was!

In time the bells ceased, and the bakers were shut up; and yet there was a genial shadowing forth of all these dinners, and the progress of their cooking, in the thawed blotch of wet above each baker's oven, where the pavement smoked as if its stones were cooking too.

"Is there a peculiar flavor in what you sprinkle from your torch?" asked Scrooge.

"There is. My own."

"Would it apply to any kind of dinner on this day?" asked Scrooge.

"To any kindly given. To a poor one most."

"Why to a poor one most?" asked Scrooge.

"Because it needs it most."

"Spirit!" said Scrooge, after a moment's thought, "I wonder you, of all the beings in the many worlds about us, should desire to cramp these people's opportunities of innocent enjoyment."

"I!" cried the Spirit.

"You would deprive them of their means of dining every seventh day, often the only day on which they can be said to dine at all," said Scrooge; "wouldn't you?"

"I!" cried the Spirit.

"You seek to close these places on the Seventh Day," said Scrooge. "And it comes to the same thing."

"I seek!" exclaimed the Spirit.

"Forgive me if I am wrong. It has been done in your name, or at least in that of your family," said Scrooge.

"There are some upon this earth of yours," returned the Spirit, "who lay claim to know us, and who do their deeds of passion, pride, ill-will, hatred, envy, bigotry, and selfishness in our name, who are as strange to us, and all our kith and kin, as if they had never lived. Remember that, and charge their doings on themselves, not us."

Scrooge promised that he would; and they went on, invisible, as they had been before, into the suburbs of the town. It was a remarkable quality of the Ghost (which Scrooge had observed at the baker's), that notwithstanding his gigantic size, he could accommodate himself to any place with ease; and that he stood beneath a low roof quite as gracefully and like a supernatural creature as it was possible he could have done in any lofty hall.

And perhaps it was the pleasure the good Spirit had in showing off this power of his, or else it was his own kind, generous, hearty nature, and his sympathy with all poor men, that led him straight to Scrooge's clerk's; for there he went, and took

Scrooge with him, holding to his robe; and on the threshold of the door the Spirit smiled, and stopped to bless Bob Cratchit's dwelling with the sprinklings of his torch. Think of that! Bob had but fifteen "Bob" a week himself; he pocketed on Saturdays but fifteen copies of his Christian name; and yet the Ghost of Christmas Present blessed his four-roomed house!

Then up rose Mrs. Cratchit, Cratchit's wife, dressed out but poorly in a twice-turned gown, but brave in ribbons, which are cheap, and make a goodly show for sixpence; and she laid the cloth, assisted by Belinda Cratchit, second of her daughters, also brave in ribbons; while Master Peter Cratchit plunged a fork into the saucepan of potatoes, and getting the corners of his monstrous shirt-collar (Bob's private property, conferred upon his son and heir in honor of the day), into his mouth, rejoiced to find himself so gallantly attired, and yearned to show his linen in the fashionable Parks. And now two smaller Cratchits, boy and girl, came tearing in, screaming that outside the baker's they had smelt the goose, and known it for their own; and basking in luxurious thoughts of sage and onion, these young Cratchits danced about the table, and exalted Master Peter Cratchit to the skies, while he (not proud, although his collars nearly choked him) blew the fire, until the slow potatoes, bubbling up, knocked loudly at the saucepan-lid to be let out and peeled.

"What has ever got your precious father, then?" said Mrs. Cratchit. "And your brother, Tiny Tim? And Martha warn't as late last Christmas Day by half an hour!"

"Here's Martha, mother!" said a girl, appearing as she spoke.

"Here's Martha, mother!" cried the two young Cratchits. "Hurrah! There's *such* a goose, Martha!"

"Why, bless your heart alive, my dear, how late you are!" said Mrs. Cratchit, kissing her a dozen times, and taking off her shawl and bonnet for her with officious zeal.

"We'd a deal of work to finish up last night," replied the girl, "and had to clear away this morning, mother!"

"Well! Never mind so long as you are come," said Mrs. Cratchit. "Sit ye down before the fire, my dear, and have a warm, Lord bless ye!"

"No, no! There's father coming," cried the two young Cratchits, who were everywhere at once. "Hide, Martha, hide!"

So Martha hid herself, and in came little Bob, the father, with at least three feet of comforter, exclusive of the fringe, hanging down before him, and his theadbare clothes darned up and brushed to look seasonable, and Tiny Tim upon his shoulder. Alas for Tiny Tim, he bore a little crutch, and had his limbs supported by an iron frame!

"Why, where's our Martha?" cried Bob Cratchit, looking round.

"Not coming," said Mrs. Cratchit.

"Not coming!" said Bob, with a sudden declension in his high spirits; for he had been Tim's blood-horse all the way from church, and had come home rampant. "Not coming upon Christmas Day!"

Martha didn't like to see him disappointed, if it were only in joke; so she came out prematurely from behind the closet door, and ran into his arms, while the two young Cratchits hustled Tiny Tim, and bore him off into the wash-house, that he might hear the pudding singing in the copper.

"And how did little Tim behave?" asked Mrs. Cratchit when she had rallied Bob on his credulity, and Bob had hugged his daughter to his heart's content.

"As good as gold," said Bob, "and better. Somehow, he gets thoughtful, sitting by himself so much, and thinks the strangest things you ever heard. He told me, coming home, that he hoped the people saw him in the church, because he was a cripple, and it might be pleasant to them to remember upon Christmas Day who made lame beggars walk and blind men see."

Bob's voice was tremulous when he told them this, and trembled more when he said that Tiny Tim was growing strong and hearty.

His active little crutch was heard upon the floor, and back came Tiny Tim before another word was spoken, escorted by his brother and sister, to his stool beside the fire; and while Bob, turning up his cuffs—as if, poor fellow, they were capable of being made more shabby—compounded some hot mixture in a jug with gin and lemons, and stirred it round and round, and put it on the hob to simmer, Master Peter and the two ubiquitous young Cratchits went to fetch the goose, with which they soon returned in high procession.

Such a bustle ensued that you might have thought a goose the rarest of all birds; a feathered phenomenon, to which a black swan was a matter of course—and, in truth, it was something very like it in that house. Mrs. Cratchit made the gravy (ready beforehand in a little saucepan) hissing hot; Master Peter mashed the potatoes with incredible vigour; Miss Belinda sweetened up the apple sauce; Martha dusted the hot plates; Bob took Tiny Tim beside him in a tiny corner at the table; the two young Cratchits set chairs for everybody, not forgetting themselves, and, mounting guard upon their posts, crammed spoons into their mouths, lest they should shriek for goose before their turn came to be helped. At last the dishes were set on, and grace was said. It was succeeded by a breathless pause, as Mrs. Cratchit, looking slowly all along the carving-knife, prepared to plunge it in the breast; but when she did, and when the long-expected gush of stuffing issued forth, one murmur of delight arose all round the board, and even Tiny Tim, excited by the two young Cratchits, beat on the table with the handle of his knife and feebly cried Hurrah!

There never was such a goose. Bob said he didn't believe there ever was such a goose cooked. Its tenderness and flavor, size and cheapness, were the themes of universal admiration. Eked out by apple sauce and mashed potatoes, it was a sufficient dinner for the whole family; indeed, as Mrs. Cratchit said with great delight (surveying one small atom of a bone upon the dish), they hadn't ate it all at last! Yet every one had had enough, and the youngest Cratchits, in particular, were steeped in sage and onion to the eyebrows! But now, the plates being changed by Miss Belinda, Mrs. Cratchit left the room alone—too nervous to bear witnesses—to take the pudding up, and bring it in.

Suppose it should not be done enough! Suppose it should break in turning out! Suppose somebody should have got over the wall of the back-yard and stolen it, while they were merry with the goose—a supposition at which the two young Cratchits became livid! All sorts of horrors were supposed.

Hallo! A great deal of steam! The pudding was out of the copper. A smell like a washing-day! That was the cloth. A smell like an eating-house and a pastry-cook's next door to each other, with a laundress's next door to that! That was the pudding! In half a minute Mrs. Cratchit entered—flushed, but smiling proudly—with the pudding, like a speckled cannon-ball, so hard and firm, blazing in half of half-a-quartern of ignited brandy, and bedight with Christmas holly stuck into the top.

Oh, a wonderful pudding! Bob Cratchit said, and calmly too, that he regarded it as the greatest success achieved by Mrs. Cratchit since their marriage. Mrs.

Cratchit said that, now the weight was off her mind, she would confess she had her doubts about the quantity of flour. Everybody had something to say about it, but nobody said or thought it was at all a small pudding for a large family. It would have been flat heresy to do so. Any Cratchit would have blushed to hint at such a thing.

At last the dinner was all done, the cloth was cleared, the hearth swept, and the fire made up. The compound in the jug being tasted, and considered perfect, apples and oranges were put upon the table, and a shovel full of chestnuts on the fire. Then all the Cratchit family drew round the hearth in what Bob Cratchit called a circle, meaning half a one; and at Bob Cratchit's elbow stood the family display of glass. Two tumblers and a custard cup without a handle.

These held the hot stuff from the jug, however, as well as golden goblets would have done; and Bob served it out with beaming looks, while the chestnuts on the fire sputtered and cracked noisily. Then Bob proposed:

"A merry Christmas to us all, my dears. God bless us!"

Which all the family re-echoed.

"God bless us every one!" said Tiny Tim, the last of all.

He sat very close to his father's side, upon his little stool. Bob held his withered little hand to his, as if he loved the child, and wished to keep him by his side, and dreaded that he might be taken from him.

"Spirit," said Scrooge, with an interest he had never felt before, "tell me if Tiny Tim will live."

"I see a vacant seat," replied the Ghost, "in the poor chimney corner, and a crutch without an owner, carefully preserved. If these shadows remain unaltered by the Future, the child will die."

"No, no," said Scrooge. "Oh no, kind Spirit! I say he will be spared."

"If these shadows remain unaltered by the Future none other of my race," returned the Ghost, "will find him here. What then? If he be like to die, he had better do it, and decrease the surplus population."

Scrooge hung his head to hear his own words quoted by the Spirit, and was overcome with penitence and grief.

"Man," said the Ghost, "if man you be in heart, not adamant, forbear that wicked cant until you have discovered what the surplus is, and where it is. Will you decide what men shall live, what men shall die? It may be that, in the sight of

Heaven, you are more worthless and less fit to live than millions like this poor man's child. O God! To hear the insect on the leaf pronouncing on the too much life among his hungry brothers in the dust!"

Scrooge bent before the Ghost's rebuke, and, trembling, cast his eyes upon the ground. But he raised them speedily on hearing his own name.

"Mr. Scrooge!' said Bob. "I'll give you Mr. Scrooge, the Founder of the Feast!"

"The Founder of the Feast, indeed!" cried Mrs. Cratchit, reddening. "I wish I had him here. I'd give him a piece of my mind to feast upon, and I hope he'd have a good appetite for it."

"My dear," said Bob, "the children! Christmas Day."

"It should be Christmas Day, I am sure," said she, "on which one drinks the health of such an odious, stingy, hard, unfeeling man as Mr. Scrooge. You know he is, Robert! Nobody knows it better than you do, poor fellow!"

"My dear!" was Bob's mild answer. "Christmas Day."

"I'll drink his health for your sake and the Day's," said Mrs. Cratchit, "not for his. Long life to him! A merry Christmas and a happy New Year! He'll be very merry and very happy, I have no doubt!"

The children drank the toast after her. It was the first of their proceedings which had no heartiness in it. Tiny Tim drank it last of all, but he didn't care two-pence for it. Scrooge was the Ogre of the family. The mention of his name cast a dark shadow on the party, which was not dispelled for a full five minutes.

After it had passed away they were ten times merrier than before, from the mere relief of Scrooge the Baleful being done with. Bob Cratchit told them how he had a situation in his eye for Master Peter, which would bring in, if obtained, full five-and-sixpence weekly. The two young Cratchits laughed tremendously at the idea of Peter's being a man of business; and Peter himself looked thoughtfully at the fire from between his collars, as if he were deliberating what particular investments he should favor when he came into the receipt of that bewildering income. Martha, who was a poor apprentice at a milliner's, then told them what kind of work she had to do, and how many hours she worked at a stretch, and how she meant to lie a-bed to-morrow morning for a good long rest; to-morrow being a holiday she passed at home. Also how she had seen a countess and a lord some days before, and how the lord "was much about as tall as Peter"; at which Peter pulled up his collars so high that you couldn't have seen his head if you had been there. All this time the chestnuts and the jug went round and round; and bye and bye they had a song, about a lost child traveling in the snow, from Tiny Tim; who had a plaintive little voice, and sang it very well indeed.

There was nothing of high mark in this. They were not a handsome family; they were not well dressed; their shoes were far from being water-proof; their clothes were scanty; and Peter might have known, and very likely did, the inside of a pawnbroker's. But, they were happy, grateful, pleased with one another, and contented with the time; and when they faded, and looked happier yet in the bright sprinklings of the Spirit's torch at parting, Scrooge had his eye upon them, and especially on Tiny Tim, until the last.

Salvation Army's Bounty

from The New York Times

December 26, 1899

THOUSANDS OF THE UNFORTUNATE FED AT Madison Square Garden.

The Rich Saw Them Feast.

Joined in Singing "Praise God, from Whom All Blessings Flow"—Food Sent to 3,200 Homes.

"Welcome to God's poor" and "Whosoever will may come" were the mottoes under which the biggest Christmas feast ever given in New York took place yesterday at Madison Square Garden. During the day nearly 20,000 men, women, and children, gathered from the highways and byways of the city in one great, surging, hungry throng, and under the glare of electric lights, amid fruits and flowers and the strains of sweet music, ate their fill without money and without price.

In the boxes and gallery of the great building during the evening, when the feast was at its height, sat many thousands of well-fed and prosperous people, among them many women who had come in carriages and were gorgeously gowned and wore many diamonds, who looked on in happy sympathy. Mingling with and flitting through the throngs everywhere were the red jackets, the high crowned caps and peculiar bonnets of the soldiers in the Salvation Army, the organizers of the undertaking, which of its kind has never been equaled in magnitude by any city.

The Salvation Army had been preparing for the event for many weeks. On street corners all over the greater city had been stationed day after day members of the organization, each with a pot swinging from a tripod bearing a placard setting forth the plans for a Christmas feast, and closing with the adjuration, "Keep the pot boiling." It was principally with the nickels, dimes and quarters dropped into these pots that was built the splendid bridge that yesterday spanned for one brief day at least the chasm that yawns between the rich and the poor. And yet after all this multitude had been fed and the tremendous stores of provisions had been exhausted to the last morsel, there still remained thousands of hungry mouths unfed, and men, women, and children were perforce turned back into the streets, hungry, friendless, and cold.

An idea of the multitudes that were fed can be obtained from the following list of articles used in preparing the feast: Twenty-two hundred turkeys, 5,000 chickens, 250 geese, 250 ducks, 1,000 pounds of beef and pork, 125 barrels of potatoes, 100 pounds of suckling pig, 10,000 pounds of vegetables, 35 barrels of apples, 10,000 oranges, 10 barrels of cranberries, and hundreds of pounds of coffee, besides 5,000 pounds of plum pudding.

COOKS WORKED FOR A WEEK.

The kitchens in the Garden had been in use for a week in preparation for the great banquet. From ten to twenty cooks were constantly employed roasting, baking, stewing, and boiling. The cooked food, however, was less than half the amount of rations served out during the remarkable day, for 16,000 uncooked dinners were served out to poor families in 3,200 baskets, each basket containing sufficient food for five persons.

Throughout Sunday night a force of more than 200 Salvation Army men and women worked at the Garden like Trojans, packing the baskets, decorating the interior of the big building, and making final preparations for the great free dinner. This force was augmented early yesterday morning, Commander and Mrs. Booth-Tucker lending a helping hand wherever needed. This labor of love was lightened by song, and many an early morning pedestrian stopped and listened outside the Garden in wonder at the sound of many voices singing sacred songs within.

Two hours before 11 o'clock, the hour set for the distribution of the baskets of uncooked food, there were fully 500 people collected outside the Fourth Avenue entrance of the Garden, waiting in long lines for their turn to come to be served. The Salvation Army has peculiar facilities for seeking out the poor in the by places of the city, and to every needy family found a ticket had been given calling for a basket of provisions. Where the army might not know of deserving cases the Charities Department and various aid societies had supplied the information, so there was no doubt the baskets would go where they could do the most good.

The whole lower tier of seats on the south side of the Garden was piled high with these baskets. Under the immediate command of Sergt. Mott of the West Thirtieth Street Station, forty policemen were present to assist in preserving order. They were rarely, if ever, needed. Capt. Price reached the Garden at 10 o'clock and took charge for an hour, stationing the patrolmen at points where the pressure would be strongest. He was enthusiastic over the affair, and said it was undoubtedly the biggest piece of charitable work ever undertaken in the history of this city. . . .

INCIDENTS OF THE FEAST.

The incidents of the great feast were so numerous and followed so quickly in succession that it was difficult to follow them. It does not take a hungry person long to eat even a Christmas dinner. Time and again army workers recognized old-timers who had some time in bygone days turned temporarily aside from their evil ways, but had fallen again by the wayside. The welcome for these prodigal sons and daughters was warmer, if possible, than for the rest.

One young man with dark shifting eyes and rather short hair stood back, as if it was his first experience at a charity dinner. For a moment he was not noticed. He turned as if about to go out, when a Salvation soldier seized him by the hand. "God bless you, Tom," he exclaimed, as he took the young fellow's hand and led him to a seat and saw that his plate was filled. The soldier, when asked, would not say who or what the man was. Capt. Price said he had but recently left prison.

There were hundreds of women among the diners. Many were bright looking and neatly dressed, with honest faces, whose only crime was that of being poor. There were entire families seated together, and here and there a woman and her children. Some of the men wore tattered clothing but had clean faces and hair nicely brushed. Others in rags still clung to a high standing collar and cravat. There were men and women who had seen better days, and others who had not. But all were hungry and all were happy, for a brief space, at least.

There was no limit in the food. The bill of fare consisted of roast turkey, celery, potatoes, vegetables, cranberry sauce, plum pudding, fruit, and coffee. The table service was first-class, and included paper napkins.

While the first 2,200 were eating Commander Booth-Tucker read the following message from Gov. Roosevelt:

"Hearty thanks. Warm Christmas greeting and good wishes to all."

It was in reply to one wishing the Governor and his family a merry day. The telegram was much cheered.

FOOD SUPPLY GAVE OUT.

The one unfortunate feature of the dinner was the exhaustion of the food supply. Twice the table capacity of 2,200 was tested, and 4,400 were fed. Then some 300 more were provided for on reduced rations: but a throng estimated at nearly 3,000 was turned away without anything. The officers of the army did their utmost to prevent this. With baskets they skirmished about the houses and hotels of the neighborhood in a vain effort to obtain the necessary food.

After the dinner Commander Booth-Tucker addressed the recipients of the army's bounty as follows:

"In the name of the citizens of New York and the Salvation Army I wish you a Merry Christmas and a Happy New Year. Whatever your circumstances, your nationality, or your religion, we wish you good luck in the name of the Lord.

"It is to this end the Salvation Army exists; it is the Church of the People, the enemy of none. So far as our Christmas efforts are concerned, I wish to give thanks to a generous public and a loyal press, and I am glad to report a victory. We started to feed 20,000, and have fed over 24,000. [This included the baskets of food sent out.] It is the most mammoth affair of the kind ever attempted.

"Neither any Continental city nor even London has ever had to do anything approaching this in magnitude. It means the dawning of a new era, the bridging of the gulf between the rich and the poor."

The Commander was frequently applauded. At the close of his speech everybody sang "Nearer, My God, to Thee," and then there was a recital in unison of the Lord's Prayer. After some more singing of hymns the "Passion Play" was reproduced by the cinematograph. This was followed by a stereopticon exhibition of Salvation Army work.

CHRISTMAS EVERY DAY

WILLIAM DEAN HOWELLS

WELL, ONCE THERE WAS A LITTLE girl who liked Christmas so much that she wanted it to be Christmas every day in the year; and as soon as Thanksgiving was over she began to send postal cards to the old Christmas Fairy to ask if she mightn't have it. In about three weeks—or just the day before Christmas, it was—she got a letter from the Fairy, saying she might have it Christmas every day for a year, and then they would see about having it longer.

The little girl was a good deal excited already, preparing for the old-fashioned, once-a-year Christmas that was coming the next day, and perhaps the Fairy's promise didn't make such an impression on her as it would have made at some other time. She just resolved to keep it to herself, and surprise everybody with it as it kept coming true: and then it slipped out of her mind altogether.

She had a splendid Christmas. She went to bed early, so as to let Santa Claus have a chance at the stockings, and in the morning she was up the first of anybody and went and felt them, and found hers all lumpy with packages of candy, and oranges and grapes, and pocketbooks and rubber balls and all kinds of small presents just as they always had every Christmas. Then she waited around till the rest of the family were up, and she was the first to burst into the library, when the doors were opened, and look at the large presents laid out on the library table—books, and dolls, and little stoves, and dozens of handkerchiefs, and ink stands, and skates, and snow shovels, and photograph frames, and little easels, and boxes of watercolors, and candied cherries, and doll's houses, and the big Christmas tree, lighted and standing in the middle.

She had a splendid Christmas all day. She ate so much candy that she did not want any breakfast; and the whole forenoon the presents kept pouring in and she went 'round giving the presents she had got for other people, and came home and ate turkey and cranberry for dinner, and plum-pudding and nuts and raisins and oranges and more candy, and then went and coasted and came in with a stomachache, crying; and they had a light supper, and pretty early everybody went to bed cross.

The little girl slept very heavily, and she slept very late, but she was wakened at last by the other children dancing 'round her bed with their stockings full of presents in their hands.

"What is it?" said the little girl, and she rubbed her eyes and tried to rise up in bed.

"Christmas! Christmas! Christmas!" they all shouted, and waved their stockings.

"Nonsense! It was Christmas yesterday."

Her brothers and sisters just laughed. "We don't know about that. It's Christmas today, any way. You come into the library and see."

Then all at once it flashed on the little girl that the Fairy was keeping her promise, and her year of Christmases was beginning. She was dreadfully sleepy, but she sprang up like a lark—a lark that had overeaten itself and gone to bed cross—and darted into the library. There it was again! The Christmas tree blazing away, and the family picking out their presents, but looking pretty sleepy, and her father perfectly puzzled, and her mother ready to cry.

"I'm sure I don't see how I'm to dispose of all these things," said her mother, and her father said it seemed to him they had had something just like it the day before, but he must have dreamed it. Well, the next day, it was just the same thing over again, but everybody getting crosser; and at the end of a week's time so many people had lost their tempers that they perfectly strewed the ground. Even when people tried to recover their tempers they usually got somebody else's, and it made the most dreadful mix.

The little girl began to get frightened, keeping the secret all to herself; she wanted to tell her mother, but she didn't dare to; and she was ashamed to ask the Fairy to take back her gift, it seemed ungrateful, and she thought she would try to stand it, but she hardly knew how she could, for a whole year. So it went on and on, and it was Christmas on St. Valentine's Day, and Washington's Birthday just the same as any day, and it didn't skip even the First of April, though everything was counterfeit that day, and that was some *little* relief.

After a while, turkeys got to be so scarce that they were about a thousand dollars apiece, and they got to passing off almost anything for turkey. And the cranberries—well, they asked a diamond apiece for cranberries. All the woods and orchards were cut down for Christmas trees and where the woods and orchards used to be, it looked just like a stubblefield, with the stumps. After a while they had to make Christmas trees out of rags, and stuff them with bran, like old-fashioned dolls; but there were plenty of rags, because people got so poor, buying presents for one another, that they couldn't get any new clothes, and they just wore their old ones to tatters. It was perfectly shameful.

Well, after it had gone on about three or four months, the little girl, whenever she came into the room in the morning and saw those great ugly lumpy stockings dangling at the fireplace, and the disgusting presents around everywhere, used to just sit down and burst out crying. In six months she was perfectly exhausted; she couldn't even cry any more, she just slammed her presents across the room.

By that time people didn't carry presents around nicely any more. They flung them over the fence, or through the window, or anything; and, instead of taking great pains to write "For dear Papa," or "Mamma," or "Brother," or "Sister," or "Susie," or "Sammie," or "Billie," or whoever it was, and troubling to get the spelling right, and then signing their names, and "Xmas 188–," they used to write in the gift books, "Take it, you horrid old thing!" and then go and bang it against the front door. Nearly everybody had built barns to hold their presents, but pretty soon the barns overflowed, and then they used to let them lie out in the rain, or anywhere. Sometimes the police used to come and tell them to shovel their presents off the sidewalk, or they would arrest them.

Well, before it came Thanksgiving, it had leaked out who had caused all these Christmases. The little girl had suffered so much that she had talked about it in her sleep; and after that, hardly anybody would play with her. People just perfectly despised her, because if it had not been for her greediness, it wouldn't have happened; and now, when it came Thanksgiving, and she wanted them to go to church, and have squash-pie and turkey, and show their gratitude, they said that all the turkeys had been eaten up for her old Christmas dinners, and if she would stop the Christmases, they would see about the gratitude. And the very next day the little girl began to send letters to the Christmas Fairy, and then telegrams, to stop it. But it didn't do any good; and then she got to calling at the Fairy's house, but the girl that came to the door always said "Not at home," or "Engaged," or "At dinner," or something like that; and so it went on till it came to the old once-a-year Christmas Eve. The little girl fell asleep, and when she woke up in the morning—it wasn't Christmas at last.

Well, there was the greatest rejoicing all over the country, and it extended clear up into Canada. The people met together everywhere, and kissed and cried for joy. The city carts went around and gathered up all the candy and raisins and nuts, and dumped them into the river; and it made the fish perfectly sick; and the whole United States, as far out as Alaska, was one blaze of bonfires, where the children were burning their gift-books and presents of all kinds. They had the greatest time!

The little girl went to thank the old Fairy because she had stopped its being Christmas, and she said she hoped she would keep her promise, and see that Christmas never, never came again. Then the Fairy frowned, and asked her if she was sure she knew what she meant; and the little girl asked her, why not? and the old Fairy said that now she was behaving just as greedily as ever, and she'd better look out. This made the little girl think it all over carefully again, and she said she would be willing to have it Christmas about once in a thousand years; and then she said a hundred, and then she said ten, and at last she got down to one. Then the Fairy said that was the good old way that had pleased people ever since Christmas began, and she was agreed. Then the little girl said, "What're your shoes made of?" And the Fairy said, "Leather." And the little girl said, "Bargain's done forever," and skipped off, and hippity-hopped the whole way home.

CHRISTMAS IN THE TENEMENTS

THEODORE DREISER

THEY ARE INFATUATED WITH THE RUSH and roar of a great metropolis. They are fascinated by the illusion of pleasure. Broadway, Fifth Avenue, the mansions, the lights, the beauty. A fever of living is in their blood. An unnatural hunger and thirst for excitement is burning them up. For this they labor. For this they endure a hard, unnatural existence. For this they crowd themselves in stifling, inhuman quarters, and for this they die.

The joys of the Christmas tide are no illusion with most of us, the strange exhibition of fancy, of which it is the name, no mockery of our dreams. Far over the wide land the waves of expectation and sympathetic appreciation constantly oscillate one with the other in the human breast, and in the closing season of the year are at last given definite expression. Rings and pins, the art of the jeweler and the skill of the dressmaker, pictures, books, ornaments and knickknacks—these with one great purpose are consecrated, and in the material lavishness of the season is seen the dreams of the world come true.

There is one region, however, where, in the terrific drag of the struggle for existence, the softer phases of this halcyon mood are at first glance obscure. It is a region of tall tenements and narrow streets where, crowded into an area of a few square miles, live and labor a million and a half of people. It is the old-time tenement area, leading almost unbrokenly north from Franklin Square to Fourteenth Street. Here, during these late December evenings, the holiday atmosphere is beginning to make itself felt. It is a region of narrow streets with tall five-story, even seven-story, tenements lining either side of the way and running thick as a river with a busy and toilsome throng.

The ways are already lined with carts of special Christmas goods, such as toys, candies, Christmas tree ornaments, feathers, ribbons, jewelry, purses, fruit, and in a few wagons small Christmas greens such as holly and hemlock wreaths, crosses of fir, balsam, tamarack pine and sprigs of mistletoe. Work has not stopped in the factories or stores, and yet these streets are literally packed with people, of all ages, sizes and nationalities, and the buying is lively. One man, who looks as though he might be a Bowery tough rather than a denizen of this particular neighborhood, is offering little three-, five- and ten-inch dolls which he announces as "genuine American beauties here. Three, five and ten." Another, a pale, full-bearded Jew, is selling little Christmas tree ornaments of paste or glass for a penny each, and in the glare of the newly-turned-on electric lights, it is not difficult to perceive that they are the broken or imperfect lots of the toy manufacturers who are having them hawked about during the eleventh hour before Christmas as the best way of getting rid of them. Other dusty, grim and raucous denizens are offering candy, mixed nuts, and other forms of special confections, at ten cents a pound, a price at which those who are used to the more expensive brands may instructively ponder.

Meats are selling in some of the cheaper butcher shops for ten, fifteen and twenty cents a pound, picked chickens in barrels at fifteen and twenty. A whole section of Elizabeth Street is given up to the sale of stale fish at ten and fifteen cents a pound, and the crowd of Italians, Jews and Bohemians who are taking advantage of these modest prices is swarming over the sidewalk and into the gutters. A four- or five-pound fish at fifteen cents a pound will make an excellent Christmas dinner for four, five or six. A thin, ice-packed and chemically-preserved chicken at fifteen or twenty cents a pound will do as much for another family. Onions, garlic, old cast-off preserves, pickles and condiments that the wholesale houses uptown have seen grow stale and musty on their shelves, can be had here for five, ten and fifteen cents a bottle, and although the combination is unwholesome it will be worked over as Christmas dinners for the morrow. Cheap, unsalable, stale, adulterated—these are the words that should be stamped on every bottle, basket and barrel that is here being scrambled over. And yet the purchasers would not be benefited any thereby. They must buy what they can afford. What they can afford is this.

The street, with its mass of life, lingers in this condition until six o'clock, when the great shops and factories turn loose their horde of workers. Then into the glare of these electric-lighted streets the army of shop girls and boys begins to pour. Here is a spectacle interesting and provocative of thought at all seasons, but trebly so on this particular evening. It is a shabby throng at best, commonplace in garb and physical appearance, but rich in the qualities of youth and enthusiasm, than which the world holds nothing more valuable.

Youth in all the glory of its illusions and its ambitions. Youth, in whom the cold insistence of life's physical limitations and the law have not as yet worked any permanent depression. Thousands are hurrying in every direction. The street cars which ply this area are packed as only the New York street car companies can pack their patrons, and that in cold, old, dirty and even vile cars. There are girls with black hair, and girls with brown. Some have even, white teeth, some shapely figures, some a touch of that persuasive charm which is indicated by the flash of an eye. There are poor dresses, poor taste, and poor manners mingled with good dresses, good taste and good manners. In the glow of the many lights and shadows of the evening they are hurrying away, with that lightness of spirit and movement which is the evidence of a long strain of labor suddenly relaxed.

"Do you think Santa Claus will have enough to fill that?" asks an officer, who is standing in the glare of a balsam- and pine-trimmed cigar store window, to a smartly dressed political heeler or detective who is looking on with him at the mass of shop-girls hurrying past. A shop-girl had gone by with her skirt cut to an inch or two below her knee, revealing a trim little calf and ankle.

"Eee yo! I hope so! isn't she the candy?"

"Don't get fresh," comes quickly from the hurrying figure as she disappears in the throng with a toss of her head. She has enjoyed the comment well enough, and the rebuke is more mischievous than angry.

"A goldfish! A goldfish! Only one cent!" cries a pushcart vendor, who is one of a thousand lining the pavements to-night, and at his behest another shop-girl, equally budding and youthful, stops to extract a penny from her small purse and carries away a thin, transparent prize of golden paste, for a younger brother, probably.

Others like her are being pushed and jostled the whole length of this crowded section. They are being nudged and admired as well as sought and schemed for.

Whatever affections or attachments they have will be manifesting themselves to-night, as may be seen by the little expenditures they themselves are making. A gold-fish of transparent paste or a half pound of candy, a cheap gold-plated stickpin, brooch or ring, or a handkerchief, collar or necktie bought of one of the many pushcart men, tell the story plainly enough. Sympathy, love, affection and passion are running their errant ways among this vast unspoken horde no less than among the more pretentious and well-remembered of the world.

And the homes to which they are hurrying, the places which are dignified by that title, but which here should have another name! Thousands upon thousands of them are turning into entry ways, the gloom or dirtiness or poverty of which should bar them from the steps of any human being. Up the dark stairways they are pour-ing into tier upon tier of human hives, in some instances not less than seven stories high and, of course, without an elevator, and by grimy landings they are sorted out and at last distributed each into his own cranny. Small, dark one-, two- and three-room apartments, where yet on this Christmas evening, one, and sometimes three, four and five are still at work sewing pants, making flowers, curling feathers, or doing any other of a hundred tenement tasks to help out the income supplied by the one or two who work out. Miserable one- and two-room spaces where igno-rance and poverty and sickness, rather than greed or immorality, have made verita-ble pens out of what would ordinarily be bad enough. Many hundreds or thousands of others there are where thrift and shrewdness are making the best of very unfor-tunate conditions, and a hundred or two where actual abundance prevails. These are the homes. Let us enter.

Zorg is a Bohemian, and has a little two-room apartment. The windows of the only one which has windows look into Elizabeth Street. It is a dingy apartment, unswept and unwhitewashed at present, where on this hearty Christmas Eve, him-self, his wife, his wife's mother, and his little twelve-year-old son are laboring at a fair-sized deal table curling feathers. The latter is a simple task, once you under-stand it, dull, tedious, unprofitable. It consists in taking a feather in one hand, a knife in the other, and drawing the fronds quickly over the knife's edge. This gives them a very sprightly curl and can be administered, if the worker be an expert, by a single movement of the hand. It is paid for by the dozen, as such work is usually paid for in this region, and the ability to earn much more than sixty cents a day is not within the range of human possibility. Forty cents would be a much more probable average, and this is approximately the wages which these several individuals earn. Rent uses up three of the twelve dollars weekly income; food, dress, coal and light six more. Three dollars, when work is steady, is the sum laid aside for all other purposes and pleasures, and this sum, if no amusements were indulged in and no sickness or slackness of work befell, might annually grow to the tidy sum of one hundred and fifty-six dollars; but it has never done so. Illness invariably takes one part, lack of work a greater part still. In the long drag of weary labor the pleasure-loving instincts of man cannot be wholly restrained, and so it comes about that the present Christmas season finds the funds of the family treasury low.

It is in such a family as this that the merry Christmas time comes with a peculiar emphasis, and although the conditions may be discouraging, the efforts to meet it are almost always commensurate with the means.

However, on this Christmas Eve it has been deemed a duty to have some diversion, and so, although the round of weary labor may not be thus easily relaxed, the wife has been deputed to do the Christmas shopping and has gone forth into the crowded East Side street, from which she has returned with a meat bone, a cut from a butcher's at twelve cents a pound, green pickles, three turnips, a carrot, a half-dozen small candles, and two or three toys, which, together with a small three-foot branch of hemlock, purchased earlier in the day, completes the Christmas preparation for the morrow. Arba, the youngest, although like the others she will work until ten this Christmas Eve, is to have a pair of new shoes; Zicka, the next older, a belt for her dress. Mrs. Zorg, although she may not suspect, will receive a new market basket with a lid on it. Zorg—grim, silent, weary of soul and body—is to have a new fifteen-cent tie. There will be a tree, a small sprig of a tree, upon which will hang colored glass or paste balls of red and blue and green, with threads of popcorn and sprays of flitter-gold, all saved from the years before. In the light of early dawn to-morrow the youngest of the children will dance about these, and the richness of their beauty will be enjoyed as if they had not been so presented for the seventh and eighth time.

Thus it runs, mostly, throughout the entire region on this joyous occasion, a wealth of feeling and desire expressing itself through the thinnest and most meager material forms. About the shops and stores where the windows are filled with cheap displays of all that is considered luxury, are hosts of other children scarcely so satisfactorily supplied, peering earnestly into the world of make-believe and illusion, the wonder of it not yet eradicated from their unsophisticated hearts. Joy, joy—not a tithe of all that is represented by the expenditures of the wealthy, but only such as may be encompassed in a paper puff-ball or a tinsel fish, is here sought for and dreamed over, an earnest, child-heart-longing which may never again be gratified if not now. Horses, wagons, fire engines, dolls—these are what the thousands upon thousands of children whose faces are pressed closely against the commonplace window panes are dreaming about, and the longing that is thereby expressed is the strongest evidence of the indissoluble link which binds these weakest and most wretched elements of society to the best and most successful.

Un Poquito de
Tu Amor

WHEN MY FATHER DIED LAST YEAR, a week before Valentine's Day, a piece of my heart died with him. My father, that supreme sentimental fool, loved my brothers and me to excess in a kind of over-the-top, rococo fever, all arabesques and sugar spirals, as sappy and charming as the romantic Mexican boleros he loved to sing. *Just a little bit of your love at least, / just a little bit of your love, just that . . .* Music from my time, Father would say proudly, and I could almost smell the gardenias and Tres Flores hair oil.

Before my father died, it was simple cordiality that prompted me to say, "I'm sorry," when comforting the bereaved. But with his death I am initiated into the family of humanity, I am connected to all deaths and to their survivors: *"Lo siento,"* which translates as both "I am sorry" and "I feel it" all at once.

Lo siento. Since his death, I feel life more intensely.

My father, born under the eagle and serpent of the Mexican flag, died beneath a blanket of stars and stripes, a U.S. World War II veteran. Like most immigrants, he was overly patriotic, exceptionally hardworking, and, above all, a great believer in family. Yet often I'm aware my father's life doesn't count, he's not "history," not the "American" politicians mean when they talk about "American."

I thought of my father especially this holiday season. The day before Christmas 1997, forty-five unarmed Mayas were slain while they prayed in a chapel in Acteal, Chiapas—twenty-one of them women, fourteen children. The Mexican president was shocked and promised to hold all those responsible accountable. The Mexican people aren't fools. Everybody knows who's responsible, but it's too much to wish for the Mexican president to fire himself.

I know the deaths in Chiapas are linked to me here in the United States. I know the massacre is connected to removing native people from their land, because although the people are poor the land is very rich and the government knows this. And the Mexican debt is connected to my high standard of living, and the military presence is necessary to calm U.S. investors, and the music goes round and round and it comes out here.

I have been thinking and thinking about all this from my home in San Antonio, Texas, as fidgety as a person with *comezón*, an itching, a hankering, an itch I can't quite scratch. What is my responsibility as a writer in light of these events? As a woman, as a mestiza? As a U.S. citizen who lives on several borders? What do I do as the daughter of a Mexican man? Father, tell me. *Ayúdame*, help me, why don't you. *Lo siento.* I have been searching for answers. On Christmas, I am reverberating like a bell.

In my father's house, because my father was my father—*Hello, my friend!*—our Christmas dinners were a global feast, a lesson in history, diplomacy, and the capacity of the stomach to put aside racial grievances. Our holidays were a unique hybrid of cultures that perhaps could only happen in a city like Chicago, a bounty contributed by family and intermarriage, multiethnic neighborhoods, and the diversity of my father's upholstery-shop employees.

To this day, a typical Christmas meal at our home consists first and foremost of tamales, that Indian delicacy that binds us to the preconquest. Twenty-five dozen for our family is typical, the popular, red tamales, the fiery, green tamales, and the sweet, pink tamales filled with jam and raisins for the kids. Sometimes they're my mother's homemade batch—*This is the last year I'm going to make them!*—but more often they're ordered in advance from someone else willing to go through all the trouble, most recently from the excellent tamale lady in front of Carnicería Jiménez on North Avenue, who operates from a shopping cart.

Father's annual contribution was his famous *bacalao*, a codfish stew of Spanish origin, which he made standing in one spot like a TV chef—*Go get me a bowl, bring me an apron, somebody give me the tomatoes, wash them first, hand me that knife and chopping board, where are the olives?*

Every year we are so spoiled we expect—and receive—a Christmas tray of homemade pierogis and Polish sausage, sometimes courtesy of my sister-in-law's family, the Targonskis, and sometimes from my father's Polish upholsterers, who can hardly speak a word of English. We also serve Jamaican meat pies, a legacy from

Darryl, who was once my father's furniture refinisher, but has long since left. And finally, our Christmas dinner includes the Italian magnificence from Ferrara Bakery in our old neighborhood on West Taylor Street. Imagine if a cake looked like the Vatican. We've been eating Ferrara's pastries since I was in the third grade.

But this is no formal Norman Rockwell sit-down dinner. We eat when we're inspired by hunger or by *antojo*, literally "before the eye." All day pots are on the stove steaming and the microwave is beeping. It's common to begin a dessert plate of cannolis while someone next to you is finishing breakfast, a pork tamale sandwiched inside a piece of French bread, a mestizo invention thanks to the French intervention.

History is present at our table. The doomed Emperor Maximiliano's French bread as well as the Aztec corn tamales of the Americas, our Andalusian recipe for codfish, our moves in and out of neighborhoods where we were the brown corridor between Chicago communities at war with one another. And finally a history of intermarriage, of employees who loved my father enough to share a plate of their homemade delicacies with our family even if our countries couldn't share anything else.

Forty-five are dead in Acteal. My father is gone. I read the newspapers and the losses ring in my heart. More than half the Mexican-American kids in this country are dropping out of high school—more than half—and our politicians' priority is bigger prisons. I live in a state where there are more people sentenced to death than anywhere else in the world. Alamo Heights, the affluent, white neighborhood of my city, values Spanish as a second language beginning in the first grade, yet elsewhere lawmakers work to demolish bilingual education for Spanish-dominant children. Two hours away from my home, the U.S. military is setting up camp in the name of bandits and drug lords. But I'm not stupid; I know who they mean to keep away. *Lo siento.* I feel it.

I'm thinking this while I attend a Latino leadership conference between the holidays. I don't know what I expect from this gathering of Latino leaders, exactly, but I know I don't want to leave without a statement about what's happened in Acteal. Surely at least the Latino community recognizes the forty-five are our family.

"It is like a family," one Arizona politico explains. "But understand, to you it may be a father who's died, but to me it's a distant cousin."

Is it too much to ask our leaders to lead?

"You're too impatient," one Latina tells me, and I'm so stunned I can't respond. A wild karaoke begins, and a Chicano filmmaker begins to preach— "There's a season to play and a season to rage." He talks and talks till I have to blink back the tears. After what seems like an eternity, he finally finishes by saying, "You know what you have to do, don't you?"

And then it hits me, I do know what I have to do.

I will tell a story.

When we were in college my mother realized investing in real estate was the answer to our economic woes. Her plans were modest: to buy a cheap fixer-upper in the barrio that would bring us income. After months of searching, Mother finally found something we could afford, a scruffy building on the avenue with a store that could serve as Father's upholstery shop and two apartments above that would pay the mortgage. At last my mother was a respectable landlady.

Almost immediately a family on the third floor began paying their rent late. It wasn't an expensive apartment, something like a hundred dollars, but every first of the month, they were five or ten dollars short and would deliver the rent with a promise to pay the balance the next payday, which they did. Every month it was the same . . . the rent minus a few dollars promised for next Friday.

Mother hated to be taken advantage of. *Do they think we're rich or something, don't we have bills too?* She sent Father, who was on good terms with everybody. *You go and talk to that family, I've had it!*

And so Father went, and a little later quietly returned.

"I fixed it," Father announced.

"Already? How? What did you do?"

"I lowered the rent."

Mother was ready to throw a fit. Until Father said, "Remember when ten dollars meant a lot to us?"

Mother was silent, as if by some *milagro* she remembered. Who would've thought Father was capable of such genius? He was not by nature a clever man. But he inspires me now to be creative in ways I never realized.

I don't wish to make my father seem more than what he was. He wasn't Gandhi; he lived a life terrified of those different from himself. He never read a newspaper and was naïve enough to believe history as told by *la televisión*. And, as my mother keeps reminding me, he wasn't a perfect husband either. But he was very kind and at some things extraordinary. He was a wonderful father.

Maybe I've looked to the wrong leaders for leadership. Maybe what's needed this new year are a few outrageous ideas. Something absurd and genius like those of my father, whose kindness and generosity teach me to enlarge my heart.

Maybe it's time to lower the rent.

Just a little bit of your love at least, / just a little bit of your love, just that . . . ever since the year began that song runs through my head. My father just won't let up. *Lo siento.* I feel it.

Papá, Buddha, Allah, Jesus Christ, Yahweh, La Virgen de Guadalupe, the Universe, the God in us, help us. *Danos un poquito de tu amor siquiera, danos un popuito de tu amor nomás* . . . just a little bit of your love at least, just a little bit of your love, just that . . .

Here We Come a-Wassailing

TRADITIONAL

Here we come a-wassailing
Among the leaves so green;
Here we come a-wand'ring,
So fair to be seen.

REFRAIN:
Love and joy come to you,
And to you your wassail too;
And God bless you and send you a Happy New Year,
And God send you a Happy New Year.

We are not daily beggars
That beg from door to door;
But we are neighbors' children,
Whom you have seen before.

God bless the master of this house,
Likewise the mistress too;
And all the little children,
That round the table go.

And all your kin and kinsfolk
That dwell both far and near,
We wish a Merry Christmas
And Happy New Year.

O Come, All Ye Faithful

O Come, All Ye Faithful

TRANSLATED BY FREDERICK OAKELEY &
WILLIAM THOMAS BROOKE
MUSIC BY JOHN FRANCIS WADE

O come, all ye faithful, Joyful and triumphant,
O come ye, O come ye to Bethlehem;
Come and behold him, Born the King of angels:
O come, let us adore him, O come, let us adore him,
O come, let us adore him, Christ the Lord.

God of God, Light of light,
Lo! he abhors not the Virgin's womb;
Very God, Begotten not created:
O come, let us adore him, O come, let us adore him,
O come, let us adore him, Christ the Lord.

Sing, choirs of angels, Sing in exultation,
Sing, all ye citizens of heav'n above;
Glory to God, In the highest:
O come, let us adore him, O come, let us adore him,
O come, let us adore him, Christ the Lord.

Yea, Lord, we greet thee, Born this happy morning,
Jesus, to thee be glory giv'n;
Word of the Father, Now in flesh appearing:
O come, let us adore him, O come, let us adore him,
O come, let us adore him, Christ the Lord.

MATTHEW 2: 1–12

Now when Jesus was born in Bethlehem of Judæa in the days of Herod the king, behold, there came wise men from the east to Jerusalem,

Saying, Where is he that is born King of the Jews? for we have seen his star in the east, and are come to worship him.

When Herod the king had heard these things, he was troubled, and all Jerusalem with him.

And when he had gathered all the chief priests and scribes of the people together, he demanded of them where Christ should be born.

And they said unto him, In Bethlehem of Judæa: for thus it is written by the prophet,

And thou Bethlehem, in the land of Juda, art not the least among the princes of Juda: for out of thee shall come a Governor, that shall rule my people Israel.

Then Herod, when he had privily called the wise men, enquired of them diligently what time the star appeared.

And he sent them to Bethlehem, and said, Go and search diligently for the young child; and when ye have found him, bring me word again, that I may come and worship him also.

When they had heard the king, they departed; and, lo, the star, which they saw in the east, went before them, till it came and stood over where the young child was.

When they saw the star, they rejoiced with exceeding great joy.

And when they were come into the house, they saw the young child with Mary his mother, and fell down, and worshipped him: and when they had opened their treasures, they presented unto him gifts; gold, and frankincense, and myrrh.

And being warned of God in a dream that they should not return to Herod, they departed into their own country another way.

THE OXEN

THOMAS HARDY

Christmas Eve, and twelve of the clock.
    "Now they are all on their knees,"
An elder said as we sat in a flock
    By the embers in hearthside ease.

We pictured the meek milk creatures where
    They dwelt in their strawy pen,
Nor did it occur to one of us there
    To doubt they were kneeling then.

So fair a fancy few would weave
    In these years! Yet, I feel,
If someone said on Christmas Eve,
    "Come; see the oxen kneel,

"In the lonely barton by yonder coomb
    Our childhood used to know,"
I should go with him in the gloom,
    Hoping it might be so.

A Christmas Carol

CHRISTINA ROSSETTI

In the bleak mid-winter
    Frosty wind made moan,
Earth stood hard as iron,
    Water like a stone;
Snow had fallen, snow on snow,
    Snow on snow,
In the bleak mid-winter
    Long ago.

Our God, Heaven cannot hold Him
    Nor earth sustain;
Heaven and earth shall flee away
    When He comes to reign:
In the bleak mid-winter
    A stable-place sufficed
The Lord God Almighty
    Jesus Christ.

Enough for Him, whom cherubim
    Worship night and day,
A breastful of milk
    And a mangerful of hay;
Enough for Him, whom angels
    Fall down before,
The ox and ass and camel
    Which adore.

Angels and archangels
    May have gathered there,
Cherubim and seraphim
    Thronged the air;
But only His mother
    In her maiden bliss
Worshipped the Beloved
    With a kiss.

What can I give Him
    Poor as I am?
If I were a shepherd
    I would bring a lamb,
If I were a Wise Man
    I would do my part,—
Yet what I can I give Him,
    Give my heart.

CAROL OF THE BROWN KING

LANGSTON HUGHES

Of the three Wise Men
Who came to the King,
One was a brown man,
So they sing.

Of the three Wise Men
Who followed the Star,
One was a brown king
From afar.

They brought fine gifts
Of spices and gold
In jeweled boxes
Of beauty untold.

Unto His humble
Manger they came
And bowed their heads
In Jesus' name.

Three Wise Men,
One dark like me—
Part of His
Nativity.

CHRISTMAS MORNING

ELIZABETH MADOX ROBERTS

If Bethlehem were here today,
Or this were very long ago,
There wouldn't be a winter time
Nor any cold or snow.

I'd run out through the garden gate,
And down along the pasture walk;
And off beside the cattle barns
I'd hear a kind of gentle talk.

I'd move the heavy iron chain
And pull away the wooden pin;
I'd push the door a little bit
And tiptoe very softly in.

The pigeons and the yellow hens
And all the cows would stand away;
Their eyes would open wide to see
A lady in the manger hay,

If this were very long ago
And Bethlehem were here today.

And Mother held my hand and smiled—
I mean the lady would—and she
Would take the woolly blankets off
Her little boy so I could see.

His shut-up eyes would be asleep,
And he would look like our John,
And he would be all crumpled too,
And have a pinkish color on.

I'd watch his breath go in and out.
His little clothes would all be white.
I'd slip my finger in his hand
To feel how he could hold it tight.

And she would smile and say, "Take care,"
The mother, Mary, would, "Take care";
And I would kiss his little hand
And touch his hair

While Mary put the blankets back
The gentle talk would soon begin.
And when I'd tiptoe softly out
I'd meet the wise men going in.

The Gift of the Magi

O. HENRY

ONE DOLLAR AND EIGHTY-SEVEN CENTS. That was all. And sixty cents of it was in pennies. Pennies saved one and two at a time by bulldozing the grocer and the vegetable man and the butcher until one's cheeks burned with the silent imputation of parsimony that such close dealing implied. Three times Della counted it. One dollar and eighty-seven cents. And the next day would be Christmas.

There was clearly nothing to do but flop down on the shabby little couch and howl. So Della did it. Which instigates the moral reflection that life is made up of sobs, sniffles, and smiles, with sniffles predominating.

While the mistress of the home is gradually subsiding from the first stage to the second, take a look at the home. A furnished flat at $8 per week. It did not exactly beggar description, but it certainly had that word on the lookout for the mendicancy squad.

In the vestibule below was a letter box into which no letter would go, and an electric button from which no mortal finger could coax a ring. Also appertaining thereunto was a card bearing the name "Mr. James Dillingham Young."

The "Dillingham" had been flung to the breeze during a former period of prosperity when its possessor was being paid $30 per week. Now, when the income was shrunk to $20, though, they were thinking seriously of contracting to a modest and unassuming D. But whenever Mr. James Dillingham Young came home and reached his flat above, he was called "Jim" and greatly hugged by Mrs. James Dillingham Young, already introduced to you as Della. Which is all very good.

Della finished her cry and attended to her cheeks with the powder rag. She stood by the window and looked out dully at a gray cat walking a gray fence in a gray backyard. Tomorrow would be Christmas Day, and she had only $1.87 with which to buy Jim a present. She had been saving every penny she could for months, with this result. Twenty dollars a week doesn't go far. Expenses had been greater than she had calculated. They always are. Only $1.87 to buy a present for Jim. Her Jim. Many a happy hour she had spent planning for something nice for him. Something fine and rare and sterling—something just a little bit near to being worthy of the honor of being owned by Jim.

There was a pier glass between the windows of the room. Perhaps you have seen a pier glass in an $8 flat. A very thin and very agile person may, by observing his reflection in a rapid sequence of longitudinal strips, obtain a fairly accurate conception of his looks. Della, being slender, had mastered the art.

Suddenly she whirled from the window and stood before the glass. Her eyes were shining brilliantly, but her face had lost its color within twenty seconds. Rapidly she pulled down her hair and let it fall to its full length.

Now, there were two possessions of the James Dillingham Youngs in which they both took a mighty pride. One was Jim's gold watch that had been his father's and his grandfather's. The other was Della's hair. Had the queen of Sheba lived in the flat across the airshaft, Della would have let her hair hang out the window some day to dry just to depreciate Her Majesty's jewels and gifts. Had King Solomon been the janitor, with all his treasures piled up in the basement, Jim would have pulled out his watch every time he passed, just to see him pluck at his beard from envy.

So now Della's beautiful hair fell about her rippling and shining like a cascade of brown waters. It reached below her knee and made itself almost a garment for her. And then she did it up again nervously and quickly. Once she faltered for a minute and stood still while a tear or two splashed on the worn red carpet.

On went her old brown jacket; on went her old brown hat. With a whirl of skirts and with the brilliant sparkle still in her eyes, she fluttered out the door and down the stairs to the street.

Where she stopped the sign read: "Mme. Sofronie. Hair Goods of All Kinds." One flight up Della ran, and collected herself, panting. Madame, large, too white, chilly, hardly looked the "Sofronie."

"Will you buy my hair?" asked Della.

"I buy hair," said Madame. "Take yer hat off and let's have a sight at the looks of it."

Down rippled the brown cascade.

"Twenty dollars," said Madame, lifting the mass with a practiced hand.

"Give it to me quick," said Della.

Oh, and the next two hours tripped by on rosy wings. Forget the hashed metaphor. She was ransacking the stores for Jim's present.

She found it at last. It surely had been made for Jim and no one else. There was no other like it in any of the stores, and she had turned all of them inside out. It was a platinum fob chain simple and chaste in design, properly proclaiming its value by substance alone and not by meretricious ornamentation—as all good things should do. It was even worthy of The Watch. As soon as she saw it she knew that it must be Jim's. It was like him. Quietness and value—the description applied to both. Twenty-one dollars they took from her for it, and she hurried home with the 87 cents. With that chain on his watch Jim might be properly anxious about the time in any company. Grand as the watch was, he sometimes looked at it on the sly on account of the old leather strap that he used in place of a chain.

When Della reached home her intoxication gave way a little to prudence and reason. She got out her curling irons and lighted the gas and went to work repairing the ravages made by generosity added to love. Which is always a tremendous task, dear friends—a mammoth task.

Within forty minutes her head was covered with tiny, close-lying curls that made her look wonderfully like a truant schoolboy. She looked at her reflection in the mirror long, carefully, and critically.

"If Jim doesn't kill me," she said to herself, "before he takes a second look at me, he'll say I look like a Coney Island chorus girl. But what could I do—oh! what could I do with a dollar and eighty-seven cents?"

At seven o'clock the coffee was made and the frying pan was on the back of the stove hot and ready to cook the chops.

Jim was never late. Della doubled the fob chain in her hand and sat on the corner of the table near the door that he always entered. Then she heard his step on the stair away down on the first flight, and she turned white for just a moment. She had a habit of saying little silent prayers about the simplest everyday things, and now she whispered: "Please God, make him think I am still pretty."

The door opened and Jim stepped in and closed it. He looked thin and very serious. Poor fellow, he was only twenty-two—and to be burdened with a family! He needed a new overcoat and he was without gloves.

Jim stopped inside the door, as immovable as a setter at the scent of quail. His eyes were fixed upon Della, and there was an expression in them that she could not read, and it terrified her. It was not anger, nor surprise, nor disapproval, nor horror, nor any of the sentiments that she had been prepared for. He simply stared at her fixedly with that peculiar expression on his face.

Della wriggled off the table and went for him.

"Jim, darling," she cried, "don't look at me that way. I had my hair cut off and sold because I couldn't have lived through Christmas without giving you a present. It'll grow out again—you won't mind, will you? I just had to do it. My hair grows awfully fast. Say 'Merry Christmas!' Jim, and let's be happy. You don't know what a nice—what a beautiful, nice gift I've got for you."

"You've cut off your hair?" asked Jim, laboriously, as if he had not arrived at that patent fact yet even after the hardest mental labor.

"Cut it off and sold it," said Della. "Don't you like me just as well, anyhow? I'm me without my hair, ain't I?"

Jim looked about the room curiously.

"You say your hair is gone?" he said, with an air almost of idiocy.

"You needn't look for it," said Della. "It's sold, I tell you—sold and gone, too. It's Christmas Eve, boy. Be good to me, for it went for you. Maybe the hairs of my head were numbered," she went on with sudden serious sweetness, "but nobody could ever count my love for you. Shall I put the chops on, Jim?"

Out of his trance Jim seemed quickly to wake. He enfolded his Della. For ten seconds let us regard with discreet scrutiny some inconsequential object in the other direction. Eight dollars a week or a million a year—what is the difference? A mathematician or a wit would give you the wrong answer. The magi brought valuable gifts, but that was not among them. This dark assertion will be illuminated later on.

Jim drew a package from his overcoat pocket and threw it upon the table.

"Don't make any mistake, Dell," he said, "about me. I don't think there's anything in the way of a haircut or a shave or a shampoo that could make me like my girl any less. But if you'll unwrap that package you may see why you had me going a while at first."

White fingers and nimble tore at the string and paper. And then an ecstatic scream of joy; and then, alas! a quick feminine change to hysterical tears and wails, necessitating the immediate employment of all the comforting powers of the lord of the flat.

For there lay The Combs—the set of combs, side and back, that Della had worshipped long in a Broadway window. Beautiful combs, pure tortoise shell, with jewelled rims—just the shade to wear in the beautiful vanished hair. They were expensive combs, she knew, and her heart had simply craved and yearned over them without the least hope of possession. And now, they were hers, but the tresses that should have adorned the coveted adornments were gone.

But she hugged them to her bosom, and at length she was able to look up with dim eyes and a smile and say: "My hair grows so fast, Jim!"

And then Della leaped up like a little singed cat and cried, "Oh, oh!"

Jim had not yet seen his beautiful present. She held it out to him eagerly upon her open palm. The dull precious metal seemed to flash with a reflection of her bright and ardent spirit.

"Isn't it a dandy, Jim? I hunted all over town to find it. You'll have to look at the time a hundred times a day now. Give me your watch. I want to see how it looks on it."

Instead of obeying, Jim tumbled down on the couch and put his hands under the back of his head and smiled.

"Dell," said he, "let's put our Christmas presents away and keep 'em a while. They're too nice to use just at present. I sold the watch to get the money to buy your combs. And now suppose you put the chops on."

The magi, as you know, were wise men—wonderfully wise men—who brought gifts to the Babe in the manger. They invented the art of giving Christmas presents. Being wise, their gifts were no doubt wise ones, possibly bearing the privilege of exchange in case of duplication. And here I have lamely related to you the uneventful chronicle of two foolish children in a flat who most unwisely sacrificed for each other the greatest treasures of their house. But in a last word to the wise of these days let it be said that of all who give gifts these two were the wisest. O all who give and receive gifts, such as they are wisest. Everywhere they are wisest. They are the magi.

THE REAL GIFTS PARENTS CAN GIVE TO CHILDREN

ROSE FITZGERALD KENNEDY

CHRISTMAS HOLIDAYS IN THE KENNEDY FAMILY . . . A tapestry of many places, people, and radiant memories. And yet, looking back, I find it difficult to recall any specific gifts we gave the children, or even that they gave to each other on their saved-up allowances. I remember we always had a tree, wherever we were, and sometimes a friend who played Santa. But the presents themselves do not seem that significant.

I suppose the reason is that to us, the actual physical gifts have always been secondary to the more spiritual gifts we tried to give our children. And now, as life patterns change, as I see in my own family and others how children exercise their options to go off alone, earlier, removing themselves from the home influence, I feel that perhaps I might speak in behalf of those old-fashioned gifts which all parents, no matter what their creed, can give their children, not just at Christmas, but throughout the year.

I refer, of course, to the principles and ideals which mothers and fathers can pass along to the next generation by example, and by teaching. And uppermost in mind, of course, is the gift of faith.

Faith is a gift truly given, and always to be cherished, guarded and nurtured. As Catholics, we of course believe deeply in the power of prayer. We know the peace of heart and mind which can come from prayer, no matter what the danger, perplexity and confusion.

Whatever his religion, with faith, a child knows exactly why he was created, he has well-defined obligations to God and man. He has sure direction, ever-courageous because he knows God is directing him for his ultimate destiny, helping him to dedicate his faculties and opportunities for best fulfilling God's plans. If he can pray, he will have that peace of mind and heart which accompanies prayers, regardless of how heavy is his cross. I have always felt and I think all my children did, too, that God never sends us a Cross too heavy for us to bear.

God wants a different thing from each of us, laborious or easy, conspicuous or quite private, but something which only we can do, and for which we were created. What a beautiful gift if only parents could pass along this concept to each of their children, and each could realize how important was his individual contribution.

Another gift which we have always tried to bestow is the gift of zest—of curiosity and interest and enthusiasm for life. Children should be stimulated by their parents to see, and touch, and know, and understand, and appreciate. At meals, we always discussed history and current events. At Christmastime, for instance, Bethlehem as it was when Christ was born, and Bethlehem as it is today with the war between Arabs and Jews; Plymouth Rock when the Pilgrims arrived, and Plymouth as it is today; what the Pilgrims might have eaten for Thanksgiving in 1620 and what we will be eating in 1969. Thus, the children's interest was stimulated at an early age, and they participated in the family conversations.

. . . I believe in explaining family rules and requests, so that the children will trust their parents' reasoning, experiences, and have confidence in their judgment. For example, they were confined to sailing only in the harbor when they were little. The reason: if heavy fogs should settle in, they might have been lost or might crash against a rock. When the small ones come to visit now, I do not simply urge them to eat the healthy foods which make strong bones and teeth. I explain that if they eat foods like popcorn and candy, they will not be able to play football or swim as well as their father or brothers do. Or I show them a drawing we keep at Hyannis Port of the President making his famous swim in the Solomon Islands in World War II, after his PT boat was sunk, rescuing a shipmate by holding the life saving belt strap in his teeth. In a few minutes all the youngsters are drinking their orange juice and showing me their white teeth.

. . . How can parents give children an interest and ingenuity to cope with life? One way is to encourage hobbies: stamps, antiques, gardening, painting, a musical instrument, sports. . . . Any sort of activity which distracts, releases tension, gives more channels to energies. There is no place for boredom in a mind that is constantly seeking new horizons.

Some people collapse under strain, discouragement, and problems. Others respond to challenges and difficulties and are excited by them. This has always been a Kennedy philosophy. I will never allow myself to be vanquished or annihilated. I have always enjoyed living and working, and I believe I have had a great life.

. . . Which brings me to my last gift: the gift of service. "God has created me to do Him some definite service. He has committed some work to me which He has not committed to another. I have my mission—I may never know it in this life, but I shall be told it in the next. I am a link in a chain, a bond of connection between persons. He has not created me for naught. I shall do good, I shall do His work."

In my case, God's work is largely concerned with the problems of retarded children. My husband and I knew what it was to have a retarded child, and now I try to save other parents from some of our anguish and heartbreak. If the knowledge which scientists and doctors have now were properly publicized, mental retardation could be reduced by 50 percent. It is my hope that it will one day be eradicated as has been polio, and that all babies will be born healthy and normal.

Women as women can contribute on many levels. Their special love, tenderness and understanding can bring about these gifts I have spoken of in the hearts of their children, their husbands, their friends. To women everywhere, I can only close with the epitome of my daily philosophy—which is not to think of what might have been, but to devote your time, efforts and energies to the living, and to the immediate challenges. In this way we turn our heartaches into constructive efforts to lighten the sorrow of others. And if you can transmit the same attitude to your children, that, too, will be a precious gift all their lives, whatever may be their destiny. They will radiate happiness and understanding and their homes will be havens of love, sympathy and peace. God has bequeathed on us pleasures as well as sorrows, laughter as well as tears. May He give us the capacity to enjoy all these gifts and to share them.

Dreams of a Black Christmas

GWENDOLYN BROOKS

WHEN I WAS A CHILD, IT did not occur to me, even once, that the black in which I was encased (I called it brown in those days) would be considered, one day, beautiful. Considered beautiful and called beautiful by great groups.

I had always considered it beautiful. I would stick out my arm, examine it, and smile. Charming! And convenient, for mud on my leg was not as annunciatory as was mud on the leg of light Rose Hurd.

Charm—and efficiency.

This delight in my pigmentation was hardly a feature of my world. One of the first "world"-truths revealed to me when I at last became a member of SCHOOL was that, to be socially successful, a little girl must be Bright (of skin). It was better if your hair was curly, too—or at least Good Grade (Good Grade implied, usually, no involvement with the Hot Comb)—but Bright you marvelously needed to be. Exceptions? A few. Wealth was an escape passport. If a dusky maiden's father was a doctor, lawyer, City Hall employee, or Post Office man, or if her mother was a Schoolteacher, there was some hope: because that girl would often have lovelier clothes, and more of them, than her Bright competitors; and her hair was often long, at *least*, and straight—oh so Hot Comb straight! Such a damsel, if she had virtually nothing to do with the ordinary black women of the class, might be favored, might be Accepted.

My father was a janitor. My mother had been a schoolteacher in Topeka before her marriage, but that did not count. Who knew it, anyhow? Of course, not many knew of my father's lowly calling. Still, there was something about me—even though in the early years I wore decent dresses because my Aunt Beulah, a sewing teacher at the Booker Washington High School in Tulsa, was making them for me, sending, on occasion, five at a time—SOMETHING—that stamped me "beyond the pale." And thereby doubly.

All I could hope for was achievement of reverence among the Lesser Blacks. Alas. Requisites for eminence among these I had not. I had not brass or sass. I did not fight brilliantly, or at all, on the playground. I was not ingenious in gym, carrying my team single-handedly to glory. I could not play jacks. I could not ride a bicycle. I did not whisper excitedly about my Boyfriends. For the best of reasons. I did not have any. Among the Lesser Blacks my decent dresses were hinderers to my advance. The girls who did not have them loathed me for having them. When they bothered to remember that I was alive, that is. When they bothered to remember that I was alive, they called me "ol' stuck-up heifer"; and they informed me that they wanted "nothin' t' do with no rich people's sp'iled chirren." Doubtless, this decision amazed the Bright and the truly rich, whom the critics openly adored.

As for the Men in the world of School—the little Bright ones looked through me as if I happened to inconvenience their vision, and those of my own hue rechristened me Ol' Black Gal.

These facts of my eight-year membership in school served to sully the truly nice delights of crayon and chalk and watercolor, of story time, and textbooks with cheery pictures of neat, gay-colored life-among-the-white-folks.

Home, however, always warmly awaited me. Welcoming, enveloping. Home meant a quick-walking, careful, Duty-Loving mother, who played the piano, made fudge, made cocoa and prune whip and apricot pie, drew tidy cows and trees and expert houses with chimneys and chimney smoke, who helped her children with arithmetic homework, and who sang in a high soprano:

> *Brighten the corner where you are!—*
> *Br-rrr-righten the corner where you are!—*
> *Someone far from harbor you may guide*
>   *across the bar—*
> *Bright-TEN the cor-nerr—*
>   *where*
>   *you*
>   *are.*

Home meant my father, with kind eyes, songs, and tense recitations for my brother and myself. A favorite of his, a wonderful poem about a pie-making lady. Along had come a man, weary, worn, to beg of the lady a pie. Those already baked, she informed him, were too large for the likes of him. She said she would bake another. It, too, was "large." And the next was large. And the next, and the next. Finally the traveler, completely out of patience, berated her and exclaimed that henceforth she should draw her own sustenance from the bark of trees. And she became, *mirabile dictu,* a woodpecker and flew off. We never tired of that. My father seemed to Gwendolyn and Raymond a figure of power. He had those rich Artistic Abilities, but he had more. He could fix anything that broke or stopped. He could build long-lasting fires in the ancient furnace below. He could paint the house, inside and out, and could whitewash the basement. He could spread the American Flag in wide loud magic across the front of our house on the Fourth of July and Decoration Day. He could chuckle. No one has ever had, no one will ever have, a chuckle exactly like my father's. It was gentle, it was warmly happy, it was heavyish but not hard. It was secure, and seemed to us an assistant to the Power that registered with his children. My father, too, was almost our family doctor. We had Dr. Carter, of course, precise and semitwinkly and effective—but it was not always necessary to call him. My father had wanted to be a doctor. Thwarted, he read every "doctor book" (and he remembered much from a black tradition) he could reach, learning fine secrets and curing us with steams, and fruit compotes, and dexterous rubs, and, above all, with bedside compassion. "Well, there, young lady! How's that throat now?" "Well, let's see now. This salve will take care of that bruise! Now, we're going to be all right." In illness there was an advantage: the invalid was royalty for the run of the seizure.

And of course my father furnished All the Money. The "all" was inadequate, felt Keziah Wims Brooks: could he not leave the McKinley Music Publishing Company, which was paying him about twenty-five dollars a week (from thirty to thirty-five when he worked overtime)? Uncle Paul, her sister Gertrude's husband, worked at City Hall—had a "snap" job—made fifty dollars a week. . . . True, during the bad times, during the Depression, when McKinley, itself stricken, could pay my father only in part—sometimes eighteen dollars, sometimes ten dollars—my family ate beans. But children dread, often above all else, dissension in the house, and we would have been quite content to entertain a beany diet every day, if necessary, and not live in Lilydale as did bungalow-owning Aunt Gertrude and Uncle Paul, if only there could be, continuously, the almost musical Peace that we had most of the time.

Home. Checker games. Dominoes. Radio (Jack Benny, Ben Bernie, and Kate Smith; *Amos and Andy;* Major Bowes's *Amateur Hour;* Wayne King, the Waltz King; and "Ladies and Gentlemen: Ea-sy Aces"). Christmases. I shall stop right here to tell about those. They were important.

The world of Christmas was firm. Certain things were done. Certain things were not done.

We did not put Christmas trees outdoors.

We did not open Christmas presents on Christmas Eve.

And we had *not* made fruitcakes two or three months ahead of time.

A Christmas tree, we felt—my mother, my father, my brother, and I—belonged in the living room. Green, never silver or gold or pink. Full-branched and aspiring to the ceiling.

Christmas presents were wrapped and hidden on Christmas Eve. Oh, the sly winks and grins. The furtive rustle of tissue, the whip of ribbon off the spool, semi-heard. The trippings here and there in search of secure hiding places. Our house had nooks and crannies, a closet, a pantry, alcoves, "the little room," an extensive basement: There were hiding places aplenty.

Fruitcakes were made about a week before Christmas. We didn't care what the recipe books said. We liked having all the Christmas joy as close together as possible. Mama went downtown, as a rule, for the very freshest supplies, for then, as now, distributors sent their worst materials to "the colored neighborhood." Candied cherries and pineapple but no citron. Mama didn't like citron (*I* did and do), so that was out. Candied orange and lemon, however. Figs galore. Dates galore. Raisins, raisins, raisins.

We children had the bake-eve fun of cutting up the candied fruit, shelling and chopping the nuts, and mixing everything together. Our fingers got tired, our teeth and tongues never. We tasted and tasted and took gay tummy aches to bed. Next day, the house was rich with the aroma of brandied fruit and spice. How wonderful. How happy I was.

It was the baking of the fruitcakes that opened our Christmas season. After that, there were the merriest playing of Christmas carols on the piano by my mother and me, with everybody singing; mysterious shopping jaunts; the lingering, careful purchase of Christmas cards; the visit to Santa Claus; the desperately scrupulous housecleaning; for my mother and myself, the calls at the beauty shop for Christmas hairdos (you had to look your very best on Christmas Day), the Christmas-tree hunt, undertaken by all, with the marvelous pungent symbol *found* and borne back triumphantly through the dusk of the third or fourth day before Christmas.

All this. So much more that fades, and fades. I almost forgot the high, high angel-food cake, made a day or two before Christmas. We were, somehow, not great Christmas-cookie advocates, but there would be a few frosted cookies about. We had Christmas candy. And filled candies and Christmas mints. Some of those dates, too, were stuffed with nuts and sugared over, to make another sort of confection.

On Christmas Eve we decorated the Christmas tree. So much silver tinsel. And ropes of fringed gold, and red, silver, blue, and gold balls, and a star on top. We children hung our stockings on the mantel—in the morning they would ache with apples, oranges, nuts, and tiny toys—over our, yes, *real* fireplace! That night we were allowed to "sample the sample"—that is, "test" fruitcake that my mother always made in a shallow pan, along with the proper proud giants—and with it we had eggnog with nutmeg on top.

With what excited pleasure my brother and I went to bed, trying to stay awake to hear Santa Claus come down our chimney, but always failing, for Santa was a sly old soul. We went to sleep with radio carols in our ears, or to the sweet sound of Mama playing and singing "Silent Night," or "Hark! The Herald Angels Sing," or "O Little Town of Bethlehem."

Next day it was so hard to wait for the sky to turn on its light. As soon as it did, out of bed we children threw ourselves and rushed into the living room. There we found, always, that Papa had turned on the Christmas-tree lights, and under the tree shone just about everything we had asked of Santa Claus. (Of course, Mama always "helped" us with our letters to Santa Claus.) My brother remembers trains and tracks, baseball equipment, wagons, skates, games. Various Christmases brought me dishes, a rocking chair, a doll house, paper dolls which I liked better than hard dolls because so much more could be done with the paper ones. My most delicate and exquisite Christmas-gift memory is of a little glass deer, dainty-antlered, slender-legged, and filled with perfume.

Of course, there were clothes—"secondary" gifts.

And BOOKS.

About books. My "book Christmas" had already begun, on Christmas Eve, soon after the Christmas tree was strung with lights. It was for long my own personal tradition to sit behind the tree and read a paper book I still own: *The Cherry Orchard*, by Marie Battelle Schilling, and published by the David C. Cook Publishing Company. It had been given me by Kayola Moore, my Sunday school teacher. I don't know why I enjoyed reading that book, Christmas Eve after Christmas Eve, to the tune of black-walnut candy crunching.

And back I went—to the back of the Christmas tree—with my new books. Late, late. After the relatives, after the Christmas turkey, after the cranberries—fresh!—none of your canned cranberries for us—and the mashed potatoes and gravy and baked macaroni and celery and candied sweet potatoes and peas-and-carrots, and the fruitcake and angel cake and eggnog. Back, while the rest of the family forgot it all in bed, to the else-dark room. The silence. The black-walnut candy. And the books that began the giving again.

It did not trouble me, then, that Santa was white and Christ and Christmas were offered as white, except for That One of the "wise men," with role ever slurred, ever understated.

Today, *my* house has not yet escaped the green-tree-fruitcake-eggnog-gifts-on-Christmas-morning "esthetic," even in this our time of black decision and ascent. The human heart delights in "celebration." Human beings delight in the Day set apart for singing and feasting and dancing and fancy dress—or "best" apparel—and the special giving of gifts and twenty-four-hour formalized love. An urgent need is a holiday for blacks, to be enjoyed by blacks everywhere. Worldwide . . .

Yes, needed is a holiday for blacks everywhere, a Black World Day, with black excitement and black trimmings in honor of the astounding strength and achievement of black people. A yearly Black People's Day—akin, perhaps, to the black concept Kwanza, which, based on a traditional African holiday, is considered by many black people an alternative to commercial Christmas; for the week beginning December twenty-sixth, homes are decorated in red and black and green, the black representing the black nation, the red representing our shed blood, the green featured as a symbol of land for nation-establishment and a symbol, too, for live faith in our young.

I see, feel, and hear a potential celebration as Africa colors—thorough, direct. A thing of shout but of African quietness, too, because in Africa these tonals can almost coincide. A clean-throated singing. Drums; and perhaps guitars. Flags or a flag. Costumery, wholesomely gaudy; costumery which, for the African, is not affectation but merely a right richness that the body deserves. Foods; not pâte de foie gras or creamed lobster de bon bon, but figs and oranges, and vegetables. . . . AND the profound and frequent shaking of hands, which in Africa is so important. The shaking of hands in warmth and strength and union.

CHRISTMAS

ST. AUGUSTINE

THE MYSTICAL MEANING OF CHRIST'S CHOICE
OF THE DAY ON WHICH HE WAS BORN.

Our Lord Jesus, who was with His Father before He was born of His mother, chose not only the virgin from whom He was to be born, but also the day on which He was to be born. Misguided men very frequently go by certain dates. One man chooses a day for setting out new vines; another, a day for starting on a journey; and sometimes, too, a man takes a special day for getting married. When they do this, they have this in mind, that anything undertaken may for that reason thrive and prosper. But no-one is able to choose the day of his own birth; whereas the Lord, who was able to create both, was also able to choose both.

Moreover, He did not make His choice of day after the manner of those silly people who think that the fates of men are bound up with the position of the stars. Obviously, He was not made happy by the day on which He was born; but the day on which He deigned to be born was made a happy one by Him. For indeed, the day of His birth also shows the mystery of His light. The Apostle indicates this when he says: *The night is passed, and the day is at hand. Let us . . . cast off the works of darkness, and put on the armor of light. Let us walk honestly, as in the day.* Let us recognize that it is day, let us be day ourselves. When we were living without faith, we were night. And, because this same lack of faith which covered the whole world like the night, had to be lessened by the growth of faith, so on the birthday of our Lord Jesus Christ the nights began to be shorter, while the days became longer.

Let us, therefore, Brethren, keep this day with due solemnity; not, like those who are without faith, on account of the sun, but because of Him who made the sun. For He who was *the Word, was made flesh,* that for our sakes He might be under the sun. Under the sun, to be sure, in His flesh; but in His majesty, over the whole universe in which He made the sun. And now, too, He, incarnate, stands above that sun which is worshipped as god by those who, intellectually blind, do not see the true Sun of Justice . . .

THE BIRTH OF CHRIST TO BE CELEBRATED.

Rightly are we carried away by the language of the Psalm, by the sound of a heavenly trumpet, as it were, when we hear: *Sing ye to the Lord a new canticle. Sing to the Lord, all the earth. Sing ye to the Lord and bless His name.* Let us acknowledge, then, let us herald the Day of Day, who on this day was born in flesh. The Day, Son of Day, the Father—God of God, Light of Light! This indeed is the salvation that is spoken of elsewhere: *May God have mercy on us, and bless us. May He cause the light of His countenance to shine upon us, that we may know Thy way upon earth, Thy salvation in all nations.* Here the phrase, *upon earth,* is repeated in the words, *in all nations.* The phrase, *Thy way,* is repeated in *Thy salvation.* We recall that the Lord Himself said, *I am the way. . . .*

He lies in a manger, but He holds the world. He nurses at His mother's breasts, but He feeds the angels. He is wrapped in swaddling clothes, but He gives us the garment of immortality. He is given milk, but at the same time is adored. He finds no room at the inn, but He builds a temple for Himself in the hearts of those who believe.

That infirmity might be made strong, strength has been made weak. Let us, therefore, admire the more also His human birth instead of looking down upon it; and let us in His presence try to realize the abasement that He in all His majesty accepted for our sakes. And then let us be kindled with love, that we may come to His eternity.

THE FIRST NOWELL

TRADITIONAL

The first Nowell the Angel did say,
Was to certain poor shepherds in fields as they lay;
In fields where they lay keeping their sheep,
On a cold winter's night that was so deep.

Nowell, Nowell, Nowell, Nowell,
Born is the King of Israel.

They looked up and saw a star
Shining in the east, beyond them far;
And to the earth it gave great light,
And so it continued, both day and night.

Nowell, Nowell, Nowell, Nowell,
Born is the King of Israel.

And by the light of that same star,
Three wise men came from country far;
To seek for a king was their intent,
And to follow the star wherever it went.

Nowell, Nowell, Nowell, Nowell,
Born is the King of Israel.

This star drew nigh to the northwest,
O'er Bethlehem it took its rest,
And there it did both stop and stay
Right over the place where Jesus lay.

Nowell, Nowell, Nowell, Nowell,
Born is the King of Israel.

WINTER
WONDERLAND

Winter Wonderland

WORDS BY RICHARD B. SMITH
MUSIC BY FELIX BERNARD

Sleigh bells ring
are you listening
in the lane
snow is glistening
A beautiful sight
We're happy tonight
walking in a winter wonderland

Gone away is the bluebird
here to stay is a new bird
He sings a love song
as we go along
walking in a winter wonderland

In the meadow we can build a snowman
Then pretend that he is Parson Brown
He'll say: Are you married?
We'll say: No man
But you can do the job
when you're in town

Later on
we'll conspire
as we dream by the fire
To face unafraid
the plans that we've made
walking in a winter wonderland

In the meadow we can build a snowman
and pretend that he's a circus clown
We'll have lots of fun with mister snowman
until the alligators knock him down

When it snows
ain't it thrilling
Though your nose gets a chilling
We'll frolic and play
the Eskimo way
walking in a winter wonderland

Walking in a winter wonderland
walking in a winter wonderland

All's Noël That Ends Noël or, Incompatibility Is the Spice of Christmas

OGDEN NASH

Do you know Mrs. Millard Fillmore Revere?

On her calendar, Christmas comes three hundred and sixty-five times a year.

Consider Mrs. Revere's Christmas spirit; no one can match it——

No, not Tiny Tim or big Bob Cratchit.

Even on December 26th it reveals no rifts;

She is already compiling her list of next year's gifts.

Her actions during the winter are conscientious and methodical,

Now snipping an advertisement from a newspaper, now clipping a coupon from a
     periodical.

In the spring she is occupied with mail-order catalogues from Racine and Provincetown
     and Richmond and Walla Walla,

Which offer a gallimaufry of gewgaws, gadgets, widgets, jiggers, trinkets, and baubles,
     postpaid for a dollar.

Midsummer evenings find her trudging home from clearance sales, balancing parcel upon
     parcel,

With blithe heart and weary metatarsal.

Soon appear the rolls of garish paper and the spools of gaudy ribbon,

And to describe the decline and fall of Mr. Revere it would take the pen of a Gibbon.

Poor Mr. Revere—such harbingers of Christmas do not brighten him,

They simply frighten him.

He cringes like a timid hobo when a fierce dog raises its hackles at him;

Wherever he steps, ribbons wind around his ankles and paper crackles at him.

He feels himself threatened by Christmas on all fronts;

Shakespeare had Mr. Revere in mind when he wrote, "Cowards die many times before
their deaths; The valiant never taste of death but once."

These are the progressively ominous hints of impending doom:

First, he is forbidden to open a certain drawer, then a certain closet, and, finally, a
certain room.

If Mr. Revere looks slightly seedy as he goes his daily rounds

It's because his clean shirts and socks are now out of bounds.

Indeed, the only reason he gets by,

He remembers previous years and has provided himself with haberdashery he can
drip and dry.

The days of September, October, November are like globules of water on the forehead of
a tortured prisoner dropping;

Each is another day on which he has done no Christmas shopping.

At this point the Devil whispers that if he puts it off until Christmas Eve the shops
will be emptier,

A thought than which nothing could be temptier,

But Christmas Eve finds him bedridden with a fever of nearly ninety-nine degrees, and
swaddled in blankets up to his neck,

So on Christmas morn he has nothing for Mrs. Revere but a kiss and a check,

Which somehow works out fine, because she enjoys being kissed

And the check is a great comfort when she sits down on December 26th to compile her
next year's list.

CHRIST CLIMBED DOWN

LAWRENCE FERLINGHETTI

Christ climbed down
from His bare Tree
this year
and ran away to where
there were no rootless Christmas trees
hung with candycanes and breakable stars

Christ climbed down
from His bare Tree
this year
and ran away to where
there were no gilded Christmas trees
and no tinsel Christmas trees
and no tinfoil Christmas trees
and no pink plastic Christmas trees
and no gold Christmas trees
and no black Christmas trees
and no powderblue Christmas trees
hung with electric candles
and encircled by tin electric trains
and clever cornball relatives

Christ climbed down
from His bare Tree
this year
and ran away to where

no intrepid Bible salesmen
covered the territory
in two-tone cadillacs
and where no Sears Roebuck creches
complete with plastic babe in manger
arrived by parcel post
the babe by special delivery
and where no televised Wise Men
praised the Lord Calvert Whiskey

Christ climbed down
from His bare Tree
this year
and ran away to where
no fat handshaking stranger
in a red flannel suit
and a fake white beard
went around passing himself off
as some sort of North Pole saint
crossing the desert to Bethlehem
Pennsylvania
in a Volkswagen sled
drawn by rollicking Adirondack reindeer
with German names
and bearing sacks of Humble Gifts
from Saks Fifth Avenue
for everybody's imagined Christ child

Christ climbed down
from His bare Tree
this year
and ran away to where
no Bing Crosby carollers

groaned of a tight Christmas
and where no Radio City angels
iceskated wingless
thru a winter wonderland
into a jinglebell heaven
daily at 8:30
with Midnight Mass matinees

Christ climbed down
from His bare Tree
this year
and softly stole away into
some anonymous Mary's womb again
where in the darkest night
of everybody's anonymous soul
He awaits again
an unimaginable
and impossibly
Immaculate Reconception
the very craziest
of Second Comings

Remembrance Is Sufficient

E. B. WHITE

IT IS NOT EASY TO SELECT the few words each year that shall serve as a Christmas greeting to our readers, wherever (like Mrs. Calabash) they are. While engaged in making the selection, we study the typewriter keys with the gravity you sometimes see in the faces of greeting-card buyers in stationery stores—faces taut with a special anguish (a sailor searching for a valentine message commensurate with his desire, a girl hunting for the right phrase to repair a broken friendship), as though all of life, all of love, must suddenly be captured on a small piece of decorative paper and consigned to the mails. This morning early, when we passed the angels in Rockefeller Center, we wished we could simply borrow a trumpet from one of them and blow our best wishes to the world in a single loud blast, instead of coming to the office and picking around among the confused shapes of a keyboard. But then, a few minutes later, gazing at the Dutch candy house in the window of KLM, we were reminded that everyone constructs a Christmas of his own, in his fashion, in sugar-candy form if need be, and that the quest for beauty, piety, simplicity, and merriment takes almost as many forms as there are celebrants, certainly too many to be covered by one note on a borrowed horn.

No one ever weeps for joy—we have this on good authority. We have it on the authority of a professor at the School of Medicine of the University of Rochester. (EXPERT DEEMS JOY NO CAUSE OF TEARS—*The Times.*) But it is true that at Christmas (season of joy, season of joy-to-the-world), tears are not unknown, or even infrequent: many find themselves greatly moved by small events—by minor miracles of home or school or church, by a snatch of music, by a drift of paper snow across a TV screen. It is, of course, not joy but beauty that is responsible for this mild phenomenon: the unexpected gift of sadness—of some bright thing unresolved, of some formless wish unattained and unattainable. Since most of the common satisfactions of Christmas are available at the stores, and for a price, we wish our readers the pleasures that are unpurchasable, the satisfactions unpredictable, the nourishment of tears (if at all convenient).

There is one member of our household who never has to grope for words as we are groping now. She is our Aunt Caroline and she is ninety-two. She has observed all her ninety-two Christmases in good health and excellent spirits, and she is in good health and spirits now. Being so old, she goes back to a more leisurely period, and when she speaks, she speaks with a precision and a refinement rare in this undisciplined century. There is nothing stiff-backed about the furnishings of her mind, but it is her nature to sit erect, to stand erect, and to speak an upright kind of English that is always graceful and exact. A few weeks ago, she said something so close to the theme of Christmas that we shall quote it here. We were sitting with her at lunch in the country, and we apologized for not having taken her for a motor ride that morning to see once again the bright colors in the changing woods. "Why, my dear," she said without hesitating, "remembrance is sufficient of the beauty we have seen."

The sentence startled us—as though a bird had flown into the room. Perhaps her statement, so casually spoken yet so poetical, is a useful clue to the grownups' strange Christmas, the Christmas that often seems so baffling at first, and then so rewarding. At any rate, it suggests the beauty that surrounds the day, the sufficiency of remembrance, the nostalgia that is the source of tears. We are in perfect agreement with the professor at this joyous season; men weep for beauty, for things remembered, for the partridge in the pear tree—the one that their true love brought them and that somehow got mislaid. So we send our greetings to all who laugh or weep or dance or sing, our love to children, our cheers to their embattled parents. To any for whom by some mischance the magical moment fails in reenactment, we give Aunt Caroline's resolute words: Remembrance is sufficient of the beauty we have seen.

For the Time Being

. . .

Well, so that is that. Now we must dismantle the tree,
Putting the decorations back into their cardboard boxes—
Some have got broken—and carrying them up to the attic.
The holly and the mistletoe must be taken down and burnt,
And the children got ready for school. There are enough
Left-overs to do, warmed-up, for the rest of the week—
Not that we have much appetite, having drunk such a lot,
Stayed up so late, attempted—quite unsuccessfully—
To love all of our relatives, and in general
Grossly overestimated our powers. Once again
As in previous years we have seen the actual Vision and failed
To do more than entertain it as an agreeable
Possibility, once again we have sent Him away,
Begging though to remain His disobedient servant,
The promising child who cannot keep His word for long.
The Christmas Feast is already a fading memory,
And already the mind begins to be vaguely aware
Of an unpleasant whiff of apprehension at the thought
Of Lent and Good Friday which cannot, after all, now
Be very far off. But, for the time being, here we all are,
Back in the moderate Aristotelian city
Of darning and the Eight-Fifteen, where Euclid's geometry
And Newton's mechanics would account for our experience,
And the kitchen table exists because I scrub it.

It seems to have shrunk during the holidays. The streets
Are much narrower than we remembered; we had forgotten
The office was as depressing as this. To those who have seen
The Child, however dimly, however incredulously
The Time Being is, in a sense, the most trying time of all.
For the innocent children who whispered so excitedly
Outside the locked door where they knew the presents to be
Grew up when it opened. Now, recollecting that moment
We can repress the joy, but the guilt remains conscious;
Remembering the stable where for once in our lives
Everything became a You and nothing was an It.
And craving the sensation but ignoring the cause,
We look round for something, no matter what, to inhibit
Our self-reflection, and the obvious thing for that purpose
Would be some great suffering. So, once we have met the Son,
We are tempted ever after to pray to the Father:
"Lead us into temptation and evil for our sake."
They will come, all right, don't worry; probably in a form
That we do not expect, and certainly with a force
More dreadful than we can imagine. In the meantime
There are bills to be paid, machines to keep in repair,
Irregular verbs to learn, the Time Being to redeem
From insignificance. The happy morning is over,
The night of agony still to come; the time is noon:
When the Spirit must practise his scales of rejoicing
Without even a hostile audience, and the Soul endure
A silence that is neither for nor against her faith
That God's Will will be done, that, in spite of her prayers,
God will cheat no one, not even the world of its triumph. . . .

Blow, Blow, Thou Winter Wind

from *As You Like It,* Act II, Scene vii

WILLIAM SHAKESPEARE

Blow, blow, thou winter wind.
Thou art not so unkind
As man's ingratitude.
Thy tooth is not so keen,
Because thou art not seen,
Although thy breath be rude.
Heigh-ho, sing heigh-ho, unto the green holly.
Most friendship is feigning, most loving mere folly.
Then heigh-ho, the holly.
This life is most jolly.
Freeze, freeze, thou bitter sky,
That dost not bite so nigh
As benefits forgot.
Though thou the waters warp,
Thy sting is not so sharp
As friend remembered not.
Heigh-ho, sing heigh-ho, unto the green holly.
Most friendship is feigning, most loving mere folly.
Then heigh-ho, the holly.
This life is most jolly.

ACKNOWLEDGMENTS

I AM GRATEFUL TO MY LITERARY AGENT, Esther Newberg, for being born on Christmas Day and bringing the spirit of Christmas to everything she does. I would also like to thank my veteran collaborator and editor, Gretchen Young, and her assistant, Greer Baxter, for inspiring me to take a new look, or many new looks, at Christmas. I am grateful to Fritz Metsch, David Lott, Anna Campbell, and Sarah Mandell at Hyperion for taking care of the complicated aspects of producing this book, Christine Ragasa in publicity, and of course, Bob Miller. And to Fred Courtright at The Permissions Company for his hard work obtaining permissions.

This book is enriched beyond measure by the genius of Jon Muth, and I am honored to work with him again. It has also been a pleasure to work with Laura Maestro, who captures the magic of Christmas in so many ways.

I am fortunate to have worked with an outstanding researcher, Elizabeth Janiak, who brought deep knowledge and meticulous scholarship to the process of gathering the material, and the amazing Janea Mathis, who keeps track of everything and never stops smiling. I am always indebted to the peerless and dedicated archivists and staff of the John F. Kennedy Library and Foundation, especially Stephen Plotkin, Tom McNaught, Megan Desnoyers, and Tom Putnam.

I am grateful to Megan Kultgen and Elizabeth Berberich for being willing to help me out with any request.

It was a special thrill to visit the Library of Congress, and I am grateful to those who helped make its treasures accessible to me: Dr. James Billington, the Librarian of Congress; Victoria Hill, Acting Chief of the Humanities and Social Sciences Division; Reference Specialists Cheryl Adams and Sheridan Harvey; Jeff Flannery and Bruce Kirby in the Manuscript Division; and Clark Evans in the Rare Book and Special Collection Division. I would also like to thank Dr. Charles Bryan and

Frances Pollard at the Virginia Historical Society; Mary V. Thompson at Mount Vernon; Dan Jordan at Monticello; and the staff of the New York Society Library for searching their collections to help illuminate the history of Christmas.

I would not have been able to include the material relating to Christmas in wartime without the help of Major General Guy C. Swan III, Lieutenant Colonel Gerald Torrence, and Specialist Linden Moya at the U. S. Army Heritage and Education Center, and Brian Whiting at the USO of New York.

A special thank you to Robin Hall, Group Vice President, Scott Rutan, and Bob Byers of Macy's Annual and Special Events and Macy's Archives, who shared fascinating material from both the archives and Santaland in New York, and their colleagues in Chicago, Jamie Becker and Michelle Mesenberg.

For those who are interested, there are a number of wonderful histories of Christmas in America, especially *The Battle for Christmas* by Stephen Nissenbaum, *Consumer Rites* by Leigh Eric Schmidt, and *Inventing Christmas* by Jock Elliott.

Though they had nothing to do with this book, I would like to thank Marta Sgubin, Sean Driscoll, and Jean Claude Nedelec for helping us create our own family Christmas every year.

And to my family, as always.

CREDITS

Langston Hughes, "Carol of the Brown King" from *Collected Poems*. Copyright © 1994 by The Estate of Langston Hughes. Reprinted with the permission of Alfred A. Knopf, a division of Random House, Inc. and Harold Ober Associates, Inc.

Garrison Keillor, "The Old Scout: The Season of Letter-Perfect Families" (December 12, 2006). Copyright © 2006 by Garrison Keillor. Reprinted with the permission of the author.

Martin Luther King, Jr., "A Christmas Sermon on Peace" (December 24, 1967). Copyright © 1967 by Martin Luther King, Jr. Reprinted with the permission of Writers House, LLC on behalf of the proprietors.

"Happy Xmas (War Is Over)" Words and Music by John Lennon and Yoko Ono. Copyright © 1971 Renewed 1999 Lenono Music and Ono Music. All Rights Controlled And Administered by EMI BLACKWOOD MUSIC INC. (BMI). All Rights Reserved. International Copyright Secured. Used By Permission.

Claude Lévi-Strauss, excerpt from "Father Christmas Executed," translated by Diana Gittins, from *Unwrapping Christmas*, edited by Daniel Miller. Copyright © 1993 by Daniel Miller. Reprinted with the permission of Oxford University Press, Ltd.

Excerpts from "Santa Guide" from Macy's Santaland, part of Macy's Annual Events. Reprinted with the permission of Macy's.

Groucho Marx, letter to Fred Allen, December 23, 1953. Reprinted with the permission of Groucho Marx Productions, Inc.

Andrew J. McClurg, "Children of the World v. Santa Claus." Reprinted with the permission of the author.

Letter from Sgt. Mike Mira, December 23, 2003. Reprinted with permission of the U.S. Army Heritage and Education Center, Carlisle, PA, and the author.

Marianne Moore, "Saint Nicholas" from *The Complete Poems of Marianne Moore*. Copyright © 1958 by Marianne Moore, renewed. Reprinted with the permission of Viking Penguin, a division of Penguin Group (USA) Inc. and Faber & Faber, Ltd.

Edwin Morgan, "The Computer's First Christmas Card" from *Collected Poems*. Copyright © 1990 by Edwin Morgan. Reprinted with the permission of Carcanet Press, Ltd.

Vladimir Nabokov, "Christmas" from *The Stories of Vladimir Nabokov*. Copyright © 1995 by the Estate of Vladimir Nabokov. Reprinted with the permission of Alfred A. Knopf, a division of Random House, Inc. and The Orion Publishing Group, Ltd.

Ogden Nash, "All's Noel That Ends Noel." Originally published in *The New Yorker*. Reprinted with the permission of Curtis Brown, Ltd.

Grace Paley, "The Loudest Voice" from *The Little Disturbances of Man*. Copyright (c)1959 by Grace Paley. Reprinted with the permission of Viking Penguin, a division of Penguin Group (USA) Inc. and the Elaine Markson Literary Agency.

"Pedida de la Posada" from *Las Christmas*. Copyright © 1998 by Cantomedia, Inc. and Joie Davidow. Reprinted with the permission of Alfred A. Knopf, a division of Random House, Inc.

"Christmas in Hollis": Words and Music by Joseph Simmons, Darryl McDaniels, and Jason